From Pregnancy to Mothe

From Pregnancy to Motherhood: Psychoanalytic aspects of the beginning of the mother-child relationship explores the mental states associated with pregnancy, birth, and the early days of motherhood from a psychoanalytic perspective. Drawing on clinical research findings and the Infant Observation method originally developed by Esther Bick, the contributors examine a range of topics which include: how women's views of motherhood are influenced by social, cultural, and biotechnological factors; how women's sense of identity changes throughout pregnancy and motherhood; how women's relationships with family, partner, and future child are shaped; and how mental health professionals can better understand ways to work with issues of maternal and infant mental health.

Gina Ferrara Mori presents the research of psychoanalysts and psychotherapists working in different settings with mothers-to-be exploring their emotions, wishes, dreams, phantasies, and fears during the "time" in which they wait for the birth of their baby and experience the various phases of their bodies' development. Their work discusses the specific and complex developmental process in female identity which the authors have termed the construction of the "internal motherhood" which becomes a "psychic container" establishing the pre-conditions for developing bonds, affection, and their relationship with the baby once it has been born.

From Pregnancy to Motherhood develops and elaborates theoretical thinking and research already available, as well as presenting new material. It will be stimulating reading for psychoanalysts, psychologists, psychotherapists, gynaecologists, paediatricians, ultrasound doctors and technicians, midwives, social workers, healthcare assistants, registered and practical nurses, teachers, and students.

Gina Ferrara Mori is a member and training analyst of the Italian Psychoanalytic Society and the International Psychoanalytic Association. She is a child and adult psychoanalyst, and supervisor of the psychoanalytically oriented psychotherapists at the Martha Harris Study Centre in Florence.

From Pregnancy to Motherhood

Psychoanalytic aspects of the beginning of the mother-child relationship

Edited by Gina Ferrara Mori

Translated by Michela Benuzzi

Routledge
Taylor & Francis Group

LONDON AND NEW YORK

First published 2015
by Routledge
27 Church Road, Hove, East Sussex, BN3 2FA

and by Routledge
711 Third Avenue, New York, NY 10017

Routledge is an imprint of the Taylor & Francis Group, an Informa business

Previously published in Italian as Un tempo per la maternità interiore. Gli albori della relazione madre-bambino, 2008 by Borla, Rome, Italy.

British Library Cataloguing in Publication Data

A catalogue record for this book is available from the British Library

Library of Congress Cataloging in Publication Data

Tempo per la maternità interiore. English
From pregnancy to motherhood : psychoanalytic aspects of the beginning of the mother-child relationship / edited by Gina Ferrara Mori.
   pages cm
   "Previously published in Italian as Un tempo per la maternità interiore. Gli albori della relazione madre-bambino, 2008 by Borla, Rome, Italy."
Includes bibliographical references and index.
   1. Pregnant women—Mental health. 2. Mothers—Mental health. 3. Mother and child—
   Psychological aspects. 4. Love, Maternal—Psychological aspects. I. Mori, Gina Ferrara.
   II. Title.
RG560.T4313 2015
618.20651—dc23   2014044980

ISBN: 978-0-415-73609-1 (hbk)
ISBN: 978-0-415-73610-7 (pbk)
ISBN: 978-1-315-74291-5 (ebk)

Typeset in Times New Roman and Gill Sans
by codeMantra

Printed and bound in the United States of America by
Edwards Brothers Malloy on sustainably sourced paper

Contents

Contributors

Maria Rosa Ceragioli, Ph.D. (Pisa) – Psychologist, psychoanalytic psychotherapist CSMH-AMHPPIA and EFPP. Head psychologist at the Family Consulting Functional Unit, in the public sector, in charge of the brief consultation service for parents of children from 0 to 5 years old. She is author, together with A. Luperini, L. Mori and G. Smorto, of the book *Aspettando. Figure della maternità*, Florence 2011.

Luigia Cresti Scacciati, Ph.D. (Florence) – Psychologist, psychoanalytic psychotherapist AFPP and EFPP. Founding member and teacher with training functions of the AFPP. For many years, she has been working on the use of Infant Observation for the training of psychotherapists and healthcare professionals, and on the extensions of the Bick Method, in particular in the field of pregnancy and internal motherhood. She has edited, together with P. Farneti and C. Pratesi, *Osservazione e trasformazione,* Roma 2001 and, together with S. Nissim, *Percorsi di crescita: dagli occhi alla mente*, Roma 2007. She is Senior Editor of the AFPP scientific journal "Contrappunto".

Gina Ferrara Mori, M.D. (Florence) – Pediatrician, full member and supervising psychoanalyst SPI and IPA. Expert in child and adolescent psychoanalysis, supervising analyst for students of CSMH in Florence. She has written many clinical papers for specialized journals as well as research studies on Infant Observation and early mother-child relationships. She is the editor of the book *Un tempo per la maternità interiore*, Roma 2008.

Isabella Lapi, Ph.D. (Florence) – Psychologist, psychoanalytic psychotherapist AFPP and EFPP. Teacher with training functions of the AFPP; she works in the public sector as head of a child mental health service, regarding in particular pregnancy, early mother-child relationship, and psychotherapeutic consultations on trauma and mourning in childhood. She is a member of the bioethics committee in Tuscany. She is the author of many papers on these topics.

Arianna Luperini, Ph.D. (Pisa) – Psychologist, psychoanalyst associate member SPI and IPA. Her special interests are the relationship between psychoanalysis and art, and the theme of the birth of internal motherhood. She edits the book series *S/Confini*. She is the author, together with T. Lorito and R. Tancredi, of the children's book *Il popolo di sopra*, Pisa 2007, and with M.R. Ceragioli, L. Mori and G. Smorto, of the book *Aspettando. Figure della maternità*, Florence 2011.

Jeanne Magagna, Ph.D. (London) – Child, adult, and family psychoanalytic psychotherapist who trained at the Tavistock Clinic in London. She was Head of Psychotherapy Services at Great Ormond Street Hospital for children. Among her publications are *Intimate Transformations: Babies with their Families* (2005) and *The Silent Child: Communication without Words* (2012).

Marco Mastella, M.D. (Ferrara) – With a specialization in medical psychology and child neuropsychiatry, psychoanalyst associate member SPI and IPA, expert in child and adolescent psychoanalysis. For a number of years, he has been leading supervision groups for healthcare public sector staff, teachers, and groups of parents. He is adjunct professor at the University Ferrara and University of Bologna. He was in charge of a mother-child service in the public sector and lay judge at the Appeal Court in Bologna, Section for Minors. He is the author of innumerable contributions on child psychoanalysis. He wrote S*ognare e crescere il figlio di un'altra donna,* Siena, 2009.

Fiorella Monti, Ph.D. (Bologna) – Full professor of Dynamic Psychology, Clinical Manager SAP (Psychological Help Service for Young Adults), Clinical Manager SUAPI (Child Psychological Help University Service), Department of Psychology, University of Bologna. Psychologist, psychoanalytic psychotherapist AFPP and EFPP, teacher with training functions of the AFPP. She is a member of the Scientific Committee of the Study Centre for Child and Adolescent Well-being in Forlì. Her interest is mainly focused on the development and pathology of the perinatal period. She is the author of many contributions and publications on early infancy for specialized journals. She edited with B. Davalli the book *Ripensare la nascita. Reti di sostegno dalla gravidanza alla genitorialità*, Bologna 2005, and with F. Agostini, she wrote *La depressione postnatale*, Roma, 2006.

Laura Mori, Ph.D. (Florence) – Psychologist, psychoanalytic psychotherapist EFPP. Founding member and teacher with training functions of the AFPP. Honorary member of AIPPI. Her special interests are sibling relationships, the birth of the internal motherhood, and the construction of the paternal parental role. Together with L. Root Fortini, she wrote the book *Sextuplets. Study of a Sibling Group*, London, 2010, and with M.R. Cerragioli, A. Luperini and G. Smorto, *Aspettando. Figure della maternità*, Florence 2011. She edited the book *Scenari dei legami fraterni,* Firenze 2012.

Cristina Pratesi, Ph.D. (Florence) – Psychologist, psychoanalytic psychotherapist AFPP and EFPP. Teacher with training functions of the AFPP; current Director of the AFPP post-graduate school in psychoanalytic psychotherapy. Psychologist working for the public sector, she heads a child mental health service and she is active in the areas of mental health, family consulting units, consulting centres for adolescence, psycho-oncology and palliative care. For many years now, she has been training staff in these areas. Since 2007, she has been in charge of the project "Assistance to the psychological distress in pregnancy and puerperium and prevention of the post-partum depression". She was a member of the Equal Opportunity Committee and the Committee for Moral Harassment in the public sector. She has edited, together with L. Cresti Scacciati and P. Farneti, *Osservazione e trasformazione,* Roma 2001.

Linda Root Fortini, Ph.D. (Florence) – Psychologist, psychoanalytic psychotherapist AFPP and EFPP. Teacher with training functions of the AFPP. She leads Infant Observation groups for postgraduate courses of the AFPP and coordinates a study group on the clinical treatment of adolescents. In the past, she taught courses in Developmental Psychology at the Psychology Department of the University of Florence. For many years, she has conducted training courses for healthcare staff working in the child-mother field, and for hospital staff of the Gynaecology-Obstetrics wards and antenatal groups for pregnant women in the public sector. With L. Mori, she wrote *Sextuplets. Study of a Sibling Group*, London, 2010.

Gabriella Smorto, Ph.D. (Pisa) – Psychologist, psychoanalytic psychotherapist CSMH-AMHPPIA, IIPG and EFPP, she is the Director of the Psychology Complex Operational Unit in the public sector and she works in the field of mental health for adolescents, women and families. She is particularly active in the implementation of interventions for the promotion and support of parenthood. She published various works on the treatment of children and the parental function. She is author, with M.R Ceragioli., A. Luperini and L. Mori, of the book *Aspettando. Figure della maternità*, Florence 2011.

Dina Vallino, Ph.D. (Milano) – With a specialization in educational psychology. Psychotherapist, psychoanalyst with training functions. Full member SPI and IPA, expert in child and adolescent psychoanalysis. Since the end of 1970s, she has been carrying out training and teaching professional study groups, mainly in the field of Infant Observation and child and adolescent psychotherapy. She wrote many contributions on child and adult psychoanalysis in journals, in various volumes with other colleagues, and three books: *Raccontami una storia. Dalla consultazione all'analisi dei bambini.* Roma, 1998; *Fare psicoanalisi con genitori e bambini.* Roma, 2008, and with Marco Macciò, *Essere neonati. Osservazioni psicoanalitiche*, Roma, 2004.

Acronyms

AFPP = Associazione Fiorentina di Psicoterapia Psicoanalitica

AIPPI = Associazione Italiana di Psicoterapia Psicoanalitica dell'Infanzia, dell'Adolescenza e della Famiglia

CSMH-AMHPPIA = Centro Studi Martha Harris – Associazione Martha Harris di Psicoterapia dell'Infanzia e dell'Adolescenza

EFPP = European Federation for Psychoanalytic Psychotherapy in the Public Sector

IIPG = Istituto Italiano di Psicoanalisi di Gruppo

IPA = International Psychoanalytic Association

SPI = Società Psicoanalitica Italiana

Figures

Foreword

Jeanne Magagna

In 1948, Mrs. Esther Bick was requested by Dr. John Bowlby at the Tavistock Clinic in London to initiate a child psychotherapy training involving a course on the weekly observations of a baby in the context of the family. Now, a group of Italian psychotherapists, psychoanalysts, psychiatrists and clinical psychologists are presenting to the English-speaking audience this very important and innovative study of the development of *internal motherhood*.

Like the gestation and ongoing development of a baby which requires time, the time of development of internal motherhood can not be precisely indicated because every pregnancy has its own pre-history. This most impressive book is not a collection of various contributions on the topic of maternity; rather it is the end result of a long-standing study group working for five years with Dr. Gina Ferrara Mori, a well-known and highly esteemed Florentine training child and adult psychoanalyst who trained as a paediatrician. The study group is composed of individual participants who have worked with mothers-to-be and babies. Its aim is to present the group's reflections to better understand and illustrate the development of internal motherhood. This five-year research project includes different areas such as psychoanalytic work, Pre-Infant Observation approaches like prenatal groups, echographic examinations, and consultations, as well as psycho-analytically informed insights and questioning regarding the nature of internal motherhood.

The study of internal motherhood presented in this book combines two methods of work: the first is Esther Bick's method of baby observation which involves close observation of sequences of interaction, detailed written description of the observation and use of the emotional experience of the observer to lend meaning to the observation itself; the second is psychoanalysis which allows the free associations of the individual to emerge spontaneously from the unconscious without leading questions by the analyst. Using a marriage of these two approaches as a base, a study group emerged to study how a woman moves psychologically from being an individual without a child and develops an identity of being a mother.

In this era, when we have become increasingly aware of the urgency in involving ourselves in preventative mental health measures for babies, this book regarding internal motherhood is essential reading. Through the detailed vignettes accompanied by enriching theoretical concepts derived from Italian, French and English clinicians, we can broaden our capacity to support the development of *internal motherhood* prior to the baby's birth. The depth of understanding portrayed enhances our interest in the enormous psychological transformational process involved in becoming a mother. Reading the various chapters also stimulates an inquiry into the complex impediments to the psychological growth of internal motherhood.

We see that a mother's anxieties and ambivalence during the pregnancy, if not resolved, can lead to further difficulties within the mother-baby relationship during the first year of life. The mother's experience of talking about the experience of becoming a mother seems *in itself* to be an opportunity for emotional growth. For this reason, some psychotherapists have set up groups for mothers and fathers to think about their emotional experience of the pregnancy.

Dr. Gina Ferrara Mori, a significant figure in the field of Infant Observation, has fostered an enriching discussion which potentially sensitizes gynaecologists, nurses, paediatricians, ultrasound technicians and mental health professionals as they work with parents-to-be encountering the announcement of a pregnancy and the ensuing months of pregnancy and childbirth. This point is highlighted when Isabella Lapi and Laura Mori in "The story has already started" (Chapter 1) describe meeting a mother in the latter months of pregnancy. It is clear from their chapter that ongoing observational meetings with the parents much earlier in the pregnancy could offer a more optimal vantage point from which to greet the baby and meet the baby's developmental needs.

Likewise, in Luigia Cresti Scacciati and Laura Mori's "The announcement in pregnancy: annunciation or verdict?" (Chapter 2), psychological aspects of the knowledge of the pregnancy are enhanced through the use of dreams, famous art works depicting "the annunciation" and observational vignettes. This chapter highlights how carrying the pregnancy to full-term involves a psycho-soma containment of both the physical and the emotional aspects concerning the mother-baby relationship accompanied by the mother's unconscious phantasies in relation to her own internalized parents and siblings. "Emotional holding" of the parents-to-be in every medical encounter seems crucial in order that the parents do not experience rage with a cold, impersonal announcement regarding the foetus. Shown in this chapter is how the doctor's empathy and concern in making any announcements regarding aspects of the presence and growth of the baby-in-the-womb can strengthen good parentality or lead to unwarranted persecutory anxieties influencing subsequent capacities to "bear the infant". Creating a narrative about the mother's relationship with the baby in her womb seems an important aspect of developing internal motherhood. Now, we are eagerly awaiting the new study group's findings from their project with Dr. Gina Ferrara Mori examining the process of *internal paternity*. Nowadays, professionals are fully convinced of the partner's effect on the mother's relationship to her "baby-in-the-womb" (Magagna, 2014).

The presence of "twins-in-the-womb" often exerts considerable psychological pressure on the mother's capacity to bear the pregnancy. One of the tasks of the parents is to build within themselves "two distinct spaces" for each of the babies. The process of embarking on the task of mourning the loss of being a couple without the burden of being parents – creating a secure space for each of the children – is painstakingly described in this next chapter (Chapter 3), "The Pre-Infant Observation" by Luigia Cresti Scacciati and Cristina Pratesi. In reading through these various chapters, one becomes aware that "Pre-Infant Observation" involves a most therapeutically useful transformational task involving supporting the mother's thinking functions (Vallino, 2007).

Linda Root Fortini's chapter (Chapter 4), "Listening to future mothers" describes a Florentine public health service project of creating "a thinking space" for 10–15 pregnant mothers who meet weekly in the last few months of their pregnancy with the obstetrician, paediatrician and several mental health staff, such as psychologists and psychotherapists. Here, the author does address how important the mother's relationship to the father is, as well as how important is the development of the mother's capacity to give voice to her anxieties and fears, hopes and wishes for the baby and her capacity to mother. I feel that it is also useful to consider "a group for parents to be" as is described by other Florentine psychotherapists Rossella Coveri and Miriam Monticelli (2009). It seems that the engagement of fathers and the building of "a couple's cradle" for emotional growth can have such an important impact on the mother's capacity to develop her internal motherhood. I see, however, that the presence of fathers in a group might also inhibit a pregnant mother's capacity to put herself into contact with her body "and gradually get closer to the phantasmatical life linked to her past as a girl ... having a mother ... and becoming a mother" (Root Fortini, Chaper 4, p. 52). In the group, the mothers give voice to their conflictual feelings, their fear of pain, their generosity, their wish to control and possess, and their self-absorption which will be interrupted by the birth of the baby. The detailed vignettes movingly describe vividly how each individual mother is able to experience transformation "from being a mother who tells a story ... to a mother who listens ... to a mother who thinks" (Ferrara Mori, 2006). Certainly, reading a book such as this will also initiate such a process, and for this reason, the book, *From Pregnancy to Motherhood: Psychoanalytic aspects of the beginning of the mother–child relationship*, is an invaluable text for "parents-to-be". I want always in this description of the development of internal motherhood to highlight the importance of the father in assisting this transformational process within the mother.

Already emphasized is the importance of each encounter that the mother and father make with the hospital staff. This interaction between "The ultrasound scan and internal processes" (Chapter 5) is aptly illuminated by Luigia Cresti Scacciati. The ultrasound scan is shown to mobilise strong emotions in the mother, as it fulfills the functions of examining the state of the baby in the womb. The phantasies of the mother interact with the ultrasound technology and the presiding doctor and accompanying partner (if present) in a way that can both enhance and detract from a benign internal motherhood. This chapter examines the French clinicians' specialised study and treatment of difficulties in the long journey towards *psychic motherhood,* and Brazilian studies of helping the parents to see the "baby-in-the-womb" at the time of the ultrasound scan and modulate their primitive fears and anxieties.

The fact that biological conception and mental conception do not necessarily coincide is stated by Maria Rosa Ceragioli, Arianna Luperini and Gabriella Smorto (Chapter 6). In "The development of the psychic womb: The weft and the warp", these authors emphasize how all places where the pregnant woman goes to be treated could contemplate how they can develop "a psychic womb" which acknowledges and protects all the processes of internal motherhood and the couple's collaborative parentality. The presence of an unwanted baby is also painfully touched upon in this chapter.

Arianna Luperini (Chapter 7) adds an important dimension to this observational project by highlighting how the psychoanalyst has the task of being ready to listen when "nothing is already known" (p. 91). Examined is the important area of "assisted reproduction" which bypasses some physical and psychological impasses to procreation. Alongside this is the usefulness of psychoanalytic encounters occurring simultaneously during the mother's nine months of pregnancy. Such psychoanalytic encounters allow the pregnant mother to experience being held in the arms of a devoted analyst who supports her psychologically to hold "the baby-in-the-womb".

Marco Mastella (Chapter 8) also invites us to consider the development of internal motherhood, but his is from the perspective of a male psychoanalyst working with a pregnant mother. He suggests that male psychoanalysts respond differently from female psychoanalysts to the mother-to-be's phantasies and anxieties. Mastella also invites us to look into a psychoanalytic encounter in which are present both love and aggressiveness towards oneself and the "baby-in-the-womb" newly sharing the analytic space. The way in which psychoanalysis, concurrent with pregnancy, might impede the transmission of transgenerational depression and trauma is an important focus of Mastella's discussion. This chapter, like other chapters in the book, provides new insights and new viewpoints which substantially augment Joan Raphael-Leff's psychoanalytic understanding described in *Pregnancy* (1993 and 2001).

Fiorella Monti's chapter (Chapter 9) reiterates how a deep transformational process in the parents occurs when the mother becomes pregnant and the baby is born. She beautifully describes how accompanying pregnancy and childbirth are unconscious maternal phantasies which mingle with internalised parents, grandparents, siblings and societal experiences. In undergoing this transformational process, the mother reactivates her childhood relationship to her own internalised mother while at the same time constructing her own maternal capacities. As well as a sense of well-being and fulfilment which are often present in the mother, loneliness, anxiety, inner conflict and fear can accompany this transformational process. This chapter provides poignant vignettes describing aspects of the pregnant mother's emotional and somatic crises requiring attunement by the mother's husband, family, doctors, friends, and her adult self. If such attunement is not possible, the mother's helpful inner dialogue with the baby-in-the-womb can be interrupted. Depression in both mother and baby can follow. On the other hand, pregnancy can represent a new birth for the mother, who can "share-contain-narrate" infantile experiences both in herself and her baby. In this way, a fuller integration of parts of the self and a deeper inner maturity and inner maternity "to hold the baby" can emerge.

Again, as one continues to read the various chapters, there can arise a wish to add more about fathers' roles and needs for consultations with them in relation to the pregnant mother and "the baby-in-the-womb". In particular, when reading Gabriella Smorto's "Having or not having a baby: Internal movements searching for new balances" (Chapter 10), it seems important to emphasize that there is often "a couple" – whether married or unmarried – who have allowed a pregnancy and who influence whether or not the child is permitted to be born. The mother's internal motherhood is significantly influenced not only by her relationships with her internalised parents and siblings but also by the nature of the ongoing relationship she has with her partner, whether it be male or female. The psychosomatic nature of maintaining or aborting a pregnancy is vividly depicted alongside depictions of important and helpful aspects of providing ongoing consultations with women who have unexpectedly become pregnant, and with those who have either miscarried or aborted "the baby-in-the-womb".

Cristina Pratesi in "Being received in consultation" (Chapter 11) describes how an unmourned, miscarried, aborted baby or baby who naturally died can become a shadow on the birth of the new "baby-in-the-womb". She once again stresses the importance of a trained clinician fully accepting the mother's ambivalent emotions and keeping an attitude of nonjudgmental empathic participation as the mother encounters her most truthful feelings in relation to her pregnancy.

The previous chapter provokes the question: "How do we train all the professionals greeting the pregnant mother in various settings?" Isabella Lapi gives one response to this question in "Training childbirth professionals" (Chaper 12). In this chapter, the author describes a work discussion project to assist obstetricians in augmenting their medical capacities. Work discussion group activities using the Bick observational method enable them to fully receive the mother, give emotional significance to both the mother's and the obstetrician's own fears and joys, and acquire a more comprehensive understanding of the development of internal motherhood, both in themselves and in the parents.

CONCLUSION

Other professionals have discussed and researched the topic of maternity, looking at maternal representations and describing and defining the external relationships of the mother-to-be. This book examines these areas, but the aim of the study group's writings is to explore more profoundly the depths of the inner world of the future mother, which consists of her unconscious relationship to herself, her mother, her father, her partner and the future baby.

This entire book embodies a meaningful dialogue within the "observatory" of experienced clinicians working closely with Dr. Gina Ferrara Mori. The fine, detailed observational vignettes and the theoretical conceptualisation of a pregnant mother's encounters with other mothers, her partner, the hospital staff, her psychoanalyst, her internalized parents and siblings and her phantasies provide the reader with possibilities to develop further insight into how we, as professionals and as individuals in the societal psychic womb, can promote the development of a healthy internal motherhood. The ongoing nature of the development of internal motherhood involving rêverie, primary maternal preoccupation, and ongoing developmental aspects of the mother's internal motherhood are later illuminated in Dina Vallino's beautiful final chapter. I consider this impressive book to be essential reading for every mental health clinician and the doctors and nurses working with mothers-to-be and their partners.

REFERENCES

Coveri, R. & Monticelli, M. (2009) "I thought I had to be the one to knock, but it's her who's knocking. ...": an experience of preparation to the birth with a group of fathers and mothers. Unpublished presentation to the Fifth International Conference for Teachers of Infant Observation: Infant Observation in a globalised world. August 2009. London: Tavistock Clinic.

Ferrara Mori, G. (2006) "The interior experience of maternity". In: La Sala G.B., Iori V., Monti F., Fagandini P. (Ed.) *Coming into the World: a Dialogue between Medical and Human Sciences,* pp. 85–102. Berlin: Walter de Gruiter & Co.

Magagna, J. (2014) "Envy, jealousy, love and generosity in sibling relations: the impact of sibling relations on future family relations". In: Beata Maciejewska, Katarzyna Skrzpek, Zuzanna Stadnicka-Dmitriew (Ed.). *Siblings: Envy and Rivalry, Coexistence and Concern.* London: Karnacs.

Raphael, Leff, J. (2001) *Pregnancy. The inside story.* London: Karnac. Originally published in 1993 by Sheldon Press, London.

Vallino, D. (2007) *La crisi della maternità interiorewe il suo riflesso nella consultazione partecipata.* Unpublished paper read during a workshop about "Internal Motherhood". Pisa, June 2007.

Introduction

Gina Ferrara Mori

It is hard to think about the publication of a new book on motherhood: it has been an object of many studies, as well as multi-disciplinary research, scientific and non-scientific publications, various types of books and vast and widespread literature. I believe the book I edited contains a particular research on the psychic processes that accompany a pregnant woman, from the stages of the project-baby to the real motherhood experienced after her baby's birth. This book stands out amongst the vast collection of writings on the theme of pregnancy because:

- it concerns a vision of today's women, in the current socio-cultural context and in the present stage of development of new biotechnologies;
- it is the result of the work of a team that made use of a specific psychoanalytic method to share thoughts;
- it is the result of a research activity and of new experiences that lasted over time (six years) with a well-defined setting and a method that was specifically chosen, and which was part of each team member's background;
- it considers motherhood across a spectrum that is made visible in its various unfolding moments and in its various meeting places.

To provide an idea about what this book illustrates, thus differentiating it from many others, I believe one may maintain that it unveils a motherhood that "flutters its psychic existence", an expression that Dina Vallino (2004, 2005) used so that "being newborn" can be understood.

The research was devised to explore that "maternal atmosphere" that sets in at the time of the pregnancy and that determines new mental events and transformations in the processes of organizing the Self. Such atmosphere may remain hidden or stifled by the investigations of necessary, and at times excessive, medical exams of preventive-health monitoring during the gestation period, while the construction of the future mother-child relationship is taking place. Without arriving to the extremes of the process of "dispossession" and "disembodying" denounced by Barbara Duden (2006) – but still sharing with her the idea that technologies, like language, are much less innocent than one believes – the exploration methodologies and, in particular, ultrasound scans (Chapter 5) to some extent prevent expectant women from "thinking", from putting themselves in contact with the baby in their minds, from listening to their feelings, including the feelings coming from their bodies.

Together with a group of psychoanalysts and psychotherapists[1] with whom I had previous experiences of shared studies and research activities devoted to the observation of a newborn baby, its first developmental stages and child psychotherapies, I reflected at length on the importance of exploring, in depth, the pregnant status and its stages, with a first project aimed at investigating the beginnings of the mother-child relationship.

In the initial stages of our work, we devoted ourselves to the definition of the organizational aspects[2] in order to create a setting that could function as the container of our experiences in the many places where we met and welcomed the mothers-to-be and as an *ensemble* of our narratives, thoughts, information, readings and, as we proceeded, the theoretical inputs and the updates that emerged thanks to the exchange with experts and professionals working with pregnancy.

The chosen methodology was Esther Bick's[3] both because it was part of every participant's background, and because we felt it to be the most suitable to approach the emotional climate and the mental environment of pregnant women in their family contexts. Therefore, we distanced ourselves from questionnaires, structured interviews with various formulations, video-recordings, and drawing-based techniques and research, even though we considered all of these ways to study the mental representations and/or narration models of pregnancy.

Since the very beginning, the group focused on the hypothesis to *extend* the Infant Observation as it had been thought and presented on the occasion of the first national conference that took place in Florence in 1999 in a contribution of mine entitled "*Apprendere dall'osservazione*" (Learning from observation). I had called it Pre-Infant Observation (see Chapter 3), suggesting to start the observation experience at the beginning of the gestation period, during the long internal path towards becoming a mother. There was the strong belief that that was the suitable model to study all the stages of the pregnancy, exploring its changes, thinking of the prenatal nature of the infant and the maternal care as developmental stages of the child and of the mother. The intent was to trace the steps back to the very first constructions of the future mother-child relationships containing forewarning signs of their developments, and to cast light on the original events that had given shape to the project-baby and put in motion the psychic processes of the pregnant status, before observing the identity changes that take place when the new mothers meet their children and during the first year of life, like in the in-depth studies by Cathy Urwin (2007, 2012).

The group members started developing the idea to create a large observatory, suitable to understand the stories that take place in the territory of motherhood. For this reason, the places and the various contexts that were chosen were meant to grant the possibility to be in contact with the gestation experience, to be able to explore, "think" and narrate it.

The Observatory was comprised of:

• the spaces devoted to the interviews preparatory to Infant Observation when the observer and the pregnant woman – in her final stage of pregnancy and in her normal life environment – meet. These interviews clearly showed many aspects of the subjectivity of the ongoing internal experience and some fore-warning signs of the qualities of the future mother-child relationship, high-lighting the idea that "the story had started already" (Chapter 1). The study material and the records of the Infant Observation experiences have already become extremely rich and vast (Vallino, 2005);

• the places and experiences of the Pre-Infant Observations, innovative and full of events illustrating the psychic path of a pregnancy, committing the group to an intense work to understand the observation sessions (Chapter 3);

• the prenatal groups which were part of the activities carried out by some of the members of the group, like the public health workers. These groups facilitated the exchanges of the future mother's subjective experiences, promoted by the fact of being together in an atmosphere of active listening and participation (Chapter 4);

• the psychotherapists' and psychoanalysts' therapy rooms which, when one of their patients plans to have a baby and then continues her therapy during the whole pregnancy and the subsequent stages, were privileged observation places of the internal motherhood and of the mother-child relationship. In these places, the therapist and the patient witness together the transformation of a really "interesting" situation, within a continuous adjustment of the clini-cal work (Chapters 7 and 8).

Over the years of our research study, other places have become observation centres, in relation to where the participants needed to be because of their work in the public health sector or because of their presence in special places like the ultrasound technician room (see Chapter 5) or the consultation rooms (Chapters 6, 10 and 11).

In the space of discussions and reflections on what had been read, observed, and experienced, many stimulating references to material from literature, art and cinema emerged. In the contributions of some of the co-authors, these references emerge with the emotional resonances that went with them. The beautiful image of the *Madonna del Parto* (Madonna of the childbirth) by Piero della Francesca (Figure 1) with its extraordinary pictorial expression of the internal motherhood (Ferrara Mori, 2006) was, for the working group, a source of inspiration and communication of very complex mental activities related to the pregnancy pro-cessing path. The contemplation of this painting representing the annunciation of the forthcoming event – the childbirth – highlights a position of concentrated self-observation in her new identity as a future mother already united to the child inside.

Monique Bydlowski[4] was for us a source of inspiration: she is a psychiatrist and psychoanalyst who, for many years now, has been carrying out in a Paris maternity ward those research and consultation activities documented in many of her writings. The group got in contact with her, and the exchange of opinions that derived from this contact was fruitful and very useful for our research project.

In her book *Je rêve un enfant* (2000), she explains the work model she devel-oped to listen to the mothers-to-be in the consultation room: "It is a question of

Figure 1 "Madonna del Parto" by Piero della Francesca.

listening to these young women and reacting to their words, always giving priority to their psychic reality, to their inner experience, as opposed to the external reality of the pregnancy, so strong in its medical aspects" (p. 113 [Own translation]).

Undoubtedly, the ideas referring to the internal psychic reality and to the complexity of the experiences of the mothers-to-be, illustrated in many sections of the book, contributed to the adoption of the expression *internal motherhood* as a specific reference to the internal experience of that process that develops in the period of pregnancy and that falls into a somato-psychic evolutionary area.

This area appeared to be vast and only in part describable through the mental representations explored by many scholars (Ammaniti, 1995), and since the very first formulation by Freud (1915), considered as categories within the field of the subjective experiences. To these we should indeed add phantasies, dreams, *rêveries*, desires, emotions and complex emerging psychic movements, promoted by that particular psychic functioning of the pregnant woman that Bydlowski

(1997) defined as "psychic transparency", characterized by a decreased level of resistance when faced with the repressed unconscious material, with a marked investment of the personal history and infantile conflicts. Furthermore, the same mental representations are continuously reprocessed and transformed, thus giving shape to a status of psychic life that determines a developing maternal identity, and constantly changing to achieve new balances (Chapter 10).

The internal motherhood, in its innumerable dimensions, is a sort of complete "mapping" that describes and defines the world of the internal relationships of the mother-to-be with herself, her own mother, her partner, and the child-to-be, from the conception to when she feels its full foetal life up to its birth.

The crises of the internal motherhood are part of the mother-child relationship, but if they are determined by painful intra-psychic events and unresolved conflicts, remote emotional tensions may resound in a mirror-like fashion with the story of the child, as Vallino (Addendum) well illustrated in a "participated" consultation experience of a little girl in the presence of both parents.

During the long period of our work, the group went from a study on Pre-Infant Observation to a wide-ranging research on the "maternal constellation", and a few "central ideas" were identified in relation to the emergence of some movements and a few psychic processes specific of the entire gestation, including:

- the *uniqueness of each construction of the internal motherhood*, already identified by innumerable studies of Infant Observation, very much influenced by the family relational dynamics and, among these, the dynamics with the partners;
- the *constant presence of situations of latent crises* that have a specific oscillating characteristic in their emergence and showing themselves in relation to anxiety-producing events, different according to the various stages of the pregnancy, in relation to the announcements coming from the biological monitoring, to particular environmental situations and, at times, depending on the transformations of the unconscious mental representations (Chapters 3 and 9);
- the *manifest need for significant and supportive figures* like one's own mother, the midwife, the gynaecologist, the partner, and the observer (Chapter 4);
- the complex *identification movement* with one's own mother (Chapter 5);
- an *early objectivity* of the baby-to-be in the mind of the mother in relation to the ultrasound scan virtual images with an ensuing induced precociousness-prematurity of the mother-child relationship (Chapter 5);
- the role of *ambivalence* in the project of having or not having a child (Chapters 8 and 10);
- the *transformation function* of the participating observer and the listening activity to the mothers-to-be, from mothers who feel, see, talk, dream, and suffer to mothers who "think" (Chapter 4).

Besides these central ideas, which have become important reference points for those who take care of pregnant women, a relevant consideration concerns the inputs that the group members offered to the pregnant women in an attentive and pleasant atmosphere that had developed in the various places of the Observatory.

It was a question, as a matter of fact, of offering, in the right moments, a containment of the emerging emotional unbalances, times to process the crises, the activation of personal resources to deal with new realities, the mobilising of the competences to give words to the experiences and to develop a sense of inner life and intimacy of great value to create an internal dialogue between the mother and her child, in preparation for the moment of the birth.

These various forms of being present and participating gave meaning to preventive modes, besides having implicitly a psychotherapeutic value, as acknowledged in the reconstructions of the stories collected and told in the context of the work group discussions.

Over the long period of time (five years) devoted to the study of the internal motherhood, with a valid methodological set-up, the group participants acquired not only competences and knowledge but also the sensitivity suitable to accompany a pregnant woman in her path to establish a new maternal identity and to train birth workers (Chapter 12).

There have been many developments and initiatives undertaken by the group members in various areas of motherhood and perinatal period to extend and convey the acquired knowledge, the tested working method and the use of specifically achieved training.

NOTES

1 The group consists of: Gina Ferrara Mori (group organiser and leader, paediatrician and psychoanalyst), Luigia Cresti Scacciati (psychologist, psychotherapist), Maria Rosa Ceragioli (psychologist, psychotherapist), Linda Root Fortini (psychologist, psychotherapist), Isabella Lapi (psychologist, psychotherapist), Arianna Luperini (psychologist, psychoanalyst), Marco Mastella (paediatrician, neuro-psychiatrist, psychoanalyst), Fiorella Monti (psychologist, psychotherapist), Laura Mori (psychologist, psychotherapist), Cristina Pratesi (psychologist, psychotherapist), Gabriella Smorto (psychologist, psychotherapist). The first period of existence of the group also featured the presence of Daniela Martignano, psychologist and psychotherapist, who left, with her premature demise, not only an emptiness in terms of her presence but also of contributions derived from her experiences in the groups for future mothers.

2 We established a schedule of two meetings a month, lasting two hours each, and they were recorded. Taking turns, each member of the group would write a report, which would then be read at the beginning of the following meeting. The collection of recordings and reports, 100 as a whole, are the records documenting the group activity, and it contains a wealth of testimonies and materials on motherhood.

3 According to Esther Bick's method (1964), Infant Observation consists in observing, once a week for an hour, the development of a newborn baby within the family, from the birth until the age of two. Afterwards, the observer writes what was observed, trying to remember as many details as possible. Then the material is read, discussed and processed during seminars in a small group with a specialized leader (psychoanalyst or psychotherapist having a personal experience of the Infant Observation) and the other observers. The method features three main stages: 1) the observation of the baby within its family; 2) the subsequent written reports of the observations; 3) the supervision seminar in the small group, following a sequence that leads the observation from

a phase of annotation to a level of initial inferences, and afterwards to the formation of meaningful concepts in relation to what has been observed in order to reach a dynamic understanding of the interactions. This observation is defined "participated" because the observer has a neutral and participating position at the same time: the observer is the witness of the uniqueness of the situation that is unfolding before his/her eyes and pays attention to his/her own personal experiences. It is the use of the observer's countertransference that offers an effective basis for a direct knowledge of the development, as it helps in grasping the emotional meaning of interactions and behaviour.

4 Monique Bydlowski has been working for many years in a maternity ward and is also the director of a research centre in Paris. She has created a professional figure that she herself defined, paraphrasing the well-known formulation by P.C. Racamier, "psychoanalyst without a couch" (Le Psychanalyste Sans Divan). The expression is due to the fact that such figure is present together with a doctor-obstetrician during the visits of the mothers-to-be in hospital during the pregnancy. "The obstetrician leads the consultation and his/her collaborator (this is how the figure of the psychoanalyst also present is introduced), assists him/her as a witness willing to take in the experience, ready to seize the chance if the mother-to-be offers it, or to stay quiet, to just let the time go by and just be present if nothing comes. Like a Trojan horse, the analyst will exploit the trust the patients place in the medical device, will take advantage of the transference that normally develops to propose an exchange to people who are not asking it *a priori*" (Bydlowski, 2000, p. 133 [own translation]). She also devised a form of psychotherapy having the same length of the pregnancy period itself, aimed at those pregnant women who request it.

REFERENCES

Ammaniti, M. (1992) (Ed.) *La gravidanza tra fantasia e realtà*. Roma: Il Pensiero Scientifico.

Ammaniti, M. (2008) *Pensare per due. Nella mente delle madri*. Bari: Laterza.

Ammaniti, M., Candelori, C., Pola, M., Tambelli, R. (1995) *Maternità e gravidanza. Studio delle rappresentazioni materne*. Milano: Raffaello Cortina.

Bick, E. (1964) "Notes on Infant Observation in Psycho-Analytic Training". In: Harris Williams M. (ed.) *Collected Papers of Martha Harris and Esther Bick*, pp. 240–256. Perthshire, Scotland: The Clunie Press, 1987.

Bydlowski, M. (1997) *La dette de vie: itineraire psychanalytique de la maternité*. Paris: P.U.F.

Cresti Scacciati, L. & Nissim, S. (2007) (Eds.) *Percorsi di crescita: dagli occhi alla mente*. Roma: Borla.

Duden B. (2006) *Il gene in testa, il feto in pancia. Sguardo storico sul corpo delle donne*. Torino: Bollati Boringhieri.

Ferrara Mori, G. (1999) "Apprendere dall'osservazione". In: Cresti, L., Farneti, P., Pratesi, C. (Ed.) (2001) *Osservazione e trasformazione, L'infant observation nella formazione; la prevenzione e la ricerca*, pp. 23–34. Roma: Borla.

Ferrara Mori, G. (2006) "The interior experience of maternity". In: La Sala, G.B.; Fagandini, P., Iori, V., Monti F., Blickstein, I. (Eds.) *Coming into the World: a Dialogue between Medical and Human Sciences,* pp. 85–102. Berlin: Walter de Gruiter & Co.

Freud, S. (1915) 'The Unconscious'. In Strachey, J. (Ed.) (1957/2001). *The Standard Edition of the Complete Psychological Works of Sigmund Freud*, Volume XIV (1914–1916), pp. 159–216. London, Vintage.

Racamier, P.C. (1993) *Le Psychanalyste sans divan. La psychanalyse et les institutions de soins psychiatriques*. Paris: Payot.

Roccato, M. (2003) "Sogni in gravidanza: immagini delle trasformazioni del Sé". In: *Rivista di psicoanalisi*, xlix, 1: 179–201.

Stern, D.N. (1995) *The Motherhood Constellation*. New York: Basic Books.

Urwin, C. (Ed.) (2007) "Editorial. Special issue: Becoming a Mother. Changing Identities: Infant Observation in a Research Project". *International Journal of Infant Observation and its Applications*, X, 3: 231–234.

Urwin C., Sternberg J. (Ed.) (2012) *Infant Observation and Research. Emotional Processes in Everyday Lives*. Hove and New York: Routledge.

Vallino, D. & Macciò, M. (2004, 2006 2ed) *Essere neonati. Osservazioni psicoanalitiche*. Roma: Borla.

Chapter 1

The story has already started

Preliminary meetings in the infant observation

Isabella Lapi and Laura Mori

THE CLASSICAL METHOD AND ITS EXTENSIONS

For Esther Bick, the Infant Observation method consisted in giving "… a unique opportunity to observe the development of an infant more or less from birth, in his home setting and in relation to his immediate family, and thus to discover how these relations emerge and develop" (Bick, 1964, p. 240). Michel Haag (2002) defines Esther Bick's method as holistic, as the observation is extended to the whole family within which the child is born and also beyond, to relatives, friends, animals, all those who spend time with the family in those days. He remembers Bick saying: "It is not just the observation of the baby, because this is simply not possible", thus adding to Winnicott's statement that there can be no baby without a mother.

Bick's interest was focused on understanding and grasping the change of identity of each family member when a new baby arrives, in particular the mother's, and on how the relationship starts from the shocking (we could say "catastrophic", using Bion's term) event of the birth of a child, that represents a true caesura.

As it is well known, the method provides for a preliminary meeting at the beginning of the observation that should take place towards the end of the pregnancy. Before the birth of the child, the observer contacts the family, preferably with the help of a go-between, and sets up a preliminary interview (Falcao, 2002). Bick considered this first interview relevant to defining the contract between the observer and the family, advising to "give a simple explanation to the parents – namely, that the observer wished to have some direct experience of babies as part of his professional development" (Bick, 1964, p. 241). The goal also was to agree on terms and define the setting, convey to the mother the sense of the presence of the observer, an unobtrusive and indeed respectful container, emotionally present but without advancing demands (Magagna, 1991). The preliminary interview offers the chance to gather some initial information that will thus not need to be discussed again in the observation setting. Haag also notes that Bick suggests a first supervision after the prenatal visit or, even better, that the observer be prepared by participating in an observation group even before starting to look for parents-to-be (Haag, 2002).

Among the criteria for the choice of a suitable case for a training observation, Bick advised that birth should not take place too far away from the first meeting. According to her, it was advisable to have just one prenatal visit so as not to set up an observer-parents relationship having too much relevance before the birth, to avoid a maternal transference and the phantasy of an observer/therapist more interested in the mother than the child, and also so that neither the observer nor the group should wait too long (Haag, 2002, p. 243). One of the drawbacks an observer might face is that "the mother may attempt to build up a strong dependence relation" (Bick, 1964, p. 242), which would interfere with the attempt of the observer to remain "detached from what is going on" (p. 241), and to assume a psychoanalytic approach of "fluctuating attention, uniformly suspended".

Therefore, the meeting is considered basically preliminary and preparatory to the actual observation, both for the choice of a suitable family and to lay the foundations of the future relationship. Bick placed a great deal of attention on the effects that the arrival of the child produces in mothers, and she described these effects with great precision and participation. There are mothers who become depressed and regress to a part object relation level, and in these cases they are not able to perform a maternal function. They offer their breast, the feeding-bottle, or their arms, but there is no mother behind them. There are mothers who cannot offer even this, such as in the following case – presented by Michel Haag (2002) – that Bick had defined as distressing.

> During the preliminary interview the mother had told the observer: "I'm gonna buy a chair, a nice chair", and the observer had thought that a baby cannot support himself/herself on a chair. When she went to observe the baby for the first time, the mother immediately handed her the baby, saying: "You are happy to look after him, aren't you?". The mother could not hold him – Bick commented – for this reason, she had thought about a chair. This baby would be put in his cot straight away, even when he was crying; from time to time the mother would go closer and touch him. By simply being touched, he would put himself back together again and the child would calm down and could spend quite a long time in his cot before starting to cry again until when, after a long time, the mother would go back and touch him. … In the rest of the observation, it was possible to observe how, luckily, this child, endowed with a strong vitality, saved himself by developing an adhesive identity. And the mother, to maintain her vitality, went on working and working, without any break. "What happened, Bick commented, is that the mother did put him on that chair!" Haag remembers how Bick showed him a photo in which one could notice the sharp contrast between the magnificent chair the mother had initially bought for the observer, which now could be used by the grown-up child, and the child's anxious stare.

Over the years, as the implementation of the Infant Observation method expanded, the preliminary interview took up a different relevance in the sense of considering it the beginning of the observation and to acknowledge its value in terms of what the future mother-child relationship was going to become. There are two areas in which this new development has become mature: the Infant Observation groups and the implementation of the method for research purposes.

In the early eighties, Gina Ferrara Mori described, in her work with observation groups, a preparatory phase that coincided with the need to wait to find the mothers-to-be and wait for the births of the babies, when the observers' resistances were made explicit and dealt with, along with their doubts, possible obstacles, and when a particular attention was devoted to getting ready for the initial meetings with the mothers. These meetings, recorded in a detailed manner and then read and discussed within the group, immediately revealed to us very interesting materials to understand the uniqueness of each relationship, but also highlighted how intense transference dynamics would strike the observer since the very beginning: "[…] The group begins to be emotionally involved and starts to project massively on the observer. These projections were not easy to recognize and were expressed by an abundance of verbalizations and enactments" (Ferrara Mori, 1981, p. 184 [own translation]).

Thus, the preliminary interviews started being considered an integral part of the observation work also because of the relational circuit that becomes activated in it and which contains aspects that are also predictive of the future relationship with the child (as we will illustrate further on); at times, though, this circuit is so intense that it might jeopardize the possibility itself of the observation.

A few problematic elements present before the first meeting with Lorena had instilled doubts about the possibility of actually starting the observation: the observer is a neighbour of the mother-to-be and she feels "in tune" with her because they both have recently experienced a loss. The preliminary interview confirms these elements: the mother-to-be is dominated by death anxieties, caused by a previous extra-uterine pregnancy but also by the regret of not having been close enough to her son, because of work commitments. The observer feels "affected by the story of the extra uterine pregnancy", she appears clearly involved in the mother's anxieties, and she thinks she has therapeutic expectations towards her and that perhaps she knows about the observer's losses. It seems apparent that in the observer too there is the therapeutic expectation to heal her own losses by taking care of Lorena's. We have therefore a symmetrical picture (perceived and put into words by the observer herself: "I felt we were in the same situation", "after all, she and I have something in common"); the observer even recalls a very peculiar dream she has had (a blue ribbon appears[1] – and that morning she actually sees one on her mother's building entrance door), which makes us suspect about the presence in her of merged or adhesive identification aspects. The situation of being on equal terms that has developed appears manifest even in the fact of sitting on the same sofa one next to the other, so much that the observer, as she herself tells us, must move away a little to be able to see the mother's face. The "sofa" is too little, there is no space for the right distance, and the observer cannot fit. This symmetry, which prevents one from understanding who the observer is and who the mother to be observed is, is clearly very distant from the asymmetry necessary to the therapist/patient relationship and observer/ observed relationship. There are many parameters that make Infant Observation contraindicated in such a situation, and the suggestion is offered to the observer to remain in contact with the mother to talk from time to time but that she should find another family for her Infant Observation.

Also in the eighties, Manuel Pérez-Sànchez recognizes the importance of the pre-liminary interview. Even if he restates that the first interview with the parents is aimed at getting to know each other and to decide whether the observation will take place, in a note he maintains that: "If the interview takes place before the delivery, we may find a reservoir of data on anxieties and expectations during the pregnancy, data which may turn out to be useful to understand specific conducts during the upbringing" (1982, p. 18 [own translation]).

The accrued importance attributed to this "observed [material]" before the birth enabled our current Infant Observation groups to always discuss the first meeting between the observer and the mother-to-be very carefully and with inter-est, because it allows sensing already a *maternal atmosphere* rich with many emotions, the immediate and complex game between the mother's projections onto the observer and the strong emotional involvement in dealing with this new experience.

In parallel to the development of training through the observation prac-tice, the extension of the method for research purposes has started to show an interest in life before birth, with a blossoming of studies that have shown the impor-tance of the psychological and relational continuity between before and after the birth.

Alessandra Piontelli for instance, conducted (1987, 1992) "trans-natal" obser-vations extending the Infant Observation to the prenatal life with the help of ultrasound techniques. They were observations of the foetal behaviour, month by month, starting from the fourth, and after observations of the newborn baby, using the classical methodology. The main conclusion of this study was *the striking behavioural continuity* between before and after the birth. This reminds us of Sigmund Freud's famous statement: "There is much more continuity between intra-uterine life and earliest infancy than the impressive caesura of the act of birth would have us believe" (Freud, 1926, p. 138). The accent in this pioneering research seems to be mostly on the child.

Some other research focused more specifically on the mother using extensions and/or implementations of Esther Bick's classical method. We will refer to two research projects carried out in Italy in the eighties.

At the Obstetrics and Gynaecology University Clinic in Turin, Livia Di Cagno's team (1984) decided to study, using a psychodynamic approach, the mother's unconscious phantasies in the last months of pregnancy and the way in which the initial stages of the relationship between mother and child developed. In addition, an in-depth research into the beginning of mental functioning was carried out (formation of the Self and first hints of Ego activity of the newborn baby). The research, which was very interesting and innovative in regard to the methodology plan, required the spontaneous collaboration of a sample of 16 first-time mothers-to-be, contacted on the occasion of their participation to a psycho-physical ante-natal course in view of the delivery. The tools used were the free interview, the technique of empathic listening, and the daily observation (lasting one hour, start-ing from the first day after the birth until discharge, at the moment of feeding). Three interviews were provided for (the first at the eighth month, the second after a fortnight, and the third three days after the delivery), close in time to foster the emergence of a transference bond and of deep themes, the possibility to project, reveal and possibly process anxieties, even the most intense ones. The observation was carried out by a different person from the one who did the interviews, to foster a different attitude in the mother. During the interview, a narcissistic concentra-tion was encouraged in the mother regarding her emotions and feelings, while the observation was focused on the relationship between mother and child.

The research confirmed the typical unconscious phantasies and the ambiva-lence of maternal experiences during pregnancy and when childbirth approaches and the way in which these elements are important in establishing a relationship with the child in his/her first days of life. The presence or absence of anticipa-tory phantasies, the intensity of anxieties, and the characteristics of related defences – the different personalities and different couple-family relationships – would become dynamically intertwined with the experience of childbirth and the newborn's characteristics. These are the final considerations of the research: the poor predictive nature of a single anamnestic note, whether positive or negative in relation to the babies' vitality; the availability and readiness to communicate; the attraction for the maternal breast and the tolerance of frustration; the precise correspondence between the content of maternal anticipatory phantasies and the elements on which the mother's perception focuses in relation to the sum of the activities and the baby's characteristics; the cyclical trend of relational patterns in the context of each observation; and the progressive evolution of the entire period under consideration.

At the University College of Literature and Philosophy in Turin, Carla Gallo Barbisio undertook a study project on the mother-child relationship, for which three typical situations had been chosen: one observation on pregnancy and the first week of life of the child, one on the first year of life, and the last one during the third year of life.

The chapter *Osservazione della madre durante i mesi della gravidanza e la prima settimana di vita del bambino (Observation of the mother during the months of pregnancy and the first week of life of the child)* by Susanna Mazzetti (1993) shows an observation experience conducted during the pregnancy. One reads about a young mother, rather ambivalent towards her pregnancy and filled with anxieties, which are clearly discernible during the preliminary meeting, the story of which definitely ends up becoming a sort of first observation. The mother welcomes the observer with a depressed expression and immediately tells her about the first two months, which she experienced in a traumatic way. The obser-vations after the birth confirmed this initial anxious state, and the baby became the new container for her maternal anxieties. Mazzetti's work was read with a great deal of interest and widely discussed within the Observatory group, which lingered in particular on the role of the young observer [female], commenting on her identification with the mother, that at times transformed her into blotting paper for the intense emotions that filled the space, reducing the emotional burden, and also a container that fostered the mother's capacity to convey her fears and guilt and allowed her to talk about her dreams.

INTERNAL MOTHERHOOD IN THE PRELIMINARY INTERVIEWS

Our study group has performed a retrospective investigation which highlighted, during the preliminary interviews, privileged aspects for *the observation of the internal motherhood.* During these first meetings, one may notice the quality of the anxieties when the time of childbirth approaches and many forewarning signs of the mother-child relationship, and of the mother-child-observer relationship, which is established later on.

As a matter of fact, the preliminary interviews normally take place shortly before the birth, when the caesura represented by the childbirth and the encounter with the real baby are drawing nearer, and it is possible to grasp a particular state of the internal motherhood dominated by the anxieties of the last quarter of pregnancy and by the fear of giving birth. During the pregnancy, a psychic path develops, featuring different stages, each of them with specific psychological tasks, anxieties, and somatic expressions.

Raquel Soifer (1973) identifies various moments to which particular types of anxieties and physical symptoms can be associated: the beginning of the gestation, during which the anxiety derives from the doubts about the reality of conception and one's own capacities to change and to be able to take care of a child; the stage of the implantation of the embryo, which is unconsciously perceived and triggers persecutory experiences; the perception of the foetal movements with phantasies of an aggressive and dangerous foetus or malformations of the foetus and ensuing Oedipal guilt; the perception of the internal movements of the foetus with anxieties of loss, of being emptied out; the fear of a premature delivery as an anticipation of the feared separation, which becomes transformed into somatic manifestations (such as collapses, cramps, etc.). In the final stage of pregnancy, the fear of giving birth emerges: a difficult separation both from a psychic and a physical point of view. The feeling of loss and separation is combined with the fear of dying in childbirth or that the child might die whilst being born. The death anxieties rotate around dangerous phantasies: of damaging the baby, or about a dangerous child who might cause damage.

Other studies as well confirm these anxieties, which become more intense as the delivery approaches; in particular, Fornari (1981) draws a distinction between *separation anxiety*, with castration and death phantasies, and *genetic anxiety*, related to the child's health. The latter can be referred to as the typical anxiety of every creative process and lays on the recognition of the foetus as a whole object;

while separation anxiety appears to be linked to a foetus that is still perceived as a part object.

The alternating of joyful phantasies and agonizing phantasies in regard to possible damage to oneself and the baby-to-be increases the maternal ambivalence and makes the mother particularly in need of support.

> Simona has recently come back to Italy after a period spent abroad and she welcomes the observer [female] with clear signs of ambivalence: she forgets about the appointment, she leaves her alone in the sitting room and does not offer her to take a seat, she talks to her with reticence and uneasiness. It is indeed ambivalence which dominates her experiences towards motherhood, and the child-to-be and the arrival of the observer seem to have made manifest the fact that the birth is drawing nearer, a dangerous and difficult event to think about. Depressive and persecutory feelings prevail: she says she has not chosen a name yet "to ward off ill-luck", and referring to the baby, she states that "until the very last moment you don't know whether he's going to be normal"; she talks at length about hospitals and says that medical care is better abroad. These feelings have probably characterized all her pregnancy but they now betray the existence of an underlying unconscious phantasy of damage coming from the child, and perhaps from herself as well.

In the last stage of pregnancy, "the psychological task of a mother-to-be is to get ready to separate from the child inside her and giving up aspects of the infantile Self" (Roccato, 2002 [own translation]), a process that might be painful in and of itself and provoke intense depressive feelings.

> Adele, whom the observer [female] meets one week before the birth, tells her about her anxiety "that is growing": Adele is a doctor who works with seriously ill children, and her anxiety is now becoming focused on the health of her future child "because I've seen children who were born in perfect health and then …". She adds she feels very "swollen" and she has difficulties breathing. After the birth, there will be no one helping her because her own mother died two years ago and her elderly father lives far away: she will only be able to count "on a few friends and a little on my mother-in-law". Adele is "swollen" also because of her thoughts and emotions about motherhood, that as the birth draws nearer, become heavier and heavier and they swell her mind; she is very much in contact with her emotions though and she is able to express them without rigid defences or ambivalence. She welcomes the observer nicely and seeks her containment. The observer senses her loneliness and her need, now that she is about to become a mother herself, to still have her own mother close to her.

In other situations, the imminent encounter with the real baby stirs up another type of anxiety: the anxiety of the stranger, a different self who has an independent life, whom the mother does not know, and she does not know whether she will be loved by the baby. To counteract these negative experiences, a creative thought emerges: the desire for a child who, defensively, is imagined as grown-up already and born without having been delivered.

> Raffaella, a young and elegant lady, with an important profession she cares a lot for, is pregnant for the first time and the preliminary interview before the observations takes place when her pregnancy time is ending. She declares she is "more than willing at the moment to do the observation"; she does not know though how she will be organized in the future: "The child is not here yet and I have no idea how my life will be organized with a child …". She immediately adds that "it's clear that at the beginning one is more open …" and that she intends to go back to work straight away. The baby's room is ready and her name has been chosen already ("a simple name"). She does not talk about her pregnancy or the delivery; on the contrary, she feels she "is afraid of finding herself with a complete stranger to be known … at the beginning all new things are frightening, then one gets used to them and one discovers they're simple …". She resumes talking about the bedroom, and she wonders whether her little baby girl will like it or "whether in the future she might say no, I don't like it". Raffaella alternates between accepting and refusing her new role as a mother. She hides her anxieties behind the organizational factors and simplifications, her anxieties. She defensively uses her attachment to her job, perhaps to escape a more intimate contact with the baby. The delivery, the pregnancy and her bodily experiences are not mentioned, they are kept out of sight; while Raffaella shows that at the moment, her main anxiety is: the anxiety of the stranger. The real baby who is about to be born and who will need her is also that baby who is about to enter her life preventing her from being well organized, the stranger who, imagined as being grown up already, might be able to criticise her choices, perhaps hinder her professional independence.

There is not always an internal space for the child in the mind of the mother-to-be.

> Rebecca is a young, foreign mother who has an alternative lifestyle and works in the rehabilitation field. During the first meeting with the observer [female], she appears very self-confident and in control of all the practical details, competent, with a strong need for having many others around: her husband, her obstetrician sister, another Italian obstetrician, the gynaecologist, the observer. On the other hand, no references are made to the child who is about to be born, neither phantasies nor expressions of desire or intimate emotions: Rebecca has not asked about the gender, neither does she mention whether she has thought about names; she has not prepared her home. There is only, in a corner of the master bedroom, a little cot, which looks more like a toy for dolls rather than a real cot for a real baby. Rebecca keeps away from her internal motherhood: she recalls how she kept on dancing until the seventh month and now she is attending "an accelerated ante-natal course"; but she is not getting ready

for the birth and her child has not got a space in her mind as yet ("I've had the chance to thoroughly witness the development of a friend's child but I've forgotten everything now", she tells the observer), or in her life with her partner ("this home is little, it's fine for two but perhaps not for three"). Rebecca seems to be locked inside a narcissistic state that prevents her from getting in touch with her internal part, and it could hinder the contact with the newborn baby as well. Only when she hints at her own mother, who lives abroad and who "will come only if there's a real need", there is a moment of silence, she is taken up in her thoughts, a shadow that allows catching a glimpse of an emotional need. At the end of the interview she asks the observer information about her job, and the observer tells her about the supervision group: "I don't know why exactly but I find myself talking about the consultations with children suffering from alopecia".

A RETROSPECTIVE READING

Analysing the preliminary meetings retrospectively from the point of view of *internal motherhood* allowed us to fully grasp how they contain, in a nutshell, elements that later on will characterize the development of the mother-child relationship and the mother-child-observer relationship. This retrospective viewpoint highlights the connection between the setting up of the internal motherhood *before the birth* and of the maternal and parental relationship with the real child *after the birth*, and in this sense the preliminary interviews contain forewarning aspects of the future relationships.

The discussion and the reflection carried out in the group on the preliminary interviews allow the construction of interpretative hypotheses, of "imaginative thinking" (Cresti, Pratesi, 2002) on the maternal experiences and the possible development of the mother-child relationship.

We would like to quote, to exemplify these hypotheses, a few short reports on the development of the relationships between the mothers, of whom we summarised the preliminary interviews with the observer [female] and their children, also showing the way in which the relationship with the observer becomes established in parallel with transference connotations.

Raffaella, who in the preliminary interview with the observer defensively does not mention childbirth and fantasizes of an already grown up and independent girl, accepts the beginning of the observation only a few weeks after the birth of her daughter, Maria, thus preventing the observing eyes from witnessing the moment of birth. Not even upon request of the observer does she manage to express her emotional experience, and she will minimize the experience of giving birth by saying "it was a beautiful experience". As announced, she goes back to work very early and she does not breastfeed her child. In the relationship with her child she will greatly enhance every single achievement of independence and Maria will grow up developing both language ability and motor coordination very early: a muscular second skin that will give her that containment, which, left by the mother to be looked after by an affective although fragile and anxious grandmother, at times she will not get. The fulfilment of independence, the quick growth and the muscularity will also characterize the child's further development: during a meeting with the observer, when Maria is just four years old, the grandmother will proudly inform her that "Maria has already won a gymnastics competition!".

Only after giving birth, the husband of Simona, a young mother dominated by damage anxieties, reveals to the observer that the mother had had an abortion years before, which she had experienced traumatically and without receiving the help she would have needed at an emotional level. Simona's need of support, already perceived in the preliminary interview, becomes even stronger after the little girl's birth, which takes place before the expected time, against the mother's wish to defer the moment of delivery and have more time to feel ready. Simona has difficulties offering a suitable emotional contact and a good *handling* of the baby, who will soon show that she does not really enjoy being held in her mother's arms, preferring a little mattress. Serena will have difficulties growing up and eating.

The anxieties connected to the theme of separation and the feelings of loneliness and pain that go with it, perceived by the observer in the preliminary meeting, characterize the relationship with little Pietro and reach their peak when, about eight months after his birth, Adele must decide about going back to work. Adele goes through a seriously difficult moment of deep sadness and uncertainty on what to do, but her capacity of contact with herself and of self-awareness helps her solve the need for care for the child and the need of support and tranquillity for herself. She changes her job, so to no longer be in contact with seriously ill children, which caused her an unbearable anxiety, and she chooses as a baby sitter for her child a mature woman, who has grown-up children, and who will be a vice-mother for her.

These brief examples illustrate how the observation approach helps us understand the connection between very early signs having a possible forewarning value and the subsequent evolution both of the child-parents relationship and the child himself/herself. The possibility to carry out this "*path forward, aimed at imagining the future* and making forecasts about it", that helps us grasp the existing *continuity* between the early stages of the mother-child encounter and between the pre- and post-natal life of the child, is according to us made possible by an analysis of these first meetings in view of the concept, of a genuinely psychoanalytic origin, of *posteriority or*, in the French expression introduced by Jacques Lacan, *après-coup*. As it is well known, this expression was used by Freud as well in his conceptualization of the psychic temporality and causality to explain how every psychic experience is reprocessed at a later stage in relation to new experiences or to access a further stage of development (thus reconciling the apparently conflicting dichotomy between the linear and genetic time of consciousness and the story and the timelessness of the unconscious). More specifically, with this concept, one refers to the fact that new experiences allow reprocessing what initially had not found a place in a meaningful context (for instance, a traumatizing event). This *a posteriori* processing is stimulated by new events or by the acquisition of a new level of maturity. It is not just a deferred action, of a cause that remains latent until it has the occasion to manifest itself, but of a retroactive causal action, from the present towards the past (Baranger, 1969). Therefore, it is an attempt to give a retrospective meaning that can illuminate the understanding of the subsequent story, helping to grasp more deeply and further on in time the aspects of uniqueness of every mother-child relationship, avoiding a too mechanistic reading of events. Such an *a posteriori* reading also allows us to fully use, and rightfully so, not just the "specular resonance"[2] of the observation group discussions, but also all the other non-verbal and counter-transference aspects experienced by the observer and the group participants – especially when such aspects and experiences are very intense:

> In the preliminary interview with Rebecca, a few days before the birth of a boy, Marco, the prevailing theme appeared to be that of a difficult contact with the emotions and the external world. In the continuation of the observation, for a long time Rebecca did not have contact with the child: she does not call the observer after the birth, in the first few observations she does not show the observer the child ("because he's sleeping") but she shows her photos and a thick book on child development. For her, Marco seems to be more a child to be trained rather than cared for by being close to him, and the child soon started having skin problems, suffering because his bottom was always red, and then a serious dermatitis which also required the child to be hospitalized: the problem of contact – perceived at a counter-transference level by the observer during the preliminary meeting when she found herself talking about alopecia! – becomes so somatically concrete.

The viewpoint of *internal motherhood* in the *après-coup* also allowed for a deeper understanding of some preliminary interviews, giving them a new meaning and allowing for a clearer interpretation of what happened in the subsequent observations. An example of this is the preliminary meeting with a mother who the observer [female] perceived as fragile and asking for help and support, while the discussion inside the observatory group highlighted the woman's narcissistic and omnipotent aspects – aspects that probably led to the interruption of the observation.

> The preliminary interview with Tiziana can take place only after a series of telephone calls, of minor misunderstandings and difficulties, such as finding the way to her house. The interview itself takes place in a confused and complicated scenario that almost makes one lose sight of who the protagonists and the aims are: the observer is welcomed *too* warmly and only afterwards

she understands she has been mistaken for someone else; the mother cannot find a place (and not even the chairs!) to sit down and talk to the observer, and for this reason the observer is forced to take the initiative. Tiziana talks a lot about her study and work experiences (she underlines the fact she holds a university degree and works for a student service) and her friendships, but the pregnancy remains in the shadows, and the observer only later notices the big belly hidden under a large shirt. The mother-to-be, already at the last month of pregnancy, talks endlessly of external facts and events but she does not communicate anything about her emotions and phantasies about her future baby, or about her expectations and the couple's plans. She seems engrossed in a cloud of external facts without a solid internal identity. Even the story, just hinted at, of her own birth (she was born after a painful delivery from a mother who always reproached her for making her suffer) is not a way, albeit displaced and defended, to communicate her own fear but rather a regression to a child Self as the daughter of an incapable mother, with whom it is impossible to identify. In the same way, the theme of the mourning for the belly is only hinted at in a slightly bizarre way: "It'll be funny to find oneself without a big belly … the women who came back to the course after giving birth without a belly were funny". The Infant Observation group that discussed this interview for the first time interpreted Tiziana's behaviour as a defence against the anxiety of the imminent motherhood, reading into her confusion a strong need for orientation and support, and an indirect request for help. From the observation notes: "We wonder what pushed the woman to accept the observation and we think it is her emotional need. The whole interview seems very much characterized by Tiziana's strong emotionality that she tries to keep at a distance by using words. The access to feeling oneself is hard and, just like we feel her emotionality, we also see her adhesive nature – the primitive defence of sticking because of the difficulty of making contact with feelings: goodbyes must be repeated five times, as if Tiziana could not bring the meeting to an end and separate from the observer". With today's eyes, being trained to grasp more in depth the internal motherhood, the observatory group did not find in the mother such a manifest need for support and a request for help: on the contrary, she presents herself as someone who knows everything (she has a university degree, she helps students, she knows about child development, she has many friends), while it is the observer who needs her to observe and learn. The adhesive approach seems determined by identity confusion, which is projected onto the observer, making everything confused, from the very first telephone call, to finding the house and the interview itself, thus inducing difficulties in understanding. A more pathological situation than had originally been perceived in the first discussion now seems to appear, which makes us fear for the development of the relationship with the baby girl about to be born. Unfortunately, what then happened confirms such worry: the baby is born after a difficult delivery and she is kept in hospital; Tiziana is openly anxious and is afraid to go home "because it's too cold for my breast". Once they are back home, the observations become more and more complicated: the baby cries a lot, she develops somatic conditions, she is more and more subtracted from the observer's eyes. Bizarre aspects and projective identifications multiply, also supported by the dominating figure of the husband: at the end, the observer is dismissed.

Working on the preliminary meetings – when the story has already begun – showed us the value that carrying out an observation from the beginning of the pregnancy might have: the value in terms of knowledge of the psychic movements that led to conception, internal vicissitudes of waiting, of being born and the establishment of a specific, unique, internal motherhood; the training value for the observer, who would find himself/herself having a new viewpoint from which to observe; the preventive value of offering the future mother a new opportunity to contain anxiety in relation to the crises of motherhood.

This led us, as indicated in the story of the observatory and as will be explained in more detail in Chapter 3, to extend Esther Bick's method of planning a Pre-Infant Observation. Ferrara Mori presents this way, at the 5th International Congress on Infant Observation (Ferrara Mori, 2002), the work initiated by the observatory:

> Mostly we would like to continue our dialogue with Esther Bick: it is a dialogue that rereads her writings and all the testimonies of her work with the observers, rethinking her central ideas and how today, after many experiences, we try to reflect on all of this. In relation to our Pre-Infant Observation project we reread and reflected on a reply that Esther Bick gave an observer (Haag, 1984) who intended to begin an Infant Observation: "Talking in general of the prenatal visit, is it just one meeting or more than one?". Her reply was: "No, no, no way, because we do not want to set up something just with the mother without the baby, we do not want to be the mother's therapist [...]". But if Bick did not intend to set up a form of therapy with the mother and we also share this view, she always believed in the support and the therapeutic contribution of the function of observation on behalf of a participating observer [...]. During an Infant Observation there is implicit but not explicit support, inherent in the method, it is not sought after or managed by the observer [...]. We are aware of the interest for the Infant Observation, as proposed by Esther Bick, which has grown, becoming research and knowledge, with developments and various types of applications which she could not have foreseen. Her "no, no ..." is definitely a warning we take in great account not to fall into a therapeutic position when observing a mother with her difficulties with her baby, and also a mother-to-be in relation to her baby inside.

NOTES

1 In Italy, when a baby is born, either a blue or pink ribbon is hung on the door of the house where the family lives [translator's note].

2 Proto-mental identifying phenomenon (Vallino, 1992) that takes place in the Infant Observation discussion groups.

REFERENCES

Baranger, M. (1969) "Regresión y temporalidad en el tratamiento analítico". In: *Revista de Psicoanálisis*, 26.
Bick, E. (1964) "Notes on Infant Observation in Psycho-Analytic Training". In: *Collected Papers of Martha Harris and Esther Bick*, edited by Meg Harris Williams. The Clunie Press, Perthshire, Scotland, 1987.
Cresti Scacciati, L. & Pratesi, C. "The use of Infant Observation as a beacon throwing light upon the future and the past". In: *Creating bonds. Proceedings of the VI Infant Observation International Congress Cracow*, 2002.
Di Cagno, L., et al. (1981) "L'osservazione dell'interazione madre-bambino nel primo anno di vita: presentazione di una esperienza, riflessioni e testimonianze". In: *Quaderni di psicoterapia infantile*, 4: 137–147.
Di Cagno, L. (1984) *Il neonato e il suo mondo relazionale*, Roma, Borla.
Falcao, L. (2002) "Esther Bick et l'observation du bébé", speech held at the VI Infant Observation International Congress following Esther Bick's method, Cracow, 2002. Unpublished.
Ferrara Mori, G., et al. (1981) "L'osservazione dell'interazione madre-bambino nel primo anno di vita: presentazione di una esperienza, riflessioni e testimonianze". In: *Quaderni di psicoterapia infantile*, 4: 179–200.
Ferrara Mori, G. (2002) "Pre-Infant Observation: una estensione della metodologia di Esther Bick", speech held at the VI Infant Observation International Congress following Esther Bick's method, Cracow, 2002. Unpublished.
Fornari, F. (1981) *Il codice vivente. Femminilità e maternità nei sogni delle madri in gravidanza*. Torino: Bollati Boringhieri.
Freud, S. (1926) 'Inhibitions, Symptoms and Anxiety'. In Strachey, J (Ed.) (1959/2001). *The Standard Edition of the Complete Psychological Works of Sigmund Freud: An Autobiographical Study, Inhibitions, Symptoms and Anxiety, The Question of Lay Analysis and Other Works*, Volume XX (1925–1926), pp. 87–170. London, Vintage.
Gallo Barbisio, C. (1993) (Ed.) *L'aggressività materna*. Torino Bollati Boringhieri.
Haag, M. (1984) *A propos des premières applications françaises de l'observation régulierè et prolongée d'un bébé dans sa famille selon la méthode d'Esther Bick: des surprises profitables*. Paris: self-published.
Haag, M. (2002) *Le méthode d'Esther Bick pour l'observation régulière et prolongèe du tout–petit au sein de sa famille*. Paris: self-published.
Magagna, J. (1991) "Tre anni di osservazione di un bambino con Ester Bick". In: *Contrappunto*, 9: 3–32.
Mazzetti, S. (1993) "Osservazione della madre durante i primi mesi della gravidanza e la prima settimana di vita con il bambino". In Gallo Barbisio, C. (Ed.) (1993) *L'aggressività materna*, pp. 65–86. Bollati Boringhieri, Torino.
Pérez-Sànchez, M. (1982) *Primi passi nello sviluppo emotivo*. Roma: Borla.
Piontelli, A. (1987) "Infant Observation from before birth". In: *International journal of psycho–analysis*, 68: 453–463.

Piontelli, A. (1992) "Dal punto vista del feto. Brevi appunti su uno studio osservativo della gravidanza e del periodo post–natale". In Ammaniti, M. (Ed.), *La gravidanza tra fantasia e realtà.* Roma: Il Pensiero Scientifico, pp. 109–120.

Roccato, M. (2003) "Sogni in gravidanza: immagini delle trasformazioni del Sé". In: *Rivista di psicoanalisi*, XLIX, 1: 179–201.

Soifer, R. (1973) *Psicología del embarazo, parto y puerperio.* Argentina: Ediciones Kargieman.

Vallino, D. (1992) Atmosfera emotive e affetti. In: *Rivista di Psicoanalisi*, XXXVIII, 3, 617–637

Chapter 2

The announcement in pregnancy

Annunciation or verdict?

Luigia Cresti Scacciati and Laura Mori

The theme of the *announcement* of pregnancy and/or *in* pregnancy indicates meta-phorically our intent to divulge the work carried out by the group Observatory of internal motherhood. In the "words that announce"[1], there exists a concentrated entanglement of contrasting and even paradoxical meanings corresponding to the complexity of the psychic path of the whole pregnancy. The paradox lies in the fact that the certainty of what is announced goes hand in hand with the uncertainty of the effects the announcement will produce. Thus "announcing" implies tolerating the unpredictable future of the meanings that it will take up in the life of the individual.

All the pregnancy process is strewn with a multiplicity of announcements (given *to* the woman or *by* the woman), capable of generating or expressing different emotional reactions, phantasies and expectations:

- the *signs-announcements* arriving to the woman by her changing body – externally and internally – and by the implantation and growth of the child-to-be (amenorrhoea, breast engorgement, changes in tastes, nausea, first movements of the foetus, etc.);
- the announcements deriving from medical investigations – first of all, the pregnancy test, ultrasound exams, genetic tests, gynaecological and obstetrical visits, etc. – that become responses bearing a verdict[2] – "Am I pregnant or not?", "Will it be a boy or a girl?", "Will it be healthy or not?", "Will it be one or twins?" – and that at times might lead to making difficult decisions, even dramatic ones;
- the announcements that during the gestation the mother-to-be delivers to her relatives, friends, acquaintances, colleagues, etc.

Various authors highlighted the importance of the moment of the announcement and its specificity in relation to the construction path of the internal motherhood. Massimo Ammaniti, investigating the woman and her partner's emotions at the news of the pregnancy, underlines how this "event [...] that makes the woman aware of another life inside her, represents a specific emotional connotation concerning the acceptance/non-acceptance of her own motherhood. When pregnancy is ascertained, it becomes a reality to cope with, both internally and externally" (Ammaniti *et al.*, 1995, p. 16 [own translation]).

It is certain that the announcement in pregnancy implies a strong emotional impact, the triggering of deep phantasies and feelings, at times conflicting, and therefore it has a possible traumatic implication which will require a time – and a space – to be worked through. This strong emotional impact is widely represented by the artistic iconography, which over the centuries reproduced the theme of the Annunciation with many different and subtle facets.

The religious texts, from which artistic iconography derives its themes, deal with the announcement of pregnancy in innumerable excerpts. It happens according to an almost fixed pattern in which, before arriving to the full acceptance by the individual receiving the announcement, various contrasting stages take place (emotional upset, fear, doubt). The biblical texts (*Genesis, Judges, Samuel*) describe the emotional reaction – mostly agitation and fear – at the announcement, both of female (Sarah, Agar) and male characters (Abraham, David, Joachim). The Gospels, though – in particular St. Luke's – mainly deal more in detail with the woman's emotional responses: *Luke*, indeed, shows us the following mental states of the internal path through which the Virgin goes, from a first stage of *conturbatio* when faced with the announcement, to *cogitatio*, then *interrogatio*, to then achieve – through *humiliatio – meritum*, the final phase of the deep and aware acceptance[3].

The latter emotional condition is beautifully portrayed by Beato Angelico in his *Annunciazione* [Figure 2.1], painted between 1433 and 1434, and currently at the *Museo diocesano* in Cortona, Italy. In this scene, the angel Gabriel expresses the great mystery to the woman that God chose: in a large and elegant Renaissance arcade, a proper dialogue takes place between the angel, whose active presence is underlined, and Maria, slightly leaning forward, as if about to stand up, her face lighted up by an internal life, her eyes showing the adaptation but also the understanding of the mystery of her conception (cf. Feuillet, 1994). The awareness of the woman's changed life and of the new responsibility after receiving the announcement of conception is marvellously expressed in the *Annunciata* [Figure 2.2], painted in 1474 by Antonello da Messina, a painting that departs from the traditional patterns of the iconography to leave the whole scene to Mary. "What happens is illustrated using facial expressions and the hands. There is no visible trace of God's messenger, but intense is the perception of something extraordinary that is taking place while we observe. The absence is an acute presence, detectable, convincing despite its mystery. Hands and eyes talk: they are replying to Gabriel decreeing the alliance with God, the 'yes' to generating Christ" (Santambrogio, 2007, p. 42 [own translation]).

The atmosphere is very different in the elegant triptych of the *Annunciazione* [Figure 2.3] by Simone Martini (1333), currently at the Uffizi Museum in Florence. On a shining, golden background, the two figures of the angel and the Virgin face each other: the angel seems to have just landed and is leaning toward Mary, gracefully offering her a branch. Mary appears to pull back and with demureness fold in herself, her body almost torn between her pelvis and legs, her shy look, ashamed[4] and lowered, as to emphasize her surprise and the subtle fear, her right hand to her neck to clasp the fastener of her long, dark cape, the other hand buried in the prayers' book to keep it half-open at the page when her reading had been interrupted by the surprising and turbulent arrival of the angel.

Figure 2.1 "Cortona Annunciation" by Beato Angelico (the central panel).

Figure 2.2 "Virgin Annunciate" by Antonello da Messina.

Figure 2.3 "The Annunciation and Two Saints" by Simone Martini (detail of the central panel).

We believe that the various narrative scenes we mentioned successfully express the ambivalence that, to a various extent, characterizes the whole pregnancy process. The etymological ambiguity of the word "*incinta*"[5] (pregnant), that may both mean "inside an enclosure" and "devoid of belt", shows it.

The various "characters" present in the iconography of the Annunciation – Mary, the archangel Gabriel, the dove representing the Holy Spirit, God Father – may illustrate each time different qualities and moments of the woman's experience and therefore be considered – as Ferro states (1992, p. 26) about the characters of the analytic dialogue – metaphors that allow for "opening of meanings" and narratives in various directions, able to combine different levels of meaning, referring to both the internal and external world of the mother-to-be. The angel, as an "outsider", or the "third", could recall the figure of the gynaecologist, the doctor performing the ultrasound scan, the observer – or symbolize different parts and aspects of the mother herself towards the changes in her body and her status; the Holy Spirit probably alludes to the generating function of the father/partner; other recurring iconographic elements, such as the flower vase or the lilies might refer to other symbolic values. As for the spatial arrangement of the characters, there are some recurring architectural elements: among them, the columns, separating the angel and Mary, almost seem to act as metaphors for the "mental space" the woman needs to cope with her status change.

The group reflection focussed at length on the manifold and contrasting implications that the announcement of pregnancy might contain. We wish to propose some of these aspects, linked to the complex emotional mobilization triggered by the announcement that attracted our attention in a particular way. They are wonderfully illustrated in the following literary excerpt:

> The test was era unequivocal, I was pregnant. I voiced that sentence without believing it too much. With shaking hands, I observed the result, immobile, astonished. For an instant I did not do a thing, I wanted to take advantage of my last moment of loneliness [...] alone with myself [...] with a strange feeling that something irreversible was about to happen [...] something that no longer depended on me. But that now still belonged to me, for a few more hours, few minutes perhaps, a secret just for me, a real mystery, huge, beautiful, overwhelming, strange. The moment of the announcement was at the same time precious and burning, because I wanted to tell and I did not want to, I would rather keep the news to myself for a little longer, save it just for me.
>
> (Abécassis, 2005, pp. 24–25 [own translation])

This poignant description by the French writer Eliette Abécassis combines many salient aspects of the issue of the announcement in pregnancy:

- the sense of irreversible change, already independent from one's own voluntary control;
- the sense of changeover, of "turning the page" in one's own existence, from daughter to mother: watershed to which the frequent presence of a book – open or half-closed – in the hands, in the lap or anyway close to Mary seems to allude to, in the iconography of the Annunciation;
- the need to collect one's thoughts and be alone to get close to this new reality: pregnancy is the experience of an intimate encounter with oneself, as Monique Bydlowski (2000) says, with one's own mysterious interior and – now – fecund; the bodily change, which makes evident, manifest, what is happening and prevents from keeping the secret; the woman must come to terms with the shocking bodily transformations through an attitude of "active submission" before being able to tell the world about "the good news".

THE ANNOUNCEMENT IN INFANT OBSERVATION AND IN THERAPY

As regards our direct experiences, we found (Chapter 1) that in some preliminary interviews before Infant Observation, the mother-to-be reacted at times with uneasiness to the arrival of the observer, almost as if the latter implicitly took up the role of "announcement bearer" and his/her visit at home somehow "strength- ened" the evidence and inevitability of the imminent delivery. The situation some- how emerged as the storming in of an upsetting announcing angel, which forces onto the woman a sudden and too close coming into contact with the reality – beyond the phantasies that might or might not have foreshadowed the event – therefore stirring up anxiety and an obscure sense of threat.

This psychological reaction is well represented in the famous *Annunciazi- one* [Figure 2.4] by Lorenzo Lotto (1527, *Pinacoteca comunale* in Recanati), in which Mary is depicted in the moment of the *conturbatio*, of perturbation, or even upsetting, provoked by the arrival of the angel and his words. He seems to be making his announcement in an assertive and lofty manner, kneeling down hold- ing a lily; Mary turns her shoulder to him lifting her hands to the sky; between the two, there is a cat that is running, arching its tail: this is a very realistic detail, which might allude to evil running away faced with the divine revelation, but which definitely also emphasizes Mary's fright because of what the angel has announced (see Zuffi, 2004).

The threatening and disquieting meaning of the arrival of the observer appears to be in line with Franco Fornari's theories (1981) about the *primary paranoia* typical of the maternal code. From the analysis of a large sample of dreams of pregnant women and women who had just given birth, at the level of

Figure 2.4 "Recanati Annunciation" by Lorenzo Lotto, circa 1527, oil on canvas.

imagination, what would emerge is a situation in which, on the one hand, the mother omnipotently identifies herself in all the three characters of the primary scene (child, mother, paternal phallus); on the other hand, she projects outside (often in the father) all the persecutory nature inherent in the delivery and the birth. "As the mother-child symbiosis can only become established in a relationship inside which the level of persecution is zero and because in reality the delivery and the birth are experienced as the peak of persecution, there exists a primary need to deviate the persecution out of the mother-child relationship, otherwise the primary symbiosis will not have a chance to get established" (Fornari, 1981, p. 272 [own translation]).

In other preliminary interviews, we were struck by the fact that the *announcement did not have any space*, in that neither the narrative of the experience of the "construction of a child", nor an imaginative anticipation of the future baby, was possible.

In a situation obsserved[6] from the seventh month of pregnancy until the eighteenth month of life of the child, the "narrative dimension" of the announcement appeared hardly present, since the very beginning.

> Deborah, a young woman at her first pregnancy, in the meeting (at home) before the birth does not communicate anything to the observer [female]: she does not talk about her representations or her feelings, she does not report anything about the ultrasound scans, or the preparations for the future baby. On the contrary, she delegates to her husband or her parents the responsibilities and expectations. The foetus seems to be experienced, from the phantasmatic point of view of phantasy, as split off from the emotional context. The aspects that emerge more clearly are the somatic ones: risk of a miscarriage and of a premature delivery; these symptoms made us think about an expression "direct" in body of deeply conflicting aspects that cannot be welcomed in the mind.

In our experience of psychotherapeutic/psychoanalytic treatment of pregnant women, we identified other aspects connected to the announcement issue. In some cases "announcing", in the sense of making one's pregnancy known to others, appears to be in itself a source of anxiety, as it re-activates the issue of the comparison with one's own internal/external mother and the connected envious drives and Oedipal phantasies, to which follow possible fears of retaliation and guilt.

> At the beginning of the psychotherapy, Elisa, 34, had talked about her difficulty in conceiving. Then, after a few months, she finally gets pregnant, and keeps this news to herself for a whole week: she wants the therapist to be the first person to know because – as it will emerge during the session – the therapist can help her find a way to tell her very intrusive mother, to whom Elisa always had to tell everything. "Otherwise I felt too bad", she recalls: her mother's eyes seemed to dig into her, read the secrets inside her, all the lies, the hidden things, and she *had* to tell her everything not to feel bad. The patient almost seems to take on her awareness of her own ambivalence towards her mother and the recurring wish

not to have children so not to give her [mother] such a joy. During this very intense session, the patient also phantasizes about a solution to the problem of announcement: it will be Christmas soon and all the family should gather at her brother's; on such occasion, she could communicate the "good news" to everyone, thus avoiding the necessity to have a moment alone with the mother ... and putting herself instead at the centre of the "nativity scene"!

In the context of the therapeutic process, sometimes the pregnancy announcement the patient gives to the therapist communicates, together with the new reality, a quality of the transference situation, like in the historical pseudo–pregnancy of Anna O[7]. that so much troubled Josef Breuer. In some cases, it may mean a sort of "triumphant healing", which vouches for the drive to end the treatment: it is then possible to have a premature and accelerated ending of the analysis, by performing a forward flight, acting as a "body healing", a biologic pregnancy that precedes the psychic work of the conclusion of the therapy. On other occasions, the announcement "I'm pregnant" may foreshadow the difficulty of starting a real contact with one's internal, emotional world.

Three months after a first interview upon her request to start the analysis, Federica, 37, comes again to start the therapy with the triumphant announcement of being pregnant. Despite her seductiveness and the analyst's counter-transference difficulties – who realizes how behind this unexpected pregnancy there is the risk of a psychotic breakdown – the therapist decides to work with the woman in a *vis-à-vis* setting, once a week, with the aim of preventing-supporting this problematic maternity. Since the very first sessions, she has appeared to be characterized by various risk factors: the emergence of an internal relationship with a cold and unwelcoming mother who triggered strong rage feelings; the primary, violent aggressiveness which seemed to evolve into foetus-centred persecutory phantasies, making one fear of unconscious abortive drives. Other significant data on this were the intents, announced by the patient, to carry out exploratory investigations, which she experienced as being laden with sadistic features. As for these aspects and the risk of a breakdown that they probably indicated, the therapist's choice of "identifying with the foetus" and to help the woman imagining the positive characteristics was of importance, with the intention of performing a support task to this difficult mother-child relationship. The therapist's technical choice – which implied a *holding* approach rather than an interpretative one – allowed for a good containment of the patient. The psychotherapy continued even after the birth of the baby girl.

In general, the reflections on the psychoanalytic psychotherapies with patients who become pregnant during the treatment allowed us to grasp the complexity and the variety of the mental processes triggered by pregnancy – including the issue of the announcement – and to value the support that a psychotherapy may offer.

THE TRANSFORMATION PROCESSES TRIGGERED BY THE ANNOUNCEMENT

We will now report on some observation moments, illustrating the internal processes triggered in a young woman faced with the announcement of her first pregnancy.

Daniela[8], a young hairdresser who had met the observer [female] in the past, entrusts the latter with an implicit task of listening to her experiences, starting from the very beginning of her pregnancy. The announcement of her pregnancy thus takes place in an atmosphere we could define as "positive pre–transference"; as a matter of fact, Daniela spontaneously communicates she is pregnant, with a smiling and moved attitude, and immediately tells a dream:

> I was inside a sort of big balloon, filled with water; it was not clear, there were many specks, it was slightly cloudy. I swam the breaststroke, I went forwards without seeing well. Then I noticed a little head, in the distance, I went closer: it was a little girl with a lovely, round face and blue eyes who was staring at me.

This dream seems to cast light on the deepest dimension of her relationship with the archaic maternal figure. On the one hand, one may notice the normal regressive identification with a foetus-girl: here, the foetus seems to be still an *internal* object, re-activating the baby that Daniela herself had been; together, though, we see the incipient taking on of a maternal function of getting closer to the intimate encounter with the potential baby. It is perhaps possible to notice some idealization (blue eyes), but also the sense of difficulty in "focusing" on the new, exciting experience.

In this case, we notice the way in which the announcement of pregnancy always goes hand in hand, in some way, with the comparison with other female figures: both in the sense of a recovery and re-definition of the internal relationship with one's mother, and as a need to refer and compare to, also at an external level, with other female models or other women able to share the experience. Monique Bydlowski explained well the way in which the motherhood becomes "real" only starting from the encounter with other women[9] (2000).

Once again, the artistic iconography derived from the Gospels makes us sense the *pathos* and the symbolic relevance of the meeting between Mary and Elisabeth, both pregnant[10]: it is a theme very much used by painters over the centuries. We have a beautiful interpretation of this meeting in the famous *Visitazione* by Pontormo (Chapter 4, Figure 4.2).

Bydlowski thus summarizes her thinking on this aspect: "The fecundated maternal body is so unthinkable for the mother-to-be, like the child in the womb, and the 'visitation' of another woman is necessary for the pregnancy to become real and for it to be possible to be represented" (2000, p.159 [own translation]).

It is actually a crucially important process in the internal motherhood, the one for which the woman manages to "represent for herself" the child who is developing inside her: this is a process that often would require time, a graduality, and at times tends to be "accelerated" in a way that is little in tune with the woman's deep needs. Some external spurs (for instance, the immediate prescription of medical examinations), the massive use of technologically advanced investigations – although useful from the diagnostic point of view – may at times make it more difficult to welcome the announcement and the processing of the traumatic elements inherent to it.

THE ANNOUNCING WORDS OF THE DOCTOR PERFORMING THE ULTRASOUND SCAN

In Daniela's case, during her pregnancy, the meanings taken up by the ultrasound investigations and the "medical announcements" that went with them, i.e. the ways in which their results were communicated, turned out to be very interesting. Since the beginning of her pregnancy, Daniela seems to invest a lot emotionally on this type of investigation. As a matter of fact, the woman, as if she unconsciously showed her impatience in relation to the encounter with the real foetus, in a dream at the third month "anticipates" the experience of the first ultrasound scan: no more just an imaginary child, but a real baby. Indeed, the ultrasound investigations, starting from the first one (carried out soon after), seem to force on her in a sudden and traumatic manner the encounter with an "external object" characterized by shocking evidence: it is not one foetus, but two. Moreover, such announcement is done by the doctor in a cold, impersonal way, devoid of empathy, so that it triggered in the woman an emotional storm, also tinged with anger.

> Daniela recalls that during the examination, the doctor had an indifferent expression and did not even look at her in the face. In an almost incidental way then, she told her: "There's two of them"! Daniela was speechless, she could not utter a word: she only had a "little tear" down the side of her face! Only when she left the unwelcoming space of the ultrasound scan room, Daniela could give vent to her intense and ambivalent feelings: with an "hysterical" laughter, and then she cried her eyes out! For the three following days, she could not sleep!

Among the significant aspects that kept emerging, besides the shock brought on by the announcement of bearing twins, what was registered in Daniela was the presence of negative feelings triggered by the "impersonality" of the doctor who performed the ultrasound scan; and vice-versa of positive experiences and gratitude towards the doctors who later on provided her with patient and precise explanations, thus carrying out the role of "good" parental images, offering a suitable *holding*, and thus strengthening the process of acquiring the maternal identity.

Next to the above mentioned situation, further reflection inputs on the possible experiences of the pregnant woman in relation to the announcement by the doctor, and on the significant role he/she may play according to the ways in which he/she conveys the information and relates to the pregnant woman, derive from an experience of "participating observation" carried out in a public healthcare outpatient clinic in Florence[11] at the moment of the ultrasound scan.

Claudia is at the twenty-second week of her first pregnancy. As soon as the scan starts, she observes in silence, with clear anxiety, the ultrasound exploration the doctor is performing. She replies in monosyllables to the doctor's questions; then as soon as the doctor tells her about the measurements, the anatomical parts, the foetus' movements, and says everything is going well, the patient asks her: "Can parvovirus have negative effects? You know, I had the flue … I heard about malformations or mental disorders …". The doctor offers more information and a reassuring answer, while showing her the foetus moving: "The little head with the brain, the spine, the little foot moving, etc."; the woman relaxes visibly. Now she starts following the examination in detail, adding personal comments on the data provided by the doctor and showing she already has a certain "knowledge" of the foetus!

Here, we witness the burden of the *genetic anxieties* (Fornari, 1981); the possibility of expressing them and being reassured – in this case, what is key is the description by the doctor of the foetus' movements and the "humanization" of the ultrasound image – nonetheless allows the woman to relax and regain the contact with her "child inside".

Isabela, a young immigrant mother, at the twelfth week of her first pregnancy, seems to feel her maternal capacity as "minimal" because of the threat linked to a previous loss of blood. Faced with the evidence of the vitality and normality provided by the response of the doctor performing the scan, the woman shows a recovery in her level of confidence.

After asking her to lay down and having started the examination, the doctor asks her: "Can you see it?". And the woman asks: "Is it really that little?". Then she mumbles something, perhaps: "Is the detachment visible?". The doctor asks her a few questions, then checks more details and concludes: "No, no more signs of detachment. Can you see? It moves by itself!". Isabela then smiles, she looks moved, she observes all the details the doctor shows to her and asks: "Everything is fine then?!". The doctor reassures her. Isabela: "Oh! Well, thank you!". She takes the "photo" of the scan, takes her leave, visibly moved.

It is interesting to analyse more in depth the extent to which the doctor's "announcing words" – in particular of the one who performs ultrasound scan examination – may contribute to the strengthening of the processes of acquisition of parental identity; we will discuss further (in Chapter 5) the hypotheses of the French authors who consider the ultrasound scan as a possible "organizer of parentality".

In our experience of observers, therapists, trainers of ante-natal course groups, etc., we have identified the importance of offering a listening ear to the pregnant woman, a participating understanding of her phantasies, her emotional states, and of the affective resurgences, more or less conflicting in her past history, thus creating the chance of a narrative *"enveloppe"* (Anzieu, 1987) – i.e. a container in which a narration can develop. This may help the woman to work through the important psycho-physical change processes and the re-organization of the Self typical of pregnancy, so as to go through her experience as a transformation process, fundamental for the definition of her female identity. Furthermore, welcoming the components of fear and persecutory anxiety triggered by the announcement in pregnancy may offer an important contribution so that the announcement can be experienced as an "annunciation" that enriches the woman, rather than a threatening "verdict".

NOTES

1 The word "Annunciation", solemn enunciation of a message, indicates par excellence the divine announcement of the Word made flesh to the Virgin Mary of Nazareth by the archangel Gabriel.
2 Verdict means "judgement with effects of decision, issued by those having competence or authority about the issue".
3 "Luke's text [...] suggested a whole exegesis on the Virgin Mary's various behaviours during the Annunciation. The Franciscan preacher brother Roberto Caracciolo (1425–1495) defined [...] five mental and spiritual states the virgin went through" (Feuillet, 1994, p. 35 [own translation]).
4 This Annunciation has always exemplified the Virgin's *conturbatio* characteristics. In this sense, also a comparison with the description of the *conturbatio* that Saint Bernardino had done in one of his sermons is helpful: "Have you seen that Lady of the Annunciation that is in Duomo at saint Sano altar? It certainly seems to me the most beautiful act, the most reverent and the most bashful one ever seen in a Lady of the Annunciation" (Castelnuovo, 2003, p. 5 [own translation]).
5 The Italian word "incinta" (pregnant) is an adjective from medieval Latin *incinta*, adaptation, because of popular etymology, of the classical Latin *inciens–incientis* (gravid), as per the past participle of *incingere,* "to enclose", perhaps because pregnant women used to wear a belt; or, on the contrary, giving *in* a negative value (*incinta=non cinta, cinta* means belt, so *non cinta* means not having a belt), to allude to the fact that they did not wear a belt (*Vocabolario della Lingua Italiana*, Treccani; vocabulary of the Italian language [own translation]).
6 For a detailed description, see Chapter 3.
7 Anna O. was the pseudonym of a patient of Josef Breuer, who published her case study in *Studies on Hysteria* (1886–1895), written in collaboration with Sigmund Freud. Her treatment is regarded as marking the beginning of psychoanalysis.
8 The experience from which they are taken is the "Pre-Infant Observation", carried out by Luigia Cresti Scacciati, of which we will discuss in detail in the next chapter.
9 The theme will be dealt with in detail in Chapter 4.
10 Soon after receiving the visit of the Angel – one may read in Luke's Gospel – Mary pays a visit to Elisabeth, the eldest cousin, to announce her miraculous conception. Her Visitation provokes joy and elation in Elisabeth's old and up to then sterile body, and makes her feel the child inside her, thus giving her the certainty of a pregnancy that she still doubted and that she had kept hidden up to that moment.
11 Experience carried out by Luigia Cresti Scacciati, which will be discussed in detail in Chapter 5.

REFERENCES

Abécassis, E. (2005) *Un hereux événement*. Albin Michel. Tr. it. *Lieto evento*. Venezia: Marsilio, 2006.
Ammaniti, M., Candelori, C., Pola, M., Tambelli, R. (1995) *Maternità e gravidanza. Studio delle rappresentazioni materne*. Milano: Raffaello Cortina.

Anzieu, D. (1987) "Cadre psychanalytique et enveloppes psychiques". In: *Journal de la psychanalyse de l'enfant*, 2: 12–24.

Bydlowski, M. (2000) *Je reve un enfant. L'experience intérièure de la maternité*. Paris: Odile Jacob.

Castelnuovo, E. (2003) *Simone Martini – L'annunciazione*. Milano: Il Sole 24 Ore.

Ferro, A. (1992) *La tecnica della psicoanalisi infantile*. Milano: Raffaello Cortina.

Feuillet, M. (1994) *Fra' Angelico, le maître de l'Annonciation*. Belgique: Nouvelles Editions Mame.

Fornari, F. (1981) *Il codice vivente. Femminilità e maternità nei sogni delle madri in gravidanza*. Torino: Bollati Boringhieri.

Santambrogio, G. (2007) "L'intensità dell'annunciata". In: *Il Sole 24 Ore*, Sunday, December 23, p. 42.

Chapter 3

The pre-infant observation

Luigia Cresti Scacciati and Cristina Pratesi

THE PRE-INFANT OBSERVATION ENTERS THE OBSERVATORY

In the introductory chapter, we illustrated one of the main ideas that animated the research work of our group: the possibility of exploring in a direct way the mental events inherent in the experience of the pregnancy in its manifold aspects of transformation, crisis, and construction of a maternal identity. Esther Bick's model, which many of us had had a long experience of, in its various applications, seemed particularly suitable to investigate the dawn of the mother-child relationship. The intention of acquiring personal experiences of Pre-Infant Observation – that is, accompanying some women, since the beginning, along their internal path towards becoming a mother – was born this way.

For this project of ours, to fine-tune a methodology that could be suitable to "narrate" the territory of the internal motherhood, we were spurred by the encounter with a pioneering experience of 1987 that, described by Susanna Mazzetti (1993), was then discussed and commented by our group (cf. Chapter 1).

Together with this reflection on experiences by others, we also came across the rather unexpected chance to follow, since its very beginning, a pregnancy, which turned out to be a twin pregnancy[1]. In a way, it was the future mother, Daniela, who implicitly showed her wish to be accompanied in her path towards motherhood. A previous knowledge between the observer and the observed, fostered by the fact that the woman was a hairdresser, prepared an unusual observation context. The occasion, though, appeared to be very favourable – a sort of serendipity – and the long shared path through this exciting experience started this way.

Daniela seems to attribute to me[2], as a customer-psychologist, the listening/ attention function for her internal movements since the beginning of her pregnancy (in this sense, we described in Chapter 2 the emotional atmosphere in which the announcement is made as "positive pre-transference"). I already knew quite a few things about her: I knew she was an active and keen girl in her work, simple, but sensitive and quiet. Although it had not been within a clinical-professional context, I had had the chance to witness, from adolescence to adulthood, her gradual path of definition of female identity and her love choices, including those critical moments of passage and change, which had meant periods of anxiety and discomfort and which were also expressed at a bodily level (gynaecological problems, mild anorexia). This evolutionary path led to a stable love balance: the pregnancy found its place in this context, as a mature choice, to have at the age of 33 a child "with the right man at the right moment".

I believe it was the emotional turmoil of her new condition that pushed Daniela to assign to me the task of *observing-listening to* her emotional states: thus, a rather peculiar observation setting developed in which, despite the absence of a proper "contract", I nonetheless felt invited by the young woman to share her experience with her, in a real "neutral but participating" atmosphere. During the first five months, I indeed took in her spontaneous accounts during my weekly visits to her shop; subsequently, I performed home visits on average every fortnight; then, after the birth of the girls, the observations took place on a monthly basis. In general, Daniela related to me with a trustful attitude of intimacy, and she demonstrated the fact that she valued the slightly special interest I was showing towards her as well as the possibility to communicate her experiences and feelings during the entire pregnancy, and afterwards as well.

This unusual opportunity turned out to be a very enriching source, both emotionally and from the point of view of knowledge. I actually had the chance to continue the observation until over the second year of life of the two girls, thus becoming a participating – and privileged – witness of the long and gradual process of construction of the *internal motherhood* in this young woman, of her shift from a relationship with "internal objects" (her child self/the foetuses) to "external objects" (the two twin girls). I also had the possibility to catch a glimpse of the girls' identities taking shape during their first years of life, also spotting interesting aspects of continuity between the pregnant woman's mental representations and her relationship with her daughters after their birth.

Among the innumerable aspects of interest under the psychodynamic profile, we would like to focus our attention here on a point that we believe to be of crucial importance: the process of *restructuring of identifications* that gestation triggers.

MATERNAL IDENTIFICATIONS

We have already seen (in Chapter 2) how in the experience of pregnancy, especially the first, there is almost always the sense of an irreversible change: the woman must go through a role change, from daughter to mother, and consequently a re-definition of the relationship that the pregnant woman has not only with her external mother, but also with the internalized maternal image, a "legacy" of her infantile and adolescent history.

This theme – the importance of the relationships with the internal parental figures and the "reshuffling of identifications"– was treated by various authoritative psychoanalysts: we may mention, for instance, among others, contributions by Helene Deutsch (1945), Grete Bibring (1961), and Dana Birksted-Breen (1975). These authors illustrate, even with different nuances, the way in which the pregnancy normally implies a "recapitulation" of the whole development of the relationship with one's mother, and the extent to which the value of the maternal "pre-history" and the role of the first mother-daughter relationships are central. Other clinicians (see, for instance, B. Cramer, 1999) enriched the understanding of the establishment of the maternal identity, identifying the *trans-generational transmission,* from mother onto daughter, of the female identification models. Gina Ferrara Mori (2006) highlighted, as a central idea concerning the processes of the internal motherhood, the "fundamental, complex identification movement with one's own mother". We would like to add here also that our experience of over ten years at a clinical (outpatient consultations) and observation level (applications of the Infant Observation in neonatology, in the ward for premature babies, and even in the delivery room) allowed us to appreciate the way in which the more or less explicit reference to the figure of one's own mother – external/internal – is constant and ubiquitous in the mothers we met, – as was also the need, in them, to have some form of exchange with the female figure of the observer.

Going back to Daniela's case, during her pregnancy, I could grasp, in general, basically positive and sound signs of a model of relationships with the maternal object. This mainly emerges, externally, from the quality of the interpersonal relationships that the young woman has with other women: she talks with affection and appreciation of her mother, feeling very confident that she will be able to count on her help; she can have good relationships with her colleagues and with the customers, she declares being very close to few girl-friends. In general, the pregnancy seems to be experienced as an important process of maturity, a completing and enriching one, thanks to the capacity to draw from the model offered her by her mother, her female identity.

The internal events on which the relationship with her is pinned emerge from a dream that Daniela had later on during her pregnancy (sixth month):

"I was dreaming about my mother as she is in reality, in her sixties. I saw her while she was in labour and very close to giving birth. She was at home and I offered to take her to have the baby in the bathroom. I saw her standing in the bathtub, with her legs slightly apart, but she told me to leave and she let dad in. After a while I saw a child walking out of the bathroom, he had curly hair and was walking already". (She adds her eldest brother is curly while the youngest is not.)

Here, Oedipal phantasies and anxieties emerge towards the mother and her procreation capacities: the "infantile sexual theory" is revealed, according to which the act of giving birth is assimilated to a defecation; there is the acknowledgement of the paternal role in the act of making babies, together with the sense of her exclusion from the primary scene; the unconscious reparative preoccupation is present, in relation to the infantile drives of Oedipal rivalry and perhaps of envy, to give back mother her fertility.

This re-emergence of the Oedipal issue is, according to Monique Bydlowski, an unavoidable stage of pregnancy: "In the psychic process that a woman goes through to get ready to motherhood there is a shift in identification with the rival mother of the Oedipal stage. One needs to recover, behind this one, the mother of back then, the one of the original tenderness. The representation of the mother in the Oedipal phase must be erased in favour of the one that preceded it" (Bydlowski, 1997, p. 175 [own translation]). In Daniela's dream, it really seems as though a significant chunk of her repressed history as a child, including the surprise for the arrival of a baby brother, resurfaces (the "psychic transparency" the French author talks about).

As for the more conflicting aspects in relation to the internal maternal image, it is perhaps possible to notice hints of it in some slightly polemic references towards various female characters (mother-in-law, accused of intruding and of not being very willing to help; sister-in-law, pregnant too, who – according to Daniela – nurtures competive feelings). The "projective" component appears all in all limited and the rivalry aspects seem well integrated, as they do not prevent the woman from maintaining in general good relations with both her "rivals". Substantially, there is a clear prevalence of the positive experiences of identification with a loving and strong internal/external mother; when I started meeting with the "real" mother, from the ninth month onwards, I was able to fully confirm the supporting and enlivening function she carried out.

In this path of positive identification with one's own mother and with the reserve of experience and affection that she can offer, I observed nonetheless how she went through various stages of "re-shuffling": the archaic identifications of the very first months were followed, as the dream at the sixth month of pregnancy demonstrates, by the re-emergence of Oedipal themes of comparison. Later on, in the period between the approaching of the delivery and the first 8–10 months of life of the girls, I noticed an increase in intense needs of dependence and *holding*, even concrete; then a gradual and progressive need of "emancipation" from her mother. I had the impression I could detect, towards the end of the first year of life of the girls, a more manifest wish in Daniela to define an area of *differentiation from her own mother*, as if to vouch for an occurred working-through of the process of individualization-separation commenced through the somatic and psychic changes of the pregnancy.

Once again, the artistic iconography helps us to grasp, in their evidence, the different levels of identification which might develop between the young woman and her mother. They correspond in Renaissance painting to the various types of vertical or horizontal *"metterze"* [from XIII–XIV century Tuscan dialect, literally, in third position; TN], in which the configuration of the relationship Saint Anne-Madonna-Child varies, as if to relate to different manners of mutual relation.

THE PROCESS OF RE-ORGANIZATION OF THE SELF

We could therefore talk of a gradual process of *re-organization of the Self*. In Daniela, it starts from the possibility of *double identification with the foetus and the mother,* of which a hint is already discernible in her first dream, described in Chapter 2: it forewarned the complex, internal transformation movement of re-definition of the young woman's female identity.

The internal "reserves", fed by the positive reference to the mother, allow Daniela to overcome without too many difficulties the initial trauma of the announcement of the twin pregnancy (cf. Chapter 2); it seems indeed to gradually become integrated in Daniela's emotional world, fuelling a "leavened" sense of the Self and the identification with a fecund mother who is strong, bestowing care and advice.

Naturally, the process to acquire the new "maternal status" will imply for Daniela going through various critical moments: she will have to cope, for instance, with having to give up important things for her (first of all, her previous condition of independent, active girl, free to travel, enjoy herself, dancing, meeting friends). The burden of these little "developmental mournings" is not openly expressed, but it shows through in a few dreams; at the fifth month, she dreams she is with her partner in the mountains: "There were just us, on holiday, we were taking a walk, there was no reference to the pregnancy".

Furthermore, especially in the last months, Daniela repeatedly expresses her need to "get some air", a need which seems to refer to claustrophobic unconscious anxieties.

This process of re-definition of the female Self is probably made more difficult by the particularly demanding pregnancy and also by a suspected Down syndrome genetic disposition, and therefore implies a "latent crisis" (cf. Vallino, 2004) of which I notice indirect signs, for instance, in slightly manic attitudes: Daniela smiles, she actually laughs a lot, at times with an over-excited tone, to the final stages, downplaying the inevitable anxieties – the genetic one at the moment of the amniocentesis, then, in the last months, the anxieties related to the delivery (on top of it, the medical staff refers, on various occasions, to the possibility of a Caesarian!). In general, Daniela looks calm, she affects confidence, all the while projecting the anxiety onto her friends and on her sister-in-law, and resorting to various denial mechanisms (she avoids attending the ante-natal course, her reason being "she does not like talking about her stuff with the other women, who are often too anxious"). In particular, during the ninth month, the defence against the anxiety for the delivery seems to become more intense through phantasies and dreams in which Daniela "by-passes" such experience, imaging her girls already born, grown and walking! ("I was at the clinic, but I knew I had given birth already: they were walking out of the hospital by themselves, like two 'goslings'!")

So we discussed the way in which Daniela manages to mobilize, starting from the first months, her psychic resources to face and process the anxiety stirred up by the ghost of the "double" implicit in the announcement that she will have twins. Perhaps the fact that at the ultrasound scan, the placenta sacs appear differentiated contributes straight away to reduce the troubling ghosts of the anomaly; faced with the following ultrasonographic images, I constantly noticed Daniela's effort to distinguish the two foetuses (by comparing weight, measurements, position, then their different kicking in the womb).

She declares, relatively early, of having a rather stable and differentiated perception of her two girls' temperaments (one is bigger, rests on top and kicks a lot, "squashing" the other, calmer and smaller). Before the eighth month, the girls' names have already been decided: she chose Serena, while her husband suggested Alessandra as a "makeshift" for the name Alessandro – the name that he would have liked to have given a boy! In this period, Daniela shows to me a compound piece of furniture, divided into two sectors, that she ordered to be made specifically for the babies, to define two separate spaces in her small home. The cabinet makes one think about the two placenta sacs, seen in a previous ultrasound scan, and at the same time, the mother's commitment in creating a double space, both physical and psychic, in the body and in the mind, for the two twin girls. The fact that she had this cabinet specifically designed seems announcing, in a concrete way, that the mother was able to build inside herself two distinct spaces for her future girls – perhaps as the beginning of that process of "de-twining" (*dégèmelliser*), i.e. considering each twin in its individuality, of which Zazzo talks about (1984).

THE RELATIONSHIP OF THE MOTHER WITH THE TWIN GIRLS AFTER THEIR BIRTH AND THE EMERGENCE OF THEIR IDENTITIES

Already, during the gestation, the maternal representation of the different characters of her two girls starts emerging: one is stronger and more active, the other smaller and calmer.

After the birth, a clear "distribution" becomes defined, between Daniela and her husband, of the emotional investments and the practical commitment in relation to the two girls: Daniela takes care more and in a preferential way of the smaller; during my home visits, I always find Serena in mother's arms, who throughout her growing up, underlines, despite her smallness, the girl's vital and positive aspects – almost as if she wanted to protect her and simultaneously justify her for her fragility and "make up for" it! The husband, on the other hand, mainly looks after and stimulates the other girl.

In the complex game of parental identifications in relation to the two girls, it seems then that mother strongly needs to confirm the differentiation between the two twins, and that she mainly recognizes herself in the "weaker" (female) aspects from the body point of view (weight, motor development), typical of Serena, delegating to her partner the identification with the "stronger" twin (the one who should have been a boy!). This clear-cut distribution of the psychic investments indeed carries out a defensive function from those fears of "confusing duplication" which seemed to hover about in the initial stages of pregnancy. What is certain is that during all the observation experience, I witnessed a sort of implicit "fight" on the part of the mother against the risk of confusion and assimilation between the two twins.

It was interesting observing how, to this parental need to differentiate the two girls, actually corresponded, during the two years of observation, the definition in the twins of different emotional *patterns* (both from the psycho-motor and relational point of view) and of *different interaction styles*: one more mature and domineering physically, the other at a slight disadvantage, but able to mobilize compensation and adaptive modes that were perhaps more efficient. It is possible maybe to even discern, in the repetition of the observed reaction and defence modes, the basis for the development of *different characters in the two children*: Alessandra "more easygoing", the other "teasing and knowing what she wants!".

I would like to conclude this presentation with a short snapshot from an observation, which gives some indication about the cyclical occurrence of the chain of the female identifications, from mother to daughter.

In a visit at the eighteenth month, during which both girls, tired because of a very full day, looked restless and whining, I was struck to observe the way in which they found a clear way to release the tension in a particular play area, undoubtedly full of "maternal values"!

> "After stepping into her mother's bedroom, Alessandra rummages in a low shelf and grasps a hair-dryer. Serena immediately follows her example. So Daniela tells me both girls really enjoy having their hair washed and dried; in the meantime, she makes the hair-dryer rotate – it's off – on their little heads, while the girls, satisfied, are busy producing a noisy 'brum brum' with their mouths, amused, and accompanying the game!"

PRE-INFANT OBSERVATION AND THERAPEUTIC IMPLICATIONS

The identification issues – actually rather common and that might derive from the comparison of the pregnant woman with her own mother – turned out to be central in all those situations in which we were able to follow the internal path of the pregnancy and, later on, the development of the mother-child relationship.

Together with the actual Pre-Infant Observation described above, we accompanied through all the gestation phases – from the "child project" until after the birth – other women as well who, despite being in psychotherapy, had the chance to experience an intervention model that took the shape of a participating, empathic, welcoming experience of listening to them, and one in which the therapist's interpretation activity was rather limited, if not absent at all.

It is already well known the extent to which the Infant Observation can perform implicit psychotherapeutic treatment. Such psychotherapeutic components of the Infant Observation – including, for instance, the contact with the non-verbal but mental functions of the observer, with his/her continuous attention and stare – foster a first transformation of the emotional experiences and help in containing painful experiences, rather than evacuating them (Ferrara Mori, 1989; Cresti Scacciati, Lapi, 1996).

Bydlowski describes this way of therapeutic working centred on "understanding and containing without interpreting" (2000, p. 133) as deriving from Winnicott's early paediatric practice. It is the psychoanalytic development of an activity with the pregnant woman that gives without any exception the priority to their psychic reality, their internal experiences, as opposed to the external, concretely physical reality of the pregnancy – which is instead privileged by the medical, family and surrounding context. This type of intervention – lasting only as long as the pregnancy because it is connected to the phenomenon of the psychic transparency and the lowering of the usual resistances towards the unconscious – fosters the development of a very much alive transference to the therapist and allows the pregnant woman to let normally repressed memories and representations emerge, to convey and share them with the therapist, but also to "listen to oneself [...] to give the woman back the echo of her own voice" (ibidem, p. 135).

All of this allowed the group "reading" and discussing these situations as if they were other Pre-Infant Observations, in which the relevance of the reference to the internal and external maternal figure fully emerged.

Elisa[3]

Elisa, the young woman we already met in Chapter 2, asked to have a psychological interview for her difficulties in relationships with others, especially her mother.

Besides this conscious motivation, she offered, at the end of the first meeting (almost incidentally) her impossibility of becoming pregnant, even though she has had the desire to have a child for years, and for this reason, she followed various gynaecological treatments: she recalls how she once managed to get pregnant, but after about four weeks, she had a miscarriage. She also adds that she feels like a "loser" in the relationship with her mother, to be wrong, to be at fault. She cannot feel adult and acknowledged as such: she thinks she will be exposed, for her whole life, to her mother's criticisms and reproaches, subject to a constant comparison with her from which she will always emerge defeated. The idea of having a child troubles her, too: in some periods she would like to have one, other times she does not. When she feels less "down", she tries to get pregnant with all her commitment, but then she cannot get pregnant. This provokes a great frustration. Sometimes she thinks not to have children so she will not have to fight with her mother for their "possession": who, between the two, would then be the *mother?*

This situation of conflicting comparison, in which the miscarriage seems to make her being a "loser" dramatically concrete, does not allow Elisa taking up the identity of a grown-up woman, taking up the place she would deserve in the generation chain.

As regards similar situations, Bydlowski (1997) talks about a mother felt as being extremely powerful, devoid of frailties and weaknesses, bearer of an eternal fecundity, a figure with whom it is impossible to identify, "a real Queen of the Night, in the eyes of the adolescent that her daughter keeps on being".

When she announces to the therapist that she is pregnant, Elisa recalls two dreams:

"My feet are inside a pair of red shoes, with high heels, elegant, very sexy and feminine".

"A friend [female] greets me and kisses me on the cheeks: I cannot sum up the courage to tell her I'm pregnant because I know this friend has just lost the child she was pregnant with".

With the vivid concreteness and transparency of the dream images, Elisa introduces the theme of the comparison between women: through a transference shift, she allows herself to start realizing in fantasy her desire for a sexualized, adult femininity and to express it to the therapist – a replacement maternal figure, no longer young enough to be able to procreate – who can help, accompany, remove the veto to sexuality and allow the procreation of a child to occur – a welcoming and reassuring therapist who in reality normally wears a pair of low and sporty, dark burgundy loafers!

The second dream also features the theme of the encounter between women, a "visitation" in which the theme of rivalry becomes intertwined though a depressive preoccupation, which leaves some space to the hope of a welcoming full of affection.

During the sessions, Elisa mainly talks about concrete events concerning her relationship with her mother, even though at times memories of situations with her that she seemed to have completely forgotten emerge. On the contrary, she does not talk about the future baby and the pregnancy. "I'm so afraid something will go wrong and for this reason I tell everyone ambiguous things, I'm vague", she explains.

Hers seems to be a way to protect her future child from the maternal intrusive stare, letting him grow secretly inside her, not showing it to anyone and even avoiding giving it a precise gender identity, a clear connotation: Elisa does not even wish to know the sex of her child, even though she has had a chorionic villus sampling, and she reacts with great irritation and annoyance when the gynaecologist tells her anyway.

This defensive mode that Elisa has adopted induces the therapist to think that – having discovered the baby is a girl – she does not want to keep her away just from "her mother's penetrating and malicious stare that roots through her", but also from her own as well.

In this trans-generational line, the mother thus seems to assimilate the baby-to-be to herself, identifying in her turn with her own mother, in a context of envy, rivalry and retaliation[4]: the conflicting mother-daughter relationship thus seems to repeat itself in the relationship Elisa will have with her future child.

The changes to the technique the therapist decided on derived from the reflection that, in this case, the interpretation activity could have triggered persecutory aspects, bringing back Elisa to a relationship similar to the one she has with her own mother, which was felt to be intrusive and critical. Taking up a *holding* role allowed the patient to experience a relationship between women in which the representation of the original mother re-emerges, "true, sufficiently weak *urmutter*, whose unconscious representation would work very naturally in the women developing harmonious motherhoods" and of whom the bent to renunciation would be an essential characteristic (Bydlowski, 1997).

As in Federica's case[5], such choice allowed the therapist to use and implement those fundamental functions of support and of being the "midwife of the thinking functions" (Vallino, 2007) typical of the Infant Observation, as described by Esther Bick[6].

Besides the "normally" difficult aspects of the establishment and consolidation of the mother-child relationship, on some occasions we had the chance to see the way in which the themes of ambivalence, mobilized by this comparison between women all inside the future mother, could at times become even more problematic.

Delia

Delia is a young, 34-year-old woman who never met her own mother, as she died completely unexpectedly a few hours after giving birth to her.

The pain for the loss of her mother and the mystery of this death that no one ever explained to her accompanied her all through her life, which had been very hard and unhappy.

At the age of 26, soon after the beginning of a psychotherapy, she gets pregnant with a baby girl, to whom she gave birth on the day and time normally set for her sessions. A few years later, shortly after her father's death from a tumour, she becomes unexpectedly pregnant for a second time. Around the fourth month of pregnancy, she suddenly starts showing worrying respiratory distress, diagnosed as asthma crises. They mainly occur in the evening when she is in bed, they manifest themselves with a suffocating feeling that leads her to even "gasp for breath", and they do not respond to the prescribed medications.

During this same period, in the sessions, Delia often talks about her mother and her feeling guilty for making her die with her birth. An aunt told her that her mother really wanted to have a daughter and that she had spent most of the pregnancy in bed for fear of losing her, as she had been advised against having children because of a miscarriage she had had a few months earlier. Delia knows that while they were suturing her after the Caesarian, her mother had gone into a severe state of shock, and that in the medical reports of the hospital, she had been described during the crisis as "agitated and cyanotic, hungry for air and gasping for breath".

In this case, the therapist felt like she was being the *observer of two pregnancies*: the current, real one, of Delia's present and the mother's, belonging to the past, but concretely re-enacted by Delia *in the present*, in an identification with the maternal image.

Like Elisa, this woman, too, seems to have unconsciously assimilated the baby-to-be to herself, loading her with destructive, aggressive and deadly meanings, as she felt she had been with her own mother.

The various situations we illustrated in this chapter thus allowed following the unfolding of manifold "identification chains" being transmitted from mother to daughter through the generations, implying the repetition of relational configurations.

They may have a structuring value for female identity, like in Daniela's case, or vice-versa, containing conflicting knots, such to hinder the continuation of the developmental processes, as we could see in Elisa and Delia.

Even though different paths, we feel that the transformation functions inherent to the observation method promoted enrichment and emotional growth.

NOTES

1 This situation has already been described in depth in Cresti Scacciati, L. (2007) and in Ferrara Mori, G. (2006).
2 This Pre-Infant Observation was carried out by Luigia Cresti.
3 The treatments of the cases were carried out by Cristina Pratesi and presented more in detail on the occasion of the seminar with Monique Bydlowski entitled "*La costruzione della maternità interiore*", held in Florence in 2003 and, that same year, in Stockholm at the 5th Conference of the European Federation of psychoanalytic psychotherapy in the public sector (EFPP), "Psychoanalytic Psychotherapy in our Time. When, Where and for Whom?".
4 See Chapter 5.
5 See Chapter 2.
6 See Chapter 1.

REFERENCES

Birsted-Breen, D. (1975) *The birth of the first child*. London: Tavistock Publications.
Bibring, G. L. et al. (1961) "A study of the psychological processes in pregnancy and the earliest mother-child relationship". In: *The psychoanalytic study of the child*, 16: 9–23.
Bydlowski, M. (1997) *La dette de vie. Itinéraire psychanalytique de la maternité*. Paris: P.U.F.
Bydlowski, M. (2000) *Je reve un enfant. L'experience intérièure de la maternité*. Paris: Odile Jacob.
Cramer, B. (1999) "La trasmissione della femminilità". In *Contrappunto*, 25, pp. 25–35.
Cresti Scacciati, L. (2007) "La Pre–Infant Observation di una gravidanza gemellare e la continuità con il successivo percorso di crescita". In: Cresti Scacciati, L., Nissim, S. (Ed.) *Percorsi di crescita: dagli occhi alla mente*, pp. 107–124. Roma: Borla.
Cresti Scacciati, L., Lapi, I. (1996) "Dall'osservazione alla psicoterapia once-a-week". In: *Contrappunto*, 19: 15–27.
Deutsch, H. (1945) *The Psychology of Women: A Psychoanalytic Interpretation. Vol. 2: Motherhood*. New York: Grune & Stratton.
Ferrara Mori, G. (2006), "The interior experience of maternity". In: La Sala, G.B., Fagandini, P., Iori, V., Monti F., Blickstein, I. (Eds.) *Coming into the World: a Dialogue between Medical and Human Sciences*, pp. 85–102. Berlin: Walter de Gruiter & Co.
Ferrara Mori, G. & Mori F. (1989) "Una difficile attesa". In: *Quaderni di Psicoterapia Infantile*, 18, pp. 76–85.
Mazzetti, S. (1993) "Osservazione della madre durante i primi mesi della gravidanza e la prima settimana di vita con il bambino". In: Gallo Barbisio, C. (Ed.), *L'aggressività materna*, pp. 65–86. Torino: Bollati Boringhieri.
Vallino D. (1984) "L'avvio della consultazione partecipata". In: Algini M.L. (Ed.) *Sulla storia della psicoanalisi infantile. Quaderni di Psicotererapia Infantile*, 55, pp. 165–182.
Vallino, D. (2004) "La consultazione partecipata: figli e genitori nella stanza d'analisi". In: *Quaderni di Psicoterapia Infantile*, 48, pp. 131–158.
Zazzo, R., Tournier M. (1984) *Le paradoxe des jumeaux*. Paris: Stock éditeur.

Chapter 4

Listening to future mothers

Linda Root Fortini

Every pregnancy is an experience of somatic and psychic transformation, particular and unique, inscribed in the biological constitution of the woman and important for the life cycle as it confirms the existence of an internal bodily space of the female anatomy. It is an experience that is impossible to know or control completely, mysterious even, as the woman experiences herself both as a carrier and protagonist of the event. It is an experience of health, of risk, of hope, of fear, of desires and of needs. There is a gradual but radical change in the body, both internal and external, and the woman feels differently from herself before, alone, faced with the unknown and at the mercy of continuous changes. In particular, in the last two months of pregnancy, characterized by the oncoming delivery, the enlargement of the body and the slowing down of the active life, the anxieties and the regressive phantasies become intensified and the emotional state is mainly dominated by fear of the delivery, of being overwhelmed by a somatic violence, by an imminent danger.

ANTE-NATAL GROUPS FOR PREGNANT WOMEN

The group is a place where one may observe the construction of the internal motherhood, and a space in which women can talk about their subjective experience of the pregnancy and give value to the female world. My experience of fifteen years of work in a public health service in the area of Florence took place in a spacious and comfortable room featuring weekly meetings with the future mothers (about 10–15 women) in the last two months of pregnancy. The group included various professional figures such as the obstetrician, the key professional figure organizing the courses, who is always present, as well as the psychologist, the paediatrician and, at times, the social worker, each of which alternate their presence. The psychologist takes part in four meetings lasting two hours each for each course. Five courses a year are organized.

The presence of the two professional figures, obstetrician and psychologist, represents, according to a reflection within our study group, two different aspects of a single body-mind reality, that of being pregnant. Women oscillate between one figure and the other alternatively, according to their need, to gather detailed information on how the delivery takes place and/or to have a place where to express their fears and anxieties. The obstetrician is historically the woman who knows everything, who survives the deliveries, the one who drives away the ghost of death, while the psychologist carries out a function of containment of the ghosts related to the experiences of the pregnancy and, in this way, helps the pregnant women to make contact with their internal motherhood: to feel the foetus-baby still inside and not just to see it through the ultrasound scan. Among the many diagnostic tests and the biological monitoring of the pregnancy, there may be the risk to prevent motherhood from being "thought," to eclipse the symbolic dimension and to alter the line between reality and fantasy.

In their approach to the experience of pregnancy, women tend to oscillate between the wish to experience it, to listen to their body, tolerating not knowing and accepting to feel dependant – that is, to be like "baby mothers" – and the need to know everything on that experience, being very active trying to fill their mind with notions and information – that is being like "premature mothers". A woman in the group says: "Here in the group they teach me what I can do and if I didn't know anything I'd panic".

In regard to this particular state of vulnerability of the woman, the room where the meetings take place often functions as an idealized, protective and reassuring space. It is furnished very nicely and it is cosy, in an almost playful style, even infantilizing: it is full of soft cushions and mats. Women lie down or sit on them as if they were nursery children. This particular care for the environment appears to be an unconscious attempt to act as a buffer between reality and phantasies, a sort of womb space of concrete containment.

As soon as the participants sit down on the mats on the floor, a woman exclaims with enthusiasm and amazement as if she had only then realized it: "It's just us women here and I feel I'm in good company!". And another one adds: "I need to be with other people and, in particular, with pregnant women like me. I thought the course would provide information and some exercise, instead I like having these conversations. I feel they're helpful".

A research study on about sixty first-time mothers (Birksted-Breen, 2000) showed that the woman able to look after her child after the birth is the one who was able to express her anxieties and fears at the end of the pregnancy. This confirms the importance of a psychological preparation for motherhood, an accompaniment in the last two months of pregnancy which gives value to the female world and one that, having an implicit therapeutic function, does not necessarily need to occur in a conscious way.

In this moment of preparation, the fathers-to-be are not present but this does not mean they have been forgotten or neglected. A few women say with pleasure that they notice a change in their partner's behaviour: "He's sweeter", "He cuddles me more", "He's more accommodating", "We fight less", they say. Others convey a sense of abandonment when they say that he "is almost indifferent", "a bit distant", "always very busy". Another woman notices the different reactions between herself and her partner at the news of the pregnancy: "While my partner was jumping for joy, the doubts and the fears started for me".

The child, the result of the union of the man-woman couple, naturally belongs to both parents but in different ways. The comment of a pregnant woman shows us the way in which discovering the baby's gender may help the father-to-be to imagine the future baby already outside the maternal body: "My husband is jealous, but after the scan and the news that it's a boy, he's happy".

For the woman, the imaginary child is strictly linked to the sensory experience of her body, while for her partner, it seems to belong to an external reality. According to Busato Barbaglio (2004, p. 1155), this difference refers to different levels of tuning: "The male is more prone to deal with what already exists, with what has been born already while the woman seems to have learnt to take care of another human being since its very first cell, that is, since when the other is not before her but still inside, when it is not born yet" [own translation]. Erikson (1968), too, observing the play of children of both genders, had noticed, in relation to the inside and the outside, different ways of organizing the space, and attributes it to their anatomical difference: girls emphasize the internal space, boys the external.

So, in the group of the future mothers, there is a sharing that is different from what exists between the mother-to-be and the father-to-be as a couple in relation to their parental functioning. Women speak a different language, the language connected to the body and not just to the word, a "belly" talking, a looking inside oneself rather than toward the other. There are, however, some psychoanalytic studies showing the importance of the relationship of the future fathers with their own father in relation to the possibility for them to find an internal reference figure that helps them to change a sense of the self (Raphael–Leff, 1993).

The woman, concentrated on the perception of her body changes and influenced by biologic events, is inevitably more introverted in the last months of pregnancy (Deutsch, 1945). She does not talk much of the psychic experience of the pregnancy; a sort of amnesia occurs in her, a forgetting not simply due to the repression but to the intensity of the experience, just like what happens to children who are not mature enough to be aware of their emotional reactions. And in that sense, the psychic experiences of the pregnancy are similar to the infantile ones.

For the psychologist leading ante-natal groups for future mothers, this experience is emotionally involving and one that requires a particular mental state to avoid projections or identifications that may make one lose sight of the pregnant women's needs. I found my experience as seminar leader of Infant Observation groups (according to Esther Bick's method) particularly useful: it is a specific training to acquire a capacity to participate as a neutral observer. It helped me, together with the future mothers, to develop the capacity to tolerate not knowing how the delivery will go, and the capacity to contain the anxieties provoked by the waiting experience. The waiting, in turn, requires a training to recognize one's own infantile parts and to develop an approach to empathic understanding, letting oneself be penetrated by the communications of the future mothers without losing oneself in them, as well as a capacity of receptive listening, allowing the woman to be in touch with her infantile experiences without making her passively dependant on the professional figure – something which might provoke a sense of impotence and the need for help. The mothers who have had a less difficult delivery experience are those who felt more active and who feel that their child really belongs to them (Birksted-Breen, 2000).

The psychologist has a taking care function of the gestation experience. It consists in the creation of an emotional space to think of the "baby-in-the-mind" (Magagna, 2005, p. 178), space into which the hope, the needs, the love and hate feelings are projected and that help, in particular, first-time mothers to perform that fundamental transition from being the daughter of one's own mother to being the mother of their child: a transformation that helps oneself to be born as a mother and to receive one's child, giving birth to a new relationship.

STAYING AMONG OURSELVES AND RE-DISCOVERING ONESELF

The pregnancy indicates a shift between the past and the future; the pregnant woman really stands between two generations: she is the daughter of her creative parents and parent of her future child. The female body that changes is psychically experienced in relation to the woman's past history and her being a daughter. While the body space becomes bigger and filled with a foetus-baby who grows, the future mother's internal reality receives mental representations centred on herself as a child; a nostalgia of the child-self with a mother is re-awakened and the lost fusion is again sought after. There is then a close connection between being a daughter and becoming a mother, as the combination of the words in Dante's lines suggests: "Virgin Mother, daughter of your son".

Besides being conditioned by the infantile relationships with one's own parents, the woman has a need/desire to have one or more close female reference figures who can accompany her affectively during the pregnancy. Such figures represent both the present and a reference to the past. Monique Bydlowski calls "infantile spontaneous regression" this natural trend of the pregnant woman to be turned to her past and her child self-daughter of her mother. "Giving birth is recognizing one's own mother inside oneself, the homosexual side of motherhood, a non Oedipal representation" (Bydlowski, 1997, p. 76 [own translation]).

Identifying with a positive maternal image is a necessity for the woman, an intense need to rediscover her daughter self in a relationship with a containing maternal object. This backwards psychic movement to infantile experiences, at a deep level of the mind of the pregnant woman, re-activates the image of the little girl she had been (or she believes she had been). In that way, she starts mentally getting closer to the foetus-baby even before creating a phantasy of her child. Let us say that the baby, not born yet, starts being thinkable first of all in relation to the infantile self of the future mother – so that the foetus already becomes a place of psychic transmission, an object of identification, a return to the past even before being experienced as an object separate from herself.

As a psychologist of ante-natal groups, besides psychotherapeutically listening to the women in relation to early peri-natal prevention, I have clear in my mind this dual theme of the spontaneous regression to infantile memories and the need to have as reference maternal figures. The aim is to create within the group of the future mothers "a maternal atmosphere" (Vallino, 2004) of meditation and intimacy. In that way, the future mothers find it easier to express themselves spontaneously, to be in contact with their bodies and to gradually get closer to the phantasies linked to their past as girls with mothers (real, ideal or negative), and to become mothers themselves. Creating that maternal atmosphere (and, at times, having to recover it when it is lost) helps women to turn their thoughts inward, looking for a connection to their own story, and to start creating a contact with the baby inside: these are the first psychic movements that predispose women to a maternal disposition and a future relationship with the child.

Some pictorial images that well illustrate these two fundamental themes of internal motherhood help us visualize the intra-psychic path to motherhood. Two paintings, one by Ghirlandaio[1] and the other by Pontormo, depict Mary visiting Elisabeth – an ideal meeting between two women, a very young one and a mature one, both pregnant [Figures 4.1 and 4.2].

The scene of the first painting takes place outside, in a well-defined space, secluded and distant from the male figures that even though present are far away and turned to the external side. We observe that a group of women is gathering around the two pregnant women, a symbolic movement representing the beginning of the gradual psycho-physical change and search for a world of women and of female things. The partition wall seems to outline the concrete space of an emerging female solidarity.

Pontormo's painting, on the contrary, is set in a much more intimate and exclusive space where an intense visual encounter between Mary and Elisabeth takes place, besides a physical contact between their two bodies, already full and made heavier by pregnancy that has almost reached its end. Despite the age difference between the two women, there is a mutual identification and one may notice a shared understanding based on the fact of expecting a child. The painter illustrates

Figure 4.1 "Visitation" by Domenico Ghirlandaio.

Figure 4.2 "Visitation" by Pontormo.

the last period of pregnancy, the one in which the woman's thinking is mainly preoccupied with her body and what is about to happen in it, while the external world is already physically and mentally distant. The two pregnant women seem to wish to remain in the suspended time of that waiting while two more female figures accompany them, staring ahead, towards the soon coming event of the delivery and the birth.

There are two paintings by Leonardo da Vinci [Figures 4.3 and 4.4] depicting a family group made up of Mary, her child and Saint Anne[2]. In the first painting, the latter has Mary in her lap and Mary, in her turn, has her child on her lap. The three figures constitute a triangle at the top of which there is the figure of Saint Anne who, with a benevolent look, supports Mary while she is playing with her son, as if she, too, had become a little girl. In the second painting, at the centre, there is the child showing an already adult behaviour while this time it is Mary looking at her son in a benevolent way, an attitude which reminds us of Saint Anne's in the previous painting. This time, Saint Anne appears more in the background and almost one with Mary's body, as if she had become her shadow. According to Bydlowski (1997), "the shadow of the mother" on her own daughter who is about to become a mother, represents the real background on which the daughter depends; she is the one who has obtained her complete trust, right when

Figure 4.3 "The Virgin and Child with St Anne" by Leonardo da Vinci.

Figure 4.4 "The Virgin and Child with St Anne and St John the Baptist" by Leonardo da Vinci.

the intense conflicts that marked their relationship have been partially overcome. These two paintings together symbolically represent that maturing movement of transformation which is part of the experience of each pregnant woman and which is fundamental in the identification process taking place through the introjection of a good maternal figure.

THE GESTATION EXPERIENCE RECALLED BY THE WOMEN

Here follow a few details of the meetings I have had as a leader of the ante-natal courses with the future mothers. Some of these meetings were discussed in our study group, where we reflected on the origins and the psychic paths of internal motherhood.

The theme of the announcement

At the beginning of the meetings with the women, I introduce the theme of the announcement (see Chapter 2), which coincides with the beginning of the pregnancy, to give meaning to a path that has started already. This allows them to reconnect to the emotional impact caused by the news of expecting a baby, within the perspective of then later on dealing with the inevitable anxieties and fears for the event of the delivery. The women talk easily and willingly, expressing their feelings of surprise, incredulity, fear, bewilderment, the desire to keep the secret or the opposite, to inform everyone immediately in an intense crescendo of memories and feelings. Then they express deeper and more painful themes such as those of the inevitable ambivalence of the conflict between wanting and not wanting a child, or jealousy about the new balance in the couple relationship dynamic while becoming parents. Lastly, some women mention experiences loaded with violent emotions such as loss and death.

Below are examples of how a group of women expressed themselves during a meeting:

- "I really wanted a child, but as soon as I discovered the news, I couldn't believe it".
- "Even after the positive result of the test, which I repeated three times, I couldn't believe it".
- "I thought I couldn't conceive [a child]; I tried and tried, only after I stopped thinking about it, it arrived".
- "I kept it secret for fear: what if it's not true?".
- "I didn't realize it until my body started transforming".
- "At the first attempt, I immediately got pregnant. I knew it straight away".
- "Even though I feel the baby and I see my big belly, I can't believe I'm carrying a child".
- "I was happy but afraid I might lose the child".

- "I don't feel ready. I didn't think I could get pregnant. The child has arrived earlier [than expected]".
- "I told everyone the news on Father's Day" (a statement which makes one think about an unconscious incestuous desire, a phallic desire from childhood [Bydlowski, 1997]).
- "I got pregnant a few months after a miscarriage. I felt happy and sad, but now I'm afraid something may happen to my husband".
- "It's my second pregnancy and I'm worried for my daughter: her life will change. Sometimes she wants to be an only child, sometimes she wants a little brother" (through the identification with her daughter, perhaps the mother is expressing her own ambiguity).
- "I was happy when I discovered the news also because after my father's death, it was a divine joy. I'm just sorry he won't be able to know the child" (introduction of the theme of death).
- A woman, moved by the recalling of a loss in the family, says: "I often think about the first few months after the delivery. I'd like to feel good, but I have many anxieties. I'd like to be strong and caring enough, but I feel lonely. It's a long time since Mum is no longer here". After a participated silence on behalf of the group, the woman, supported by the others, expresses with tears in her eyes a deep sense of loneliness: "Now I'm feeling the emptiness and the absence of a support".
- Then another woman wants to share with the group the burden of her terrible loss that, even though it is a shock for the women, does not destabilize the group. "My daughter died when she was eight because of a disease. Now I'm expecting a boy who's going to carry the name of our dead daughter's preferred toy. We conceived him as a little brother and not as a replacement, because she will always be our first child".

Once the maternal atmosphere has been created, the group itself can have a containing function for the emotional impact of these last narrations without falling to pieces; indeed, it seems to be able to contain within itself the suffering of others.

The search for a significant maternal figure

Some interventions by women who have good memories of their mother help us to understand that to become a mother and feel good about it, there is the need to make contact with one's own internal mother.

> "I'd like to be a mother like mine. I felt well with her. When I was little, she always explained why I couldn't do certain things. She always tried to understand me. Even though when I was an adolescent, I didn't tell her everything, I then discovered she basically knew almost all. Since her illness, she's more anxious. We talk on the phone and often spend time together. From the outside she may seem intrusive, but she isn't; she's there if I need her. She had the same type of relationship with my grandmother".

"I grew up in a family of females. My father died young and my mother raised me and my sisters, demonstrating she was a competent and strong woman. If I hadn't had such a mother, I wouldn't have been able to have my own family. My mother's tenderness has been very important".

A woman says, as if she felt more like a sister than a mother to her future child:

"My biggest wish is that my child can spend as much time as possible with his grandparents and that he manages to have a good relationship with them. I felt well with my parents and I want this child to be with his grandparents not because I need help but because he needs the same type of relationship I've had with them".

Then a completely different type of comment follows, which shows a strong sense of confusion, of emptiness and loneliness: "I can't imagine my relationship with a small child because I can't remember how mine was with my mum".

A pregnant woman declares, almost as if she is passing a verdict of guilty: "I don't want to be like my mother who, when I was little, was always absent because of her job and then too present when I was an adolescent".

Another woman, worried for the future, needs to project outside the group her persecutory feelings in reference to her possessive mother-in-law:

"My problem is my mother-in-law who torments me. She knocks at the door without notice; she tries to plan everything. My partner is very close to his mother and he doesn't realise that contrasts may arise between her and me".

Others say they feel besieged and defenceless when faced with intrusive relatives who think they know everything and even want to decide the child's name.

The mothers-to-be do not talk much about the child who is about to be born; rather spontaneously, they recall memories of the past linked to their experiences as little girls and daughters. In the dreams they sometimes mention, they cannot see the baby well: "I dreamt about the child while I was breastfeeding him, but I can't see his face well".

"I dream about a four or five months old baby who speaks; the image is blurred".

"I dream I see the body of the child from behind; I can't see his face".

In a pregnant woman's recurring dream in which "there is a child who wakes up without crying and when I walk to the cot he smiles at me", one may notice the need to have a child who is content and thus reassures the mother making her feel adequate.

Ilaria: A woman who has always been pregnant

In another group, it is necessary to recover the maternal atmosphere that was abruptly lost when a dissonant voice has brought in that idealized image of motherhood that the group cannot share. "My desire to have a child has always been very strong, so much that I always thought nothing could go wrong. Even when I was a child, I constantly thought about it; it was a fixed idea. Since the beginning of my engagement, I had done all the required tests and examinations, and my husband says *I've always been pregnant*".

There is a heavy and unpleasant silence circulating in the group, as if the women could not recognize themselves in these words. After a while, the same woman adds that she has a sister thirteen years her junior to whom she has practically been a mother. "I used to look after my little sister, so my mother seemed the grandmother. I remember when I was little that I prayed my parents would make a little brother or sister".

At this point, the discussion is stuck. As the leader, I try to mend the tear that has taken place in the group and I say: "I acknowledge the fact that the desire to have a child can be very strong and the idea of conceiving a child may take up a lot of space in the mind, but it may also arise, besides the uncertainty on feeling or not being up to the task, the need to be helped by other people". The comments by the pregnant women that follow are centred around the fact of not feeling ready – of not thinking about it all the time and not really understanding what is happening to them – show they can bear the brunt and differentiate themselves. Underneath a defensive show of omnipotence, one may notice in this woman a fragility, probably due to the denial of the need to depend and the lack of a maternal figure available to allow her to be a little girl. (One could guess that the pregnancy has stirred up an unresolved conflict with the mother.)

A few months later, this same woman asks me for an individual meeting to tell me about a dramatic event: her child died a few hours after the birth. She talks with a great deal of suffering and in detail about her experience of loss, of the child they wanted to take a photograph of while waiting for his death, and her and her husband's desire to try again to have another child. The will to fix a still vital image of the newborn baby through a photograph helps us to understand the extent to which the parents have been deprived of that sensory experience that makes the child representable and that is necessary to work through the bereavement (Bydlowski, 1997).

The idea of resorting to the psychologist of the group she attended at the end of her pregnancy seems to indicate that besides the need to find consolation and to share the pain of the loss, Ilaria needs to be listened to over time, to express the desire for another child and a hope in the future. According to Birksted-Breen (2000), in the professional practice, it may happen that the pregnancy and the post-natal phase are treated not as a total experience, but as if they were separate moments. The professionals helping the woman during the pregnancy consider their work concluded with the birth of the child, and if afterwards more help is needed, it is often provided by different people. This operational modality re-proposes that sense of break and loss that the woman often experiences after the birth of the child. Furthermore, if the different professional competences operating in the Obstetrics-Gynaecology wards manage to cooperate together, they may act as a real and specific support to the nascent mother-child relationship (Root Fortini, 2000).

The fear of pain

One of the meetings of the group of the future mothers is devoted to the theme of suffering physical pain during childbirth. The difficulty of talking about the pain is linked to unconscious phantasies undermining the need to be reassured about their survival. If this theme can take up in the collective imagination the representation of a punishment, of a sentence of biblical scale ("in sorrow thou shalt bring forth children"), on other occasions, what may be present is a misleading phantasy that, in the attempt of driving the suffering away, exalts the "happy" event and the birth of an "angel" child. In the middle of these two extreme possibilities lays the woman's need to talk about the pain, to account for its presence and to be able to start thinking about it in order to be mentally prepared for it.

Thinking about the physiological pain that accompanies the delivery means entering a real context and acknowledgement of an event, including a work for which both mother and child participate jointly (giving birth and being born), and activates a sense of trust in oneself, in one's own capacities and in the child's competencies. Being able to manage and bear the pain fosters, from the very beginning, the creation of a psychic space to receive the child, to let oneself be born as a mother in order to develop a capacity for care and an empathic understanding of the newborn baby that foster the mother-child relationship.

Faced with the theme of the fear of the delivery, women gradually manage to give support to each other. In the discussion that follows, they talk of other experiences of physical pain (a disease or an accident) as something that may be useful to recognize one's own capacity to face unpleasant and difficult situations.

One woman talks about her difficulties in doing the exercises at home: "I tried but I'm afraid of the dark and the exercises must be done with eyes closed. In theory I relax with eyes closed but in practice I can't do it".

Another woman suggests she should try and think about something pleasurable, to have a positive thought, while a third comments it is like being little children who are afraid of the dark. "I'm not happy because I've been told I'll have to give birth before the due time (about two weeks) because there isn't enough amniotic liquid. This upsets me because I don't feel I'm ready" (not feeling ready = fear of not controlling the event).

"There are three weeks left but I'd be ready to have the baby tomorrow".

A woman laughs: "How different we are!".

At this point in the discussion, the women are invited to talk about the delivery and to say what they usually do when they feel physical pain.

"I need to be alone and curled up. I don't want other people around".

"As for me, I prefer to talk about my pain with others".

"I ask the doctor what medication I can take to have some relief".

"I scream and shout".

"I trust the techniques I've learnt during the course".

One of the future mothers seems to be carrying out a leading function in the group to make the group understand that the physical pain can be bearable. She recalls her pulmonary disease, her hospitalization, the complicated surgery she underwent, the physical suffering. "I tried to be strong by telling myself the following day would be better. I realized the more anxious I was, the more the drainages hurt. Unfortunately, my experience left a mark, but my husband says that, according to him, I've matured a lot and this really gratified me. Now I think I can face physical pain".

A woman recalls she suffered because of an accident that "wasn't completely negative, even though not pleasurable. I had a serious accident falling off a horse. The first few days, I would cry all the time, then I surrendered to the fact and I comforted myself trying to get the most out of the situation. I built myself a book rest to use my time". Then another woman, moving from the theme of the physical pain to the coming theme of a child who is about to become an external child, says: "I can't wait to hold my child in my arms". Another, almost responding to the latter and holding her belly with her hands, declares she is sorry she is about to lose the biological union with her child.

Thus, spontaneously, the theme of the discussion moves from the physical to the psychic pain: that is, the fear of a relationship that is already developing and the experience of the mental suffering that is at the basis of the mother-child relationship: the inevitable maternal task of raising one's own child to then separate from him/her.

ENCOUNTERS WITH CONFLICTUAL MOTHERHOOD

During the group meetings, one may notice in the future mothers the forewarning signs of a particular difficulty in accepting their maternal status and a project called "baby", with possible risks for the relationship between the mother and the future baby. Here follow two situations of pregnant women asking, for different reasons, individual help for those needs caused by the pregnancy and that could not be dealt with in the group. As a matter of fact, both women decided not to take part in the group. It was very helpful for me discussing these cases in our study group.

Chiara: A childbirth loaded with death fantasies

At the eighth month of her second pregnancy, a young woman asks to have individual help from the psychologist who leads the group of future mothers. She adds that she does not feel the need to attend the course; indeed, she is aware she needs individual help for a far more urgent and explosive problem: she is terrified of "dying during the delivery". At her first delivery, she had a Caesarean section with general anaesthesia because of a panic attack (somatic manifestation of her anxiety). At that time, she had not been able to psychically elaborate the accumulation of emotions linked to her being pregnant, and the delivery was experienced as an imminent danger. This time, she says, the surgeon has planned another Caesarean with local anaesthesia, and she is afraid of "losing the sensitivity in her legs".

She recalls her painful family history: because of a very serious accident when she was four months old, her father lost the use of his legs and lived twenty more years on a wheelchair without being able to work. Her mother had been very strong, working hard to support the whole family. One may see that there has been, since her childhood, a sort of inversion of the parental roles, figures that had become hybrids, partial and confusing. The father was open and welcoming but an invalid, while the mother, becoming the head of the family, was always out of the house.

Three months after her father's death, she marries and immediately gets pregnant. The speed with which these events take place makes us think that marriage and pregnancy express adolescent modes to enact Oedipal bonds of the past.

During the sessions before the delivery, the woman never talks about her first child, and when, in the last session before childbirth, she did, she only said that the child had an accident at school and he had to be taken care of and brought to the hospital by others – an episode which recalls more the traumatic story of her childhood rather than a real maternal worry. At an unconscious level, one can imagine how, besides the fear of retaliations which prevent the identification with a significant maternal figure that could have reduced her death anxiety, there is a deep sense of guilt for not wanting children if not with her father. This woman seems to be saying that only sleeping with general anaesthesia may placate her dread.

She recalls a dream: "I see the future child's face and one of his feet. Mum helps me put back into my uterus the parts of the baby that are coming out". Our study group attributes to this dream, even though disturbing, a positive thoughtful movement that will allow the pregnant woman to let the medical staff perform the epidural and be happy about it, as everything will go well. After the birth, even though she had positively valued the sessions with the psychologist, she decides she no longer needs them.

Chiara wants to be accompanied during the last weeks of her pregnancy because, reminiscent of her previous experience, she feels she may lose her self-control at the moment of the delivery, and needing to find support and containment for her death anxiety, she turns to a benign female figure (the psychologist). Our study group discussed the ways in which this woman could make use of the psychological help offered by the public health services and about how the somatic trauma of the delivery, intensified by an infantile traumatic experience, was connected to an unconscious incestuous representation.

Noemi: A motherhood conceived as a revenge

A single woman comes to the course only once, but she is noticed by everyone. With a bitter tone, she says she deeply despises her mother and then she adds, talking indirectly of her own lack of capacity to love and more explicitly of a refusal of the foetus: "I know it's a girl but I wanted a boy. Until the fifth month, I tried not to become attached to the baby because I'm afraid she may have a heart malformation".

Since the very beginning, one feels that this woman lacks a capacity for transformation of the Self and an affective space to think about a project called "baby". Motherhood is experienced in an antagonistic way with her female identity. Noemi immediately appears as someone full of rage who does not want anyone to come close to her.

The women respond to her words by defending themselves from what is sensed as a treacherous attack – that is, the projection outside herself and into the group of the image of a bad mother. Their reactions show that they are able to contain the phantasm of a negative mother. "I don't want my child to be neglected". "I want to be serene but I know there are parents who make mistakes".

Before the birth, Noemi asks for an individual session and stops attending the group of future mothers. She recalls her family history: her parents are divorced, but they keep on fighting. Her father has a relationship with another woman, but her mother does not know it, and Noemi is forced to keep the secret and to tell lies. When she comes to me three months after the birth, this relational situation of pretences and deceits with her divorced parents seems to be tragically mirrored in her present situation involving her baby girl and the baby's father. As a matter of fact, the father is a work colleague; he is married with children and does not want to reveal his paternal identity to the little girl. Because of this, the mother must keep the truth hidden and again tell lies. She would like to be able to meet with her daughter's father, but he tends to be evasive. She cries because her daughter has no father, but at the same time, she feels like a blackmailer – that which, according to her, her own mother has been towards her father. She tries to use the baby as bait to attract the father, but when her attempt fails, she experiences her daughter as an impediment to the relationship with the man, and the baby becomes an enemy, a stranger, a predator. Paradoxically, it will be the maternal grandmother who takes care of the little girl when the mother goes back to work. "Just what I always wanted to avoid because I could never bear to depend on my mother. We never got on well together". She admits she has even considered the possibility to give up her daughter for adoption.

The future mother-daughter relationship appears to be jeopardized during the pregnancy. The mother appears mentally absent in relation to her motherhood, as if she could not go through the experience of gestation and the birth of a human being other than herself. This story recalls the image of a destructive maternal aggressiveness that Gallo Barbisio (1993, p. 39) distinguishes from those, less pathologic, that have "aggressive behaviour characterized by an alternation of different forms and nuances [...] [that alternate] in a mobile way the manifestations of a refusal and an estrangement from the child followed by attempts of reconciliation".

Our group reflected on the deep causes of this motherhood, on the reason why this woman wanted to have a child, on how she used her body to express unconscious conflicts. We are faced with that "dark side" of motherhood (Alizade, 2006) that challenges the universal idea that every woman would like to have a child. We believe this motherhood has been used, unconsciously, in a perverse project and that this woman "knows that when she becomes a mother she will have the total and complete control over a new human being who will be at her mercy" (Welldon, 2006, p. 60). The birth of a girl seemed to have reawakened in this woman the awareness of her own unsatisfied needs when she herself had been a little girl.

CONCLUSION

By observing and listening to groups of pregnant women where they talk about their needs, anxieties and fears underlying the psychic experience of pregnancy, one may start exploring and understanding some themes of internal motherhood. The passage from being a woman to becoming a mother, full of physical and psychic changes, needs an accompaniment that, in particular in the final months of pregnancy, when the woman needs to feel "held in someone's arms" and to have a containing object available, that functions as a mental holding. An empathic listening and understanding can perceive those difficulties emerging from latent and unspoken experiences of the body, and reduce its emotional load, fostering the development of specific female resources: an internal sense of vital potentiality, and the capacity to bear and understand the pain as a meaningful aspect of the human experience, in general, and in particular of the female role. In such a way, the future mothers, together in the place where they are welcomed, communicate and share their bodily and psychic experiences. Thus, they amplify the emotional resonance and mutual mirroring, fostering an experience of transformation: from a mother who tells a story, to a mother who listens, to a mother who thinks (Ferrara Mori, 2006).

NOTES

1 Ghirlandaio's painting was commissioned by Giovanni Tornabuoni, the de' Medici's banker, whose wife died in childbirth.
2 Saint Anne, Mary's mother, is considered a protective figure for pregnant women who turn to her for three favours: a happy delivery, a healthy child and enough milk.

REFERENCES

Alizade, A.M. (2006) "The non-maternal psychic space". In: Alizade, A.M. (Ed.), *Motherhood in the twenty-first century*, pp. 45–58. London: Karnac.

Birksted-Breen, D. (2000) "The experience of having a baby: a developmental view". In: Raphael-Leff, J. (Ed.), *Spilt milk: perinatal loss and breakdown*, pp. 17–27. London: The Institute of Psychoanalysis.

Busato Barbaglio, C. (2004) "Setting e disposizione materna dell'analista". In: *Rivista di psicoanalisi*, i, 4: 1149–1166.

Bydlowski, M. (1997) *La dette de vie. Itinéraire psychanalytique de la maternité*. Paris: P.U.F.

Deutsch, H. (1945) *Psicologia della donna adulta e madre. Studio psicoanalitico,* Torino: Bollati Boringhieri. 1985.

Erikson, E.H. (1968) "Womanhood and the inner space". In: *Identity: youth and crisis,* pp. 261–294. New York: Norton.

Ferrara Mori, G. (2006) "The interior experience of maternity". In: La Sala, G.B., Fagandini, P., Iori, V., Monti F., Blickstein, I. (Eds.) *Coming into the World: a Dialogue between Medical and Human Sciences,* pp. 85–102. Berlin: Walter de Gruiter & Co.

Gallo Barbisio, C. (1993) *L'aggressività materna:* Torino: Bollati Boringhieri.

Magagna, J. (2005) "Teaching Infant-Observation: developing a language of observation". In: Magagna, J. et al., *Intimate transformations: Babies with their families,* pp. 177–188. London: Karnac.

Raphael-Leff, J. (1993) "The place of paternity". In: *Pregnancy. The inside story.* London: Karnac, 2001.

Root Fortini, L. (2000) "Reaching Insight in a Maternity Ward Working Group". In: *The Psychotherapy Review,* vol. 2, pp. 161–167.

Vallino, D. (2004) "La consultazione partecipata: figli e genitori nella stanza d'analisi". In: *Quaderni di psicoterapia infantile,* 48, pp. 131–158.

Welldon, E. V. (2006) "Why do you want to have a child?". In Alizade, A.M. (Ed.), *Motherhood in the Twenty-First Century.* London: Karnac.

Chapter 5

Ultrasound scan and internal processes

Luigia Cresti Scacciati

A FEW INTRODUCTORY REMARKS ...

Ultrasound scan is undoubtedly one of the most revolutionary advancements in the medical-obstetrical practice of the last decades: it was used for the first time in 1964 by a gynaecologist from Glasgow, Ian Donald, and it was originally an application of the sonar, a tool that had been used since World War I to detect submarines in the North Sea. Luckily the technique was transformed and developed, replacing the original war-strategic function with precious medical-diagnostic-preventive functions: the ultrasound scan, perfected so as to be able to acquire three- and four-dimension visions of the foetus, has thus become a fundamentally important examination in the path of motherhood for every woman in today's civilized society.

Everyone is aware of the extraordinary possibility of gaining early knowledge as to the state of health or suffering of foetus and mother, as well, that this technique allows, and the fact that, consequently, this has an impact on the subsequent stages of the pregnancy and also on the decisions, at times difficult and painful, that the woman might then take. It is therefore evident that the ultrasound scan procedure itself is a moment of strong emotional mobilization. Even in the most common and normal situations, the trepidation, the emotional jumps, joyful or painful, or the fear, the disappointment, and so on, of the woman and her partner can be easily observed and constantly accompany the medical examination. Ultrasound scan cannot then be simply considered a routine technical moment, but vice-versa: it is an experience loaded with emotional and psychological issues, very significant for all those involved – first of all, the mother, but also her partner and the other family members, the doctor performing the ultrasound scan himself/herself and, perhaps, the future baby[1]! Of course, the image that the ultrasound scan reduces the foetus to is not *the baby* and in any case there is a gap between the image (objective) and the phantasies (subjective). The discovery of this image, though, has inevitably important effects on the parents' phantasies; the ultrasound scan has in fact come to be defined as a "revolution of representations", meaning that it provokes an important readjustment of the representations themselves.

In the eighties, a very interesting activity of investigation and reflection started around these aspects, and it took place in various fields and geographical areas.

The inputs from France are particularly enriching: for decades in France they have been studying, through a psychoanalytic-psychodynamic perspective, the very early relational events starting from foetal life, with the intent of overcoming the caesura between the pre- and the post-natal. With the improvement of investigation techniques and the ensuing discovery of the foetus' sensory capacities, a specific strand of studies has arisen on *foetal psychiatry* and a marked interest for mother-foetus relationship[2]. Within such context, an intense multidisciplinary activity of reflection on ultrasound scan has developed, which includes the integrated co-participation of the doctors performing the ultrasound scans, gynaecologists, psychologists, and psychoanalysts. Further on, I will illustrate the most significant contributions produced on such themes, especially in France, but also in other countries. Actually, the French research, even though of extreme interest, tends at times to construct a sort of *anthropology of the foetus*[3], at the same time emphasizing the relevance of the ultrasound scan as a *psychic organizer of parenting*, thanks to the function that may be played in such sense by the doctor performing the ultrasound scan; therefore these works often tend to leave slightly aside *the listening/observation of the subjective resonances* in the future mother.

On the contrary, such perspective has been a priority in our investigation that, centred on a study model derived from Infant Observation – as described in the Introduction – was focused especially on the personal narrative of the women we listened to in our ante-natal courses, in the therapy room, or of those followed in their internal path all along their pregnancy or, again, of those observed in the outpatient clinic at the moment of the ultrasound scan. Through the recollections of these experiences, carried out in the various fields by the group members – "internal motherhood observatory" – a rich gallery of future mothers with their anxieties, expectations, phantasies, and memories has thus populated and animated our meetings, spurring in us thoughts, reflections and hypotheses on the complex internal implications – feelings, phantasies, etc. – that the ultrasound scan can stir up, and pushing us to look for comparison with experiences and theoretical formulations by other clinicians and researchers.

FROM THE GROUP ARCHIVES

Leafing through the pages recalling the "records" of our meetings, we may see how the psychodynamics of the ultrasonographic investigation have been the object of a particular attention on our part, since the very beginning. Here follow some reflection hints that emerged in relation to our group discussions.

Already at our third meeting the project to accompany some women during their pregnancy is outlined. The model to be used is the one learnt with Infant Observation, observing in a longitudinal way what happens on the occasion of the obstetrical-gynaecological control visits and the scans; which could be, we wondered, the phantasies attached to the presence and the words of the medical specialist on such occasions?

A few answers to these questions will come up very soon after, thanks to the observation of the pregnancy of a young hairdresser (the *Pre-Infant Observation*, already described in the previous chapters); the records show, over a continued and prolonged period of time, our comments on the manifold and different internal reactions of the woman in relation to ultrasound investigations: in an early stage of her pregnancy, one may witness the future mother's shock, triggered by the traumatic communication modes of the twin pregnancy by the ultrasound scan doctor (see Chapter 2). During the pregnancy, we observed in the hairdresser the alternation of different feelings of anxiety and reassurance in response to the different attitudes of the different doctors: at the beginning, one may notice her criticism towards the cold impersonality of the first doctor she met, who performed the ultrasound scan, while then we saw her appreciation for a different doctor who she characterized as "good and patient". Subsequently, we grasp the pregnant woman's agitation when faced with the presentation "in bits" of the two foetuses in the morphology ultrasound scan. Another element, which turned out to be a topic of discussion in the group, was that after the third month of pregnancy, the young mother's dream activity was temporarily reduced, perhaps in response to the evidence of the foetuses seen with the scan. Later on, in the records, space is given to the reflection on the "maternal interpretations" that the woman attributes to the ultrasound scan images, aimed at differentiating the two foetuses; the group is struck by her need to set up for herself representations that are "humanized" and loaded with relational meanings of the foetuses.

In parallel with this Pre-Infant Observation, which was followed and emotionally shared by the group, we encounter on various occasions in the history of our meetings, short but vivid snapshots from cases of women who were pregnant during the psychoanalytic or psychotherapeutic treatment. For instance, we see a situation of a "pregnancy at risk" (Federica's, presented in Chapter 2), in which the information provided by the pregnant woman on the investigation procedures – including the ultrasound scan – appears to be full of sadistic components so that the therapist (and the group) fear unconscious abortive drives. The experiences triggered by the ultrasound scans in other cases we discussed seem to be very different: a patient in analysis describes an "ecstatic" emotion faced with the vision of her baby-girl in uterus at her third ultrasound scan; so the examination promotes an important movement of emotional approach to the foetus, allowing her to enter her new Self as a mother. Then another patient in analysis is presented to the group: she is experiencing the pregnancy with a great deal of ambivalence and with a strong narcissistic investment (she is afraid of bodily changes, labour pains, difficulties in breastfeeding, etc.); in this case, too, the third ultrasound scan triggers a strong emotion in the future mother, faced with the image of "a big, very beautiful girl", that the woman contemplates for long: while she tells this to her analyst, she places her hand on her belly, and then remains silent in that position. In this case, the ultrasound scan, playing a very different role from the "perturbing" effect Michel Soulé talks about, helps the pregnant woman to leave her narcissism, through a sort of "aesthetic impact" (Meltzer, 1988).

Other particular aspects of emotional resonances stirred up in the women by the ultrasound scans have been highlighted during a few meetings with a gynaecologist, who told us about her experience with small groups of patients, followed from pregnancy until *post partum*: they talked, for instance, of the meaning that the 3D ultrasound scan may have, which seems to be experienced by some of the women as "the first real encounter with the child". What to say then of the control ultrasound scan that is sometimes carried out after the birth? A woman expressed her sense of loss, saying "it was nicer before". In other situations, the complex problem of informing the woman about anomalies of the foetus, detectable with the ultrasound scan, emerged: the value of the doctor's words and emotional attitude, as well as his/her empathic skills, which turned out to be crucially important elements in such delicate moments.

Further hints for reflection on the pregnant women's experiences faced with the ultrasound scan images are derived from an experience of "participating observation" that I personally carried out in a public out-patient clinic in Florence, at the moment of the examination: from this unusual observation "viewpoint", it has also been possible to cast a light on the partner and/or other family members' emotional reactions and on the meaningful role played by the doctor performing the ultrasound scans, depending on the ways in which he/she conveys the data he/she has found and how he/she relates to the woman.

IN THE ULTRASOUND SCAN ROOM: AN UNUSUAL EXTENSION OF INFANT OBSERVATION

Very soon, while carrying out our research on internal motherhood, the idea emerged that direct experiences on the field, whenever possible, would have undoubtedly enriched our possibilities of understanding the responses stirred up in women faced with the innumerable medical check-ups that characterise every pregnancy, even the most normal and physiological. Therefore we felt that the opportunity, offered by a gynaecologist with a long experience in ultrasound scanning, to let me witness the routine examinations in the public out-patient clinic she heads would be a precious one[4]. Of course, there were various problems in accessing this type of experience, which was rather new and definitely loaded with many methodological, emotional and ethical issues: for instance, how to be part of the context of the ultrasound scans in a way not to interfere with them? How could I have justified my presence to the women – and their relatives – in such an intimate moment? If, on the one hand, an approach consistent with the model of the *neutral and participating observation* by Esther Bick seemed adequate, I also considered the "risks of intrusion in the privacy", which had been a topic of discussion during a recent international congress in relation to these *extensions of* Infant Observation[5].

Last but not least, I also considered the strong emotional effects, the personal resonances that would have been entailed for me because of my being a spectator of the fascinating but "perturbing" process of growth of babies in their mothers' wombs! Anyway, the group encouraged me, and considering that other important colleagues in other countries as well had already performed similar observations, I started this experience of co-presence in the ultrasound scan room, which lasted for almost a year, with a periodical calendar, allowing me to witness, up to today, a total of 41 ultrasound scans (over half of which have been performed in the first trimester of pregnancy); besides Italian patients, I have met many non-EU women (from Morocco, South America, Albania, China, etc.), therefore different in terms of mentality, age (between 24 and 41 years of age), socio-economic conditions and the quality of their surrounding environment.

I will briefly describe the context in which the examination would take place: the gynaecologist welcomes the pregnant woman, helped by a nurse who lets the woman in and then helps the doctor transcribe the personal data, the date since the last menstruation and the calculation of the gestation week. The pregnant woman's relatives, if present, may enter, too; the observer, who remains seated to one side, mostly silent, is introduced by the gynaecologist as "a colleague interested in observing the ultrasound scan". The women's and their partners' reaction to this communication was varied: from the seeming indifference of some of them, who appeared to assimilate me *tout court* to the nurse, to the questioning, interested attitude of other women who addressed me, during the scan, as the interlocutor appointed to take care of their emotional states or educational problems (for example, how to inform the older siblings about the result of the ultrasound scan). Here follow only a few observation excerpts that are added to Claudia and Isabela's situations already presented in Chapter 2.

Valentina, 39, first pregnancy, twelfth week, with her husband

The gynaecologist explains why I am there, the couple glances at me, they both smile. The patient lays down on the bed and the doctor, soon after starting the examination and – I believe – focusing on the foetus' head, tells the woman: "Here it is, can you see it is moving? I'll take a look now and then I'll explain to you".

The husband, who had taken a seat to one side, stands up and walks closer to the bed and leans forward, towards the screen, very attentive. The patient turns her head to the screen and asks: "Is it in a horizontal position?".

Doctor: "Yes. Look at its little head".

Patient: "The big head!".

Then the doctor starts describing in detail the foetus' movements; the mother smiles, but I think she is also weeping at the same time, moved. The doctor then explains all the details of the images (head, beating heart, hands, feet, movements). The father leans further forward, the mother keeps on smiling.

Patient: "Which week is it then?".

Doctor: "We're at the thirteenth". Then she asks the woman's age and whether this is her first child; the woman answers diligently (day, month, year of birth). So the doctor asks her whether she is thinking about doing an amniocentesis and the patient, who in the meantime has stood up and is getting dressed again, replies she does not know, because they have decided to accept it anyway. Then she addresses me and she tells me: "We're so happy ... I wasn't expecting it, it was a surprise!".

The doctor repeats: "Oh yes, a very nice surprise!".

While the two partners wait to receive the photos, the woman glances at me, as if she would like to go on talking to me; then, with a happy expression, they take their leave, thanking us.

Does the couple seem to attribute to the psychologist the task of receiving their emotions? The "humanized" description of the foetus and its vitality that the doctor has given stirs up a strong emotion in both members of the couple; the father, as usual, comes closer after the foetus has been identified and its movement detected!

Manuelita, 25, first pregnancy, unsure about weeks of gestation; she comes alone (she is from a South American country)

She walks in in silence, wearing a woollen beret that she keeps also during the examination; she is expressionless. She answers the doctor's questions and confirms two abortions, indicated in her clinical records. She makes no comments, nor asks questions after the explanations that the doctor provided her on the foetus and its movements, and she does not show any reaction even when the doctor tells her everything is going well. She quickly puts her clothes back on and leaves without uttering a word.

One may sense here an emotional dis-investment and a lack of participation, perhaps connected to the previous experiences of her abortions.

Teresa, 39, first pregnancy, eleventh week, she arrives late, with her mother

When the nurse goes to the waiting room to call the patient at the time of the appointment, she has not arrived yet; there is her mother, though, impatient, asking to be let in, while waiting! But here at last Teresa is arriving. She looks a bit lost, she is dressed like a "good girl", wearing a pleated skirt and a shirt; the doctor invites her to lie down on the bed and she does it a bit tensely.

The gynaecologist asks her, routinely, the date of her last menstruation; Teresa hesitates, trying to say the date. Her mother intervenes, and she mentions the date herself, and in the meantime she comes closer to the bed, then she goes back to sit to one side. The patient answers diligently the questions about her address and age (she says she is 39 – but she does not look like it);

this is her first pregnancy. The "future grandmother" intervenes again and adds their town of origin.

In the meantime, the doctor, having started the exploration on Teresa's belly, says: "Here it is! Can you see it, *Madame*?".

The grandmother jumps up, as if the question had been addressed to her, and goes next to the bed again; the doctor shows the anatomical parts indicated and describes them.

At this point, Teresa asks: "What is the *real* size now?".

"About five centimetres [about 2 inches]", the doctor replies after measuring it; then she shows the little head, a little arm, the other little arm. The grandmother exclaims: "It's incredible!" and she touches her face, as if she were agitated. She then adds that Teresa is an only child and this is her first grandchild.

The doctor completes the measures, then concludes: "As far as we can see now, everything's fine". While the two women, standing, wait for the photos, the "grandmother" adjusts her daughter's handbag string on her shoulder.

The interactions I could observe during the examination let one sense that there is an emotional situation of strong infantile dependency of the pregnant woman on her mother. One might wonder: "Whom does this baby belong to, in their phantasy? To the young mother or to the grandmother?". Perhaps the description offered by the doctor seems to help the former to think that she *really* has a baby of her own inside.

Alessandra, 36, third pregnancy (two miscarriages), twenty-second week; with her sister and two older children

The woman comes in with her sister and two pubescent sons, who sit to one side. Laying down, as soon as the gynaecologist asks her how many pregnancies she has had, Alessandra replies, "Five!", and she starts heatedly recalling her two miscarriages that she has had a few months before: she had had a first miscarriage, then some time later she got pregnant again, but she had to have D&C again because – she says – of a mistake of her gynaecologist: he had wrongly diagnosed the death of the foetus in the womb and indicated that it would be better to have the surgery; it had then been found that the embryo was actually alive. The doctor now tries to inquire into the reason why at that moment another ultrasound scan had not been performed; the woman replies in a rather conceited and angry way, saying she will not mention the name of the gynaecologist and the hospital where all of this happened: "Anyway, it's no use now talking about it". (This new pregnancy has started a few weeks after the second miscarriage.) In the meantime the doctor has started the examination and conveys the initial data ("the little head … the little heart"). The woman though seems to be hardly listening, as she is taken up in the heat of her account. The doctor notices it is difficult to see the foetus well, as it is turned downwards and the fattish abdomen of the woman (she is actually obese) does not allow to see it properly. The doctor asks her whether she knows already the sex of the baby. Alessandra answers that, on the basis of a previous scan, perhaps it is a girl; but she adds that anyway "it's a bit naughty, it's not showing itself! In the past too it had the 'closed legs syndrome'". Answering the doctor's question about which sex she would prefer, she says she would be okay with another boy, as she knows already she gets on well with boys. In the meantime, her two sons are silent in the darkness: the older is standing staring at the screen; the other, sitting, leafs through a magazine and lifts up his head when the baby's gender is discussed and, in particular, when the gynaecologist shows in detail the foetus' spine. The mother adds that the family members now would like a girl. The gynaecologist tries to see more details, but the foetus is difficult to see and does not allow precise measuring. Therefore she suggests the woman should come back in a week, hoping the foetus has changed its position. Alessandra seems slightly vexed, but then she says it is all right. While she is waiting to receive the photos, she has the attitude of a practical, resolute person who does not lose heart. Her silent sister looks more touched than her; her sons are silent.

The woman does not appear to have worked through the trauma of her recent double miscarriage, and she cannot really pay "internal attention" to the new pregnancy (perhaps started under the pressure of conflicting components, a sort of "spite" to the gynaecologist who had "castrated" her?). Is she imagining a "foetus-girl-contentious child"? What appears to be predominant in her is the need to give vent to the bitterness and anger because of the painful experience she has had. How to explain the completely silent presence of her older children?

COMMENTS

This experience in the ultrasound scan room allowed me to come across a great variety of situations, not only under the sociological-cultural and trans-cultural profile, but also as for the *internal reactions* stirred up in the women and their partners by the ultrasound scan.

The different internal "emotional atmosphere" with which women face the examination appears to be linked, at least in part, to the chronological stage of pregnancy: that is, their reactions during the scans at the early stages of pregnancy were different from the second scans, the morphology scans, and the third, performed near the date of the delivery. For instance, it appears one may notice, in a few cases of first scan, the signs of a so-called "prematurity of mother/child relationship" (Ferrara Mori, 2006) as a consequence of the early "objectification"[6] of the future baby; in some situations, it seems the internal child cannot actually be "thinkable" and "visible" (perhaps the experience of previous abortions, like in the case of Manuelita, may play a role)[7]; very often, on the contrary, what emerged is the woman's capacity to think about the foetus as a child, an individual with its own characteristics, and also imagining it looking like the mother herself or a family member.

In general, fathers seem present and participating in the scan examination within our cultural context (the majority of Italian women came with their partners), thus playing an important *holding* function for the woman in her process of acquisition of their maternal identity; also Islamic husbands are present, even though at times with more controlling modes, aimed at depriving the woman of her decision-taking power. Eastern European, Albanian, and Chinese women, or women coming from South American countries, always came alone or with another woman; therefore, it is perhaps not by chance that in some of them one could see nuances of refusal and reduced emotional participation to the examination.

What about the fathers' internal reactions? In many of them – especially those at their first child – I often noticed a sort of hesitation in getting close to the reality of the foetus; the doctor seems to encourage them to do so thanks to the description of the foetus' movements and its size (big enough), as if this helped the future father's identification with a baby, unconsciously felt as a strong and vital penis.

Both in women and in their partners, I noticed a strong need to receive minutely detailed explanations, often aimed at placating their anxiety; the *humanization of the foetus*, through the words chosen by the doctor, contributes to dampen the turmoil that the ultrasound scan image seems to provoke. For instance, in Daniela's (the hairdresser) pregnancy, we have already seen the different reactions to different communication modes of the doctors performing the ultrasound scan.

I also wondered which of the aspects highlighted by the doctor (for instance, identifying the beating heart, the movements of the foetus, the hands, the face, etc.) seem to be more significant for the woman and her partner. In my experience, the importance of the *vitality* of the foetus emerges, in agreement with André Soler (2005), who thinks the image of the foetus' *face* is the one that always mobilizes emotionally both parents, as it allows for a *personalization* of the baby. Furthermore, as we have already seen in the hairdresser's case, for the parents, the perception of the baby in its *wholeness* is very important: the child needs to be whole for the parents to be reassured[8]. Another cause for intense anxiety for the parents is the possible discovery of *multiple embryos*, which perhaps feeds phantasies of a dangerous invasion. (Also in relation to this aspect, we saw the hairdresser's anxious response when faced with the sudden announcement of a twin pregnancy.)

It is interesting to further analyse the emotional reactions stirred up in the other family members present at the examination: what the elder brothers may feel, for instance? (see Alessandra's case). Their participation may be positive, as it implies complete information by the parents who, in a way, include the older child in their creative project? Or should one consider more the possible unfavourable aspects, as some French authors suggest? They argue in fact that the older child is a witness to a representation of the "primal scene" and experiences, in a way more disquieting than the adult, the mysterious and anxiety-provoking effect of the ultrasound scan image (comparable to the anatomic tables of Rorschach's test). Furthermore, the older child must face his/her own ambivalence, but at the same time, is implicitly invited to remove the aggressiveness against his/her future rival! So, one might wonder whether the older child's participation to the ultrasound scan might not be advisable. This "break-in" into the secrets of mother's body, according to Michel Soulé, André Soler and others takes up the meaning of crossing the threshold of the taboo of parental sexuality, thus reactivating phantasies regarding the primal scene; there is also something paradoxical, as the older sibling on the one hand witnesses the sudden revelation of the "mystery", but within a context devoid of affective intimacy, and one in which the "blunt" information, without an adequate comment and an affective reassurance, may constitute for the sibling a psychological violence.

The themes hinted at so far have been analysed in depth mainly by Michel Soulé and his collaborators (among them Marie-José Soubieux, Luc Gourand, and Bernard Golse), who have, as well, widened the reflection on the place that the ultrasound scan occupies within the *family context*; about this, they even suggest that the ultrasound examination might become an *organizer of parentality*. We also wondered to which extent one might see, in the cases we observed, the contribution of the ultrasound scan to the strengthening of parenting, or whether it is possible to identify the so-called "warning signs" in relation to the process of acquisition of the "parental" identity.

An answer to these questions requires making reference to the clinical-theoretical hypotheses formulated on these aspects by the French researchers and also from other geographical areas; I will therefore propose a brief overview, starting with a short digression, to foster a better understanding of the deep implications of the ultrasound scan.

ECHOGRAPHY AND MYTHOLOGY: THE IMPLICATIONS OF ULTRASOUND SCAN IN PARENTS' PHANTASY

The term "*ultrasound* scan", also known as *echography*, contains metaphorical meanings and implications referring, first of all, to mythology: the denomination of this technical-medical procedure, being based on the sending, reflection, and repetition of the sound waves (ultrasounds), is actually linked up with the story of the nymph Echo, narrated by Ovid in the *Metamorphoses*: the nymph is condemned by the unfair power of a furious Hera to live in a cave and to simply repeat the last sounds of other people's voices, and this prevents her from expressing and realizing her love for Narcissus, who was too much taken up by his own image. André Soler[9] suggests the idea that the triangle *Echo-Hera-Narcissus* could be seen as a metaphor of the *echographed baby-doctor performing the ultrasound scan-parent* relationship: the foetus/baby, enclosed in the cavity of the maternal womb, must remain silent, limited to simply repeating, reflecting the waves being directed at it; but the foetus/baby needs love, which perhaps it is not receiving, as the doctor performing the ultrasound scan is mainly after its defects and anomaly; the parent, like Narcissus, looks in the reflected image mostly as an image of herself/himself. The problem is then to make an encounter possible, make receiving possible, creating the space for an affective relationship: the doctor performing the ultrasound scan may then become like Eileithyia, Hera's compassionate daughter, who takes care of women, assisting them during labour.

As for the fact of *looking inside*, it implies many different deep meanings that once again mythology, linguistics, and anthropology help us to unveil[10]. The display of the intimate content of the woman's body may be experienced as an intrusion, inquisition, wanting to discover the most hidden secrets; the idea of the maternal womb recalls a sense of something mysterious, concealed, a sort of holy haven, but one that at the moment of the ultrasound scan is penetrated, revealed: according to Mireille Kohn-Feist (1996), one could talk about *phantasies of violation*, meant as a lack of respect for a holy place (etymologically "worthy of an absolute respect"), that is, something sacrilegious that might bring evil upon the foetus or the family. In actual fact, with the ultrasound scan, a sort of "break-in" into the home of the foetus/baby occurs, a home that the technique runs the risk of "unhallowing", but that may be re-consecrated through the affective relationship with the child.

In general, one might say that while the tactile contact fosters affective closeness and intimacy, the vision presupposes a distancing[11]: the look that the doctor casts on the baby in the womb cannot, after all, have the same value of an encounter through the tactile contact. The image is not enough in itself to promote an encounter: it may have a positive effect, but also a disorganizing, even traumatic, effect; it may be *organizing* as it grants an immediate emotional investment, but it becomes *disorganizing* when for instance it suddenly presents a series of distressing information.

About this, Michel Soulé suggested the notion, of Freudian origin, of the *"uncanny"*[12]; it implies the *repetition automatism*, which accompanies the death instinct: in the ultrasound scan, the woman witnesses, as a viewer, the manufacturing of the baby under the inexorable push of her genome's programme; she experiences her passiveness compared to the vital but uncontrolled force that develops in her, and she must bow to the fact of the "automatic repetition" (Fr. *Automatisme de répétition*) which is implied in the ultrasound scan images of the foetus during the nine months.

The *uncanny* also presupposes the "return of the repressed": the ultrasound scan vision may, for instance, re-trigger the infantile curiosity for the content of the maternal womb and the primal scene and, as a consequence, the infantile anxiety of being punished for one's own scoptophilia; so the phantasies of unconscious guilt would be reactivated, bringing back to the surface mother's "prehistory" and the role of the first mother-daughter relationships; thus, archaic phantasies of "abduction of the baby" may be rekindled by way of the look (the envious eye of the doctor performing the ultrasound scan would then be experienced as depriving the woman of her foetus); perhaps then the woman may feel seen, watched by the foetus, assimilated to the archaic omnipotent mother? (Such an idea would be proved by the fact that sometimes, as I have had the chance to witness personally, the pregnant woman avoids looking at the echographic screen). In addition, disturbing phantasies of the "double" may be re-awakened, as the woman sees at the same time her foetus and her womb: me/my baby-me/my mother. There may then be a reminiscence of traumatic unresolved experiences that have not been metabolized, that reawaken anxiety both in the woman and in her partner and, at times, in the doctor as well.

Soulé repeatedly suggested the idea that the ultrasound scan, as it "reifies" the product of the primal scene, entails the risk of inhibiting the free development of the imaginary baby: in this sense, he has suggested an expression that in English would read as *"voluntary termination of phantasies" (Fr. I.V.F = interruption volontaire des fantasmes)*. Of course, the fact that the phantasies on the life inside the maternal body are in a way "re-activated" thanks to the ultrasound scan entails the risk, if not to put an end to phantasies, at least to give them limiting or altered outlines; the evidence of the morphological reality of the echographic image always changes phantasies in some way, provoking a continuous re-adjustment of them. The baby is perceived through its reconstructed image, in a strictly imaginary dimension; the image would represent a "screen", in the sense of a *projective surface*[13], but perhaps also in the sense of *obstacle to the encounter*, which does not always facilitate a real encounter with the baby itself.

FURTHER RESEARCH AND THEORETICAL-CLINICAL CONTRIBUTIONS

At this point, the multiplicity and complexity of the psychological-psychodynamic issues inherent in ultrasound scan examination appear evident. To what has just been illustrated, I will add a short overview on the inputs that contributed more to their understanding.

Michel Soulé

This famous psychoanalyst, supported by a lively group of collaborators, has boosted a rich research work on the psychology and psychopathology of the "maternal-foetal relationship" and on the meanings that in such context the ultrasound scan may have[14]. If on the one hand, as we have seen already, he has investigated the disturbing implications in phantasy of the ultrasound scan (the ultrasound scan may trigger pathological projective identifications, cause persecutory feelings to arise, thus inducing a sort of psychic paralysis), he also highlighted the structuring value that the ultrasound scan often has in relation to family dynamics. According to him, the examination often induces a dynamic confirmation of the parenting process, thus being a potential *psychic organizer*: for instance, the first scan, as encounter with a real foetus – while until then the woman has experienced a relationship with an imaginary foetus – takes up the value of a "pregnancy certificate", thus representing an important step in the process of "becoming parent". The task of the doctor is then to become a "translator-nursing person-container", helping the future mother in re-organizing and give meaning to the blunt images of the examination, as it provides a precise idea of the foetus' life in the womb.

Therefore, ultrasound scan plays a very important role not just at the level of the anatomical investigation, but also at the psychological level. Thus, a very careful reflection is required from ultrasound scan professionals, through training in multi-disciplinary discussion groups. Soulé's investigation on the "perturbing" implications of the ultrasound scan also contains a reflection, devoid of prejudices, on the problem of "hate" towards the foetus: he notices how often there is the tendency to deny it, through idealization, but in reality "hostile" feelings are part of "normal" maternal experiences[15]; they become more intense when the foetus can no longer be the object onto which to project the imaginary baby, as it no longer meets the parental expectations and the trans-generational remit[16]. At times, it happens that mother's hate for her foetus is diverted towards the medical staff, and especially the doctor performing the ultrasound scan, when he/she discovers possible imperfections; the doctor, too, may hate the foetus when he/she must announce its abnormality, and this may lead him/her to formulate the diagnosis in a hasty and "violent" way.

Sylvain Missonier

By developing some of Soulé's ideas, Missonier devised a methodology of "peri-natal therapeutic consultation" as a clinical psychologist in the maternity ward. According to him, the ultrasound scan is a crucially important moment because it allows the foetus-parents-medical professionals encounter, but it also offers a possible space of exchange between specialists in body and in psyche. He enhances the psychologist/psychoanalyst function, within the multi-disciplinary group discussing on ultrasound scan, as the "narration receiver", who then fosters the shift from acting to symbolic processing. The ultrasound scan, if performed in a containing context, thus becomes a *psychic organizer of the parenting process*, as it fosters the establishment of parents-baby bonds. In short, Missonier emphasizes the possible role of *psycho-social prevention* of ultrasound scan (prevention of parenting disorders and of early mismatching in interaction), but next to this, he also considers the traumatic potential of the examination (due to the "transient effusion of phantasies") and the risks of psychic paralysis or of pathological identifications because of the re-surfacing of deep traumas (perception of the foetus as a scary or dangerous object); indeed, the ultrasound scan spurs resonances both in relation to the real and the imaginary foetus that reflect the parents' individual, marital and generational story.

THE ULTRASOUND SCAN AS A MEETING PLACE FOR DOCTORS AND PSYCHE SPECIALISTS

Even though, according to us, in French researches one could infer an excessive emphasizing of the importance of ultrasound scan and that, to a certain extent, the "maternal perspective" is neglected – that is, the investigation on the subjective experiences and resonances of the pregnant woman – we should nonetheless acknowledge an undoubted value to the flurry of multi-disciplinary reflection on ultrasound scan that has developed in France over the last few years[17]. The papers presented by doctors performing ultrasound scans and other healthcare professionals, on the occasion of various scientific meetings, actually showed the spreading among them of a remarkable psychodynamic training, aimed at accompanying with

sensitivity the moment of the encounter with the foetus; they showed their convic-
tion that ultrasound scan is not just a technical fact, but something that can offer
an emotional container to the future parent, with a structuring effect on the parents' attention towards the future baby, fostering the continuity among pregnancy,
birth and the establishment of relationships. On various occasions also, the need to
humanize the foetus has been underlined, abandoning the logic of the "fragmented
presentation" and instead including it in a "story that can be represented".

It is worthwhile mentioning, in this context of fecund integration between the
medical-healthcare and psychic-humanistic perspective, the fact that Jean-Marie
Delassus, paediatrician and psychiatrist with a psychoanalytic background, has created a new specialization – "*maternology*" – dealing with the study and treatment
of the difficulties women have in their "long journey" towards psychic motherhood.

Monique Bydlowski

The innovative contribution offered by this "couch-less psychoanalyst" to
the understanding of internal problems in pregnant women has already been
illustrated in the Introduction. As for the ultrasound scan specifically, she underlines its meaning as a "virtual test" proposing "a reality in the moment when the
baby for the mother cannot be represented yet at a psychic level" (Bydlowski,
2000, p. 22 [own translation]). The images of the child before its birth do not lend
themselves to containing specific and familiar traits.

> "Nonetheless they have the merit of giving the mother [...] the evidence
> that the movements she perceives inside herself correspond to a real baby.
> Image-synthesis of reconstructed plans that may be interpreted only by
> the specialist, the ultrasound scan in itself stirs up a little emotion if com-
> pared to the enormous emotion the new mother feels when she takes her
> baby into her arms [...]. The future mother humanizes, with her phanta-
> sies and memories, the blurred representation that the technique offers
> her [...]. There is no continuity between the virtual echographic repre-
> sentation and the real baby, as the image proposed before the birth has not
> yet a sensory model [...]. The non-possibility of representing the child
> before its birth also refers back to old terrors about the inside of the preg-
> nant woman's womb, disquieting and strange, which evades the sensory
> experience and cannot find mental images to transform into". (*ibidem*,
> pp. 22–23 [own translation])

THE OBSERVATION OF ULTRASOUND SCAN
EXAMINATION IN BRAZIL: THE "VISIT TO THE CAVES"

A very interesting research has been carried out over the years in Porto Alegre,
Brazil, by the psychoanalyst Nara Caron and her collaborators: they have applied
the Infant Observation method to the study of ultrasound scan. They christened
this experience "visit to the caves" because of the primitive aspects and the

intense emotions connected to the life-death dualism that the context of the ultra-sound scan investigation stirs up. The environment itself in which the examina-tion takes place promotes this return to the origins: semi-darkness, silence, closed windows, woman laying down and with bare abdomen, comparable to a naked internal space. The methodology of this Brazilian research, carried out by three separate teams, with a cross-comparison of data, allowed following the develop-ment of the foetus in parallel with the phantasies and the mental representations of the mother in pregnancy and their impact on the mother-child relationship. Every examination features the specificity of each foetus, through the parents' percep-tions, mirroring each couple's story. The observer plays an important role in help-ing the parents to see the baby and modulate their primitive fears and feelings; parents tend to use him/her as an object that can help them fixing attention and keeping bits of feelings together. One may also grasp the importance of intrauter-ine environment and life in the development of the child's emotional life, starting from the physical *holding* he/she has already experienced inside mother's body.

OTHER OBSERVATION STUDIES ON THE FOETUS

I will briefly mention also the original contributions by Alessandra Piontelli (see also Chapter 1), who mainly assumes the "foetus' point of view" (Piontelli, 1992). Even though the latter researcher presents interesting observations and com-ments on the mother's reaction when faced with the display of the foetus that the ultrasound scan allows, her *focus* is mainly to assess the importance of pre-natal life – that to an extent anticipates and "foresees" the individual's subsequent development – and the likely active role played by the foetus, considered in its individuality. In this context, Piontelli doesn't totally agree with the observations that only consider the mother's point of view and inner experience, as the reality of the child is mediated through the mother's phantasies and words.

CONCLUSIONS

Through what has been illustrated so far, we may understand how the ultrasound scan represents a moment of strong emotional mobilization primarily for the future mother, whose internal experiences were the main object of our investigation. We cannot neglect, though, the importance of the complex and manifold psychologi-cal resonances even inside those who, for various reasons, share the experience – fascinating and disquieting at the same time – of the encounter with the life of a baby since the dawn of his/her existence: the father and the other family mem-bers; the doctor performing the ultrasound scan, whose unconscious motivations and expectations may be reflected on the "human" quality of the encounter with the pregnant woman; and the observer who, as I have personally experienced, cannot escape coming to terms with her own memories, desires, expectations and "losses". Our group, too, continuing with the analysis of these themes, has often gone through moments of emotional and learning flurry, by way of identification movements with the various "actors" of the ultrasound scanning scenario. In a nutshell, I believe a new frontier has opened up to observe the development of "its majesty the foetus" and to create an atmosphere of higher attention and care around it.

NOTES

1 Various French authors (Jean Bergeret, Michel Soulé, André Soler, etc.) tried to demonstrate how, in psychotherapeutic practice, a few situations illustrate the traces left in the psychism of the emotions experienced in the intrauterine life. The hypothesis that the maternal emotions exert an influence on the behaviour of the baby in the womb has also been demonstrated experimentally by Yvonne Masakowsky in 1996. After all, the foetus' reaction to the maternal emotion is also mentioned in Saint Luke Gospel! It is actually plausible that the maternal emotions triggered by the ultrasound scan examination, especially if intense and unpleasant, become alterations of the physiological cardiac, respiratory rhythms, etc., for the foetus as well.

2 Formerly, Sigmund Freud, Donald Winnicott, Wilfred Bion and Marion Milner had guessed the continuity between the intrauterine life and the subsequent development of the individual psychism.

3 "*Antropologie du foetus*" was actually the title of an international conference that took place in Lyon in November 2004.

4 I am grateful to Doctor Maria Bianchini, head of the ultrasound scan outpatient clinic facility at the Public Healthcare Unit no. 10 in Florence, for letting me take part in her activity.

5 The concept of *extension* was discussed by Dina Vallino on the occasion of the First National Conference on the Infant Observation that took place in Florence in 1999, and further analysed during the Seventh International Conference on Infant Observation (Florence, 2004). *See* Cresti, Farneti, Pratesi (2001) and Cresti & Nissim (2007).

6 Bernard Golse and Monique Bydlowski (2001) described the gradual process of "objectification" the mother does of her own foetus/child in four stages: 1) purely internal object; 2) physically internal object but already psychically externalized; 3) physical external object but psychically still internalized; and 4) definitely external object.

7 For the problem of the emotional repercussions of previous abortions, see Chapter 10.

8 In his writing on *The uncanny,* Freud writes, among other things: "Dismembered limbs, a severed head, a hand cut off at the wrist [...] feet which dance by themselves [...] all these have something peculiarly uncanny about them, especially when they prove able to move of themselves in addition" (Freud, 1919, p. 244). At the basis of such anxieties, there could be the phantasies on the interior of the maternal body and the connected castration anxieties.

9 French clinical psychologist and haptotherapist, author of a short but valuable text on *L'écographie obstétricale expliquée aux parents,* 2005.

10 The myth of the Egyptian god Horus is a good metaphor of the importance of look, in all its aspects. The theme of the eye and its protective/malign functions can be found also in many Muslim cultures.

11 Soler underlines that our culture is much more *optical,* than *haptic,* it is more *scopic,* than *tactile*; the culture of the *nearby* leaves space to the culture of the *far away,* the *stranger.* The *distality* (distance) puts, by definition, the *being* at a distance.

12 The French expression *inquiétante étrangeté* corresponds to the Freudian concept of *Unheimliche.*

13 As already mentioned, the ultrasound scan image provokes phantasy/projections in phantasy similar to the Rorschach test.

14 This research work has been used not only in many publications, conference speeches, etc., but also for an interesting "multimedia kit" on the obstetrical ultrasound scan.

15 Donald Winnicott (1947) states that the mother hates her infant from the word "go", meaning she first invests her foetus – and then the child – in ambivalence.

16 François Sirol, in the article *La haine de la mère enceinte pour son foetus* (1998), illustrates in detail the reasons that may explain this type of feeling, more or less conscious, in the pregnant woman.

17 In Paris there are, as a matter of fact, various groups of echographists, gynaecologists, psychotherapists, psychoanalysts, based on modes such as Balint Groups, besides a study group "Médicine et psychanalyse" directed by Danièle Brun, that organize biennial conferences with the aim of exchanging views and opinions.

REFERENCES

Bydlowski, M. (2000) *Je reve un enfant. L'experience intérièure de la maternité.* Paris: Odile Jacob.

Bydlowski, M., Golse, B. (2001) "De la transparence psychique à la préoccupation maternelle primarie. Une voie de l'objectalisation". In: Le carnet/PSY, 63: 30–33.

Cresti, L., Farneti, P., Pratesi, C. (2001) (Eds.) *Osservazione e trasformazione.* Roma: Borla.

Cresti, L., Nissim, S. (2007) (Eds.) *Percorsi di crescita.* Roma: Borla.

Delassus, J.M. (1995) *Le sens de la maternité.* Paris: Dunod.

Ferrara Mori, G. (2006) "The interior experience of maternity". In: La Sala, G.B., Fagandini, P., Iori, V., Monti F., Blickstein, I. (Eds.) *Coming into the World: a Dialogue between Medical and Human Sciences,* pp. 85–102. Berlin: Walter de Gruiter & Co.

Freud, S. (1919) "The Uncanny". In Strachey, J (Ed.) (1955/2001). *The Standard Edition of the Complete Psychological Works of Sigmund Freud,* Volume XVII (1917–1919), pp. 219–249. London, Vintage.

Kohn-Feist, M. (1996) "Echographie et fantasmes parentaux". In: *La maternité et le sacré.* Paris: Spirale, pp. 63–70.

Meltzer, D. & Harris Williams, M. (1988) *The Apprehension of Beauty. The role of aesthetic conflict in development, art and violence.* The Clunie Press for The Roland Harris Library No. 1.

Piontelli, A. (1992) "Dal punto vista del feto. Brevi appunti su uno studio osservativo della gravidanza e del periodo post–natale". In: Ammaniti, M. (Ed.) *La gravidanza tra fantasia e realtà.* Roma: Il Pensiero Scientifico: 109–120.

Sirol F. (1998) "La haine pour le fœtus". In Soulé, M. (Ed.) *L'échographie de la grossesse.* Toulouse, ERES, 2011: pp. 215–241.

Soler. A. (2005) *L'échographie obstétricale expliquée aux parents.* Ramonville-Saint-Agne: Editions Erés.

Soulé, M., Gourand, L., Missonier, S., Soubieux, M.J. (1999) *Ecoute voir ... L'échographie de la grossesse. Les enjeux de la relation.* Toulouse: Editions Erés.

Winnicott, D.W. (1947) "Hate in the Counter-Transference". In: *International Journal of Psycho-analysis,* vol. XXX, 1949, pp. 69–74.

Chapter 6

The development of the psychic womb

The weft and the warp

Maria Rosa Ceragioli, Arianna Luperini, Gabriella Smorto

In England in 1935 a group of mothers created a multi-author correspondence magazine. Everything started thanks to one of them who, living in a situation of isolation, had launched an appeal on a magazine: "Can any mother help me?". This is how the Cooperative Correspondence Club was founded. Every month, every mother would send a letter on a topic of interest for all the others. The editor, once collected the letters under the form of a magazine, would send them to the first woman of a previously agreed upon list who would add her comment before sending the magazine to the second and so on until the magazine returned in the hands of the first. "This way everyone was going to read and comment on what everyone else had written". One of the women in the group, Elettra, has recently described the situation of mothers in our times: many things have changed, some have become simpler, but this has not made love simpler, which keeps on being a mystery, a terribly complex issue.

(From "la Repubblica", April 8, 2007)

We felt we could see in this activity of the group a good example of the coming together of a *psychic womb*[1], the same as we experienced in the observation group on the internal motherhood. The different observation experiences that were recalled and discussed in the group have spun threads of thought that, once woven into the participants' minds, allowed the surfacing of different aspects in the pregnant women's experiences. Our attention was addressed to the container itself, allowing the woman to process the pregnancy experience, thus weaving the weft and the warp of her womb. In this work, we think about the womb as the psychic fabric supporting and protecting the pregnancy somato-psychic processes. Monique Bydlowski, talking about the work of the mothers in the *internal motherhood*, writes: "The work of the gestation is one of the residual forms of craftsmanship linking up the modern human being to ancestral forms of work" (Bydlowski, 2000, p. 77 [own translation]).

In the film by Eleonore Faucher entitled *A Common Thread* (2004), we encounter again the image of the fabric woven by two women in the work rooms of a pregnancy. Claire, a very young adolescent, is pregnant, although it is not a wanted pregnancy, and her mother does not know about it. Claire is slightly confused but she decides to continue her pregnancy in secret, thinking to give birth anonymously, but at the same time she decides to make one of her desires come true: becoming an embroiderer. So she meets Madame Melikian, a mature woman who has recently lost her son and who shares with her the passion for embroidery. Both women are suffering because of what has happened to them, they refuse it, and live a suspended situation in which there is no contact with a thought that allows ways out. Interweaving in the embroidery room the refusal with the mutual attention, the two women, besides their ages, will manage to be mothers one for the other. Madame Melikian, overcoming a suicide attempt, will regain her will to live and the joy to be of help to other young people; Claire will slowly develop the capacity to love herself and will find the desire to keep the child.

In her comment to the film, Paola Golinelli (2007) writes: "In the silence of the workroom, where only the sound of the sewing machine resounds, the machine being the symbol of the work that joins them, the two women process their losses, mirroring one in the other, in a continuous interweaving, in which one puts something of herself in the other" [own translation]. In the encounter with the other woman, inside a womb-workroom, Claire may thus "face the mysterious nature of what is happening in her womb" (op. cit., p. 5 [own translation]) and set up the psychic cloth that will support her pregnancy.

Our experience listening to women before, during and after their pregnancies leads us to re-state, as already highlighted by other authors (Bibring, Winnicott, Racamier, Meltzer, Bydlowski, Bergeret-Amselek), that the biological conception does not necessarily coincide with the possibility of a mental conception. Only if the mental conception goes hand in hand with the biological conception is the woman in the condition of developing the capacity to hold and contain, allowing for the harmonious development of the mother-child relationship.

The exploration of the pregnant women's mental states shows us the way in which the developing psychic womb requires the implementation of a creative process that stirs up emotions that are very close to the turbulence that occurs in the aesthetic conflict (Meltzer, 1988). What can be more beautiful than being joined with the child as experienced during the pregnancy? At the same time, though, what can be more uncanny than the parallel idea of the inevitable dimension of separateness of the child in the womb? Pregnant women experience in their bodies and minds the uncanny beauty of being joined – and separated – which is the matrix of every form of biological and mental life.

We have already seen (Chapter 2) how the moment of the announcement takes place when the mother is in a condition of immaturity-prematurity, and is therefore accompanied and followed by big uncertainties, both in the internal experience and in the external manifestations. "As soon as I discovered it [being pregnant], I immediately felt as if I were on the clouds, it was like this for a week", says a woman during an ante-natal course. As it happens in some Renaissance paintings of Madonnas, at the beginning the woman may find herself staring into space, she may show the need to take some distance from emotions that are too strong, or, as if trying to put order in the disruption-chaos that has emerged, to put a more rational, cognitive aspect close to the intense emotion by analysing processes and events. If one thinks about the opening of the book of *Genesis* ("In the beginning God created the heavens and the earth. Now the earth was formless and empty, darkness was over the surface of the deep, and the Spirit of God was hovering over the waters"), one can clearly see the efficacy with which the chaos that heralds the creative act is illustrated.

From an undifferentiated emotion to the possibility to differentiate, to take in the significance of what is happening, to its whole extent – this is the shift that mothers do. A drive to look may appear, and so the woman steps into the "dark wood"; but a reaction of fear, of closure against knowledge may intervene. This block, this interruption of the knowledge-gaining path, when it occurs, may hinder the access to all those processes that anticipate the experience that can, vice-versa, promote the new bonds with the nucleus child, with the partner, with one's own mother and father. As Bydlowski again writes (Bydlowski, 2000, p. 27 [own translation]), "when the foetus develops [...] a weft takes shape in the unconscious of the future parents, a cloth of dreams, of secret desires, of memories, of words" (cf. also Soulè, 1990).

The visible and the non visible parts of the weft, with the grey areas representing the reverse side of the fabric, effectively embody that simultaneous presence of opposed feelings, love and fear, desire and rejection making up "the womb cloth". The thought that is conceived around the foetus-child nourishes the child, builds up the mother and feeds their relationship, acting as a second placenta. The possibility of being intimate with herself in her different aspects is the yarn used to weave the mother's psychic container.

The ambivalence is an unavoidable element of the pregnant woman's psychic state. The foetus may be experienced as a love object but also, just like with feelings of fear and mistrust, "other" from oneself, "an indiscreet witness of unknown parts of one's own self that one did not wish to be revealed" (Bydlowski, 2000, p. 28 [own translation]). The partner and the family members, too, may be invested with similar feelings, in a flexible coming and going of emotional states.

The popular culture shows both the great affective value of joy and pleasure in having children and the aspects of sacrifice and difficulty that are inherently part of this experience. The lyrics of some lullabies clearly show, as Gabriella Bartoli says (2006), mother's affective ambivalence. Here is one such lullaby[2]:

> Lullaby, lullaby, ooh,
> Who will I give this baby to?
> If I give him to the bogeyman,
> For a whole year he'll keep him,
> If I give him to the old hag,
> For a week she will keep him, ahh.
> I will give him to the little angel
> Who will keep him until morning.
> Lullaby, lullaby, oh.

Taking the ambivalence in the mind and sharing it facilitates the pregnancy development, the relationship with the child and the knowledge of the woman by herself. An experience based on the denial of the ambivalence may instead lead to idealization or the prevailing of a technical vision of the process. Therefore, we may see mothers who are extremely dedicated to their family and children, mothers only preoccupied to do what needs to be done, mothers who only allow themselves to think already thought-about thoughts (or what we could call *borrowed thoughts*) – so much so that the encounter with the child at birth may turn out to be like a sudden event that could leave them devoid of resources.

The denial of the ambivalence may take on other forms. Donald Meltzer (1973, p. 168) describes what he calls "delusion of pregnancy" as that situation in which "the pregnancy has been apprehended in psychic reality" *and* the woman does not express a real maternal capacity, but rather, she "acts up" as a mother. In these situations, the woman appears to be motivated more by competition with other women, with her own mother, rather than by the desire to become like her, a mother.

In the *Bible* episode of the Judgement of Solomon on the two mothers, one may find many aspects of the internal motherhood. And we also find there the dimension described by Meltzer. Two women gave birth on the same day and in the same place. One of the two children dies. Both mothers claim that the child who is alive is hers. Solomon orders to cut the child in two, but the mother of the living child, spurred by a deep compassion for her son, tells the king: "Give her the living child and by no means kill him". While the other replies: "Let him be neither mine nor yours, but divide him". The king answers and says: "Give the first woman the living child, and by no means kill him; she is his mother!". The first mother is ready to give up her child, the other cannot access the separation. She is competing with another woman, rather than being a mother: she wants an object that shows her superiority and therefore she is not willing to give up on it. As she is imprisoned in a narcissistic dimension, it is impossible for her to mourn over the separation. The mother is the one who, having thought her own child, has the possibility to start the process of separation from her child, a fundamental element of the maternal identity.

Donald Meltzer (op. cit., p. 168) observes that "in so far as a woman experiences her pregnancy as her own, she is free [...] to mourn. [...] from among her many internal babies a mother is phantasied to 'select' the baby to be nurtured for birth. And inasmuch this 'gift of life' is from her, its confiscation or destruction involves her in a task of mourning whereby the child is received back inside and restored to its place among her internal babies". Within this framework, a voluntary interruption of the pregnancy may, too, be part of the development of the internal motherhood.

Bergeret-Amselek (2005) underlines that often along the path to acquire *maternality,* to use Racamier's[3] words, the conception of an unwanted child is an acting out of the desire to enter a crisis to become a mother, and the pregnancy interruption is a second acting out, as a refusal of the activation of that same crisis.

In these cases, it is possible to see, in the psychological work around the request for an interruption, the dynamics of the psychic womb taking shape.

> A young couple of students requested an interruption of pregnancy: Livia, 19, is at week four of her pregnancy and does not seem to be convinced about the step she is about to take. She would like not to interrupt the pregnancy because, she says, "this child has proved to be very resistant to everything". Actually, immediately after intercourse, she thought of the possibility of having got pregnant and, despite not having used the day-after pill, she tried in many ways to stop this pregnancy. But she was not able to self-induce a miscarriage. Her boyfriend is against continuing the pregnancy: he would feel forced to stop studying to care for the child and he does not know how their relationship would go; they have only been together for seven months! Only their respective mothers know about the pregnancy and they agree about the decision to voluntarily interrupt the pregnancy, even though the girl's mother, initially, would have liked her daughter to keep this child. Thanks to the meetings, we could witness a progressive shift from the critical adolescent dimension in which the pregnancy is located and of which it was a result, to the emerging of unresolved issues and conflicts – for instance, Livia's relationship with her mother and father, who have separated, the rivalry with her mother, the ambivalence towards the child.

This pregnancy makes one think of a "test" the girl underwent, to see whether she could get pregnant, look after children, be a woman like her [female] cousins who are mothers already: they told her "now it's your turn". It seems this baby is functional to an identity definition for Livia, and that – at least at the beginning – there is not any thinking of a child-separate-from oneself to be looked after. It is indeed the possibility to talk together of this experience in the consultation sessions that allows the emergence of guilt and an ensuing atonement need, with the development of an increasing awareness of the need to leave the infantile dimension to think and therefore decide. The access to a depressive position allows Livia to become aware that every choice – whatever it is – implies giving up on something, but this is growth.

Eleonora, seen for an analysis, can show us the developments of an experience that like Livia's starts with an interruption of pregnancy. Outside the narcissistic dimension, the woman may look at what happens to her and choose to enter the pregnancy dimension in intimacy with herself, looking at herself and little by little managing to fix her stare on the event.

> Eleonora, 36, arrives to her analyst's office saying "the world seems devoid of colours". She has just experienced a voluntary interruption of pregnancy. She recalls how in the days before the interruption, she was worried not to drive on bumpy roads and at the same she was absolutely positive about the interruption. She accepts the proposal of a four-session-a-week analysis, but the day after she phones and says: "It's too much, when I left I felt

disorientated". The analyst and the patient decide together to start with two sessions. During the sessions, the analyst often finds herself thinking that the expression of Eleonora's aggressiveness is inhibiting and she cannot intervene to say something. It is the same aggressiveness that the analyst herself experiences inside in the form of feelings of annoyance, boredom, repetitiveness, and lack of interest. She has the impression that with Eleonora, her interpretation capacities are very much reduced and she feels guilty for that. This relationship seems to her just a taking away, from both parts. After a few years, the hypothesis of suggesting to the woman to end the treatment starts developing in the analyst's mind, but it is accompanied by a substantial dissatisfaction, the feeling of not having been able to help her patient more. It is only in that moment that Eleonora seems to start using the cure differently: silence appears as a new dimension of this relationship, and the feelings of sadness can now be conveyed and fully felt, without having to shut their mouth with a constant but mellow anger. The analyst starts thinking that *ending* may perhaps mean re-proposing to Eleonora the offer of four sessions, as a symbol of an entire work that may contain the patient's different aspects. The cure process started anew and the time past that the analyst had experienced as wasted and unused was re-thought as necessary, preparatory time. One day, Eleonora steps in the room and the analyst phantasizes that she is pregnant. Two weeks later, the patient tells her she is pregnant. At the fifth month of pregnancy, on the occasion of the amniocentesis, Eleonora has contractions and she is told it is better for her to rest; therefore she cannot continue with the analysis. The child is born when due. Eleonora went back to visit the analyst, saying she feels the need to restart the work, but in reality, she never resumed her sessions. At Christmas, she gave the analyst a little beautiful poinsettia. The analyst thinks about the flower as an image that well describes that "vital minimum" achieved with the analysis.

We keep on observing at the 0–5 Service the continuation of the bewilderment in the acquisition of the psychic womb. The 0–5 Service has been devised in England at the Tavistock Clinic and it offers psychotherapy through short consultations with young children and their parents.

We meet Sara there, who is four months old, and her parents. The mother, cultivated and knowledgeable, remembering the initial moments with her daughter, says: "I was alone faced with the problems". As her words highlight perfectly ("the little girl is taking shape based on my responses"), she felt the newborn baby was totally and exclusively dependant on her. Sara's mother feels she carries a milk that is not nourishing and, faced with the child's needs, anxious thoughts surface about her maternal function, felt as being totally devoid of resources. All the nourishing and caring functions are shifted outside, projected onto an outside that, instead, seems to be rich in resources and knowledge. This mother is wondering, alarmed, and repeatedly asks the outside: "Is what I'm doing OK?". On the other hand, the father, who is trying to support her, says regretfully: "I haven't read enough about children". The first consultations were tinged with a sense of dismay, revealing much deeper anxieties: this mother felt persecuted by her child because she had kept in herself a maternal image forced to function at levels of excellence. She was asking for help to find a place for all those fierce and aggressive feelings that she had for her daughter, despite loving her. Probably old bonds were resurfacing. The tolerance for her oscillatory processes, determined by the presence at the same time of contrasting emotions – ambivalence indeed – allowed this mother to have a more solid rooting in this experience. During the last but one meeting, Sara's mother is able to allow herself to say: "I can't be a perfect mother!". It is only after finding the opportunity to say the unspeakable, to talk about her grey areas, that this mother discovered the joy of letting herself go to the spontaneity in the relationship with her daughter; therefore she manages to say, "I'm more able to accept the unexpected".

We can see also by way of these experiences that the taking shape of the psychic womb requires the mental conception and the processing of the destructive drives towards the child, meant as "other", that comes to be in a possible conflict with the progression of mother's life. By widening our perspective, we may say that all the places where the pregnant woman goes to be treated or that she attends should be able to develop and express a psychic function that acknowledges and protects all the processes we described. In this sense, as Marinopoulos says (2005, p. 170), the "social fabric" may itself be a womb in which children are born together with their mothers and fathers. Indeed, "if the psychic cure lays in the hand of the psychologist, taking in the emotions of the future parents lays in everybody's hands" and "if we tried to put together a 'non-judgemental, empathic, social shell', we would be able to pay an authentic attention to all these births" [own translation]. As a way of conclusion, we believe one of the conditions to protect health in fathers' and mothers' primary relationships with their children is the existence of a social body – that is, all of us – that by expressing its primary maternal preoccupation, becomes mothers' mother.

NOTES

1   The authors use here a rather old-fashioned word, "grembo", that has a wider meaning than the English "womb", one that focuses on the features of containment. The Italian word literally means the concave space that, in a sitting person, exists between their knees and chest, with a particular reference to women: il grembo materno; la mamma tiene in grembo il suo piccino, avere (o portare) in grembo = expecting, being pregnant (with), (fam.). By extension, it refers to the internal part of something: in (o nel) grembo a (o di) = in, inside (sth), within. From grembo, the word "grembiule" (apron) developed, that is, a piece of fabric used to cover the front of a person, worn over clothes to protect them when working.

2   Popular Italian lullaby: *Ninnananna, ninna-oh!/Questo bimbo a chi lo do?/Lo darò all'uomo nero / che lo tenga un anno intero./ Lo darò alla befana / che lo tenga una settimana./ Lo darò all'angiolino / che lo tenga in sul mattino. /Ninnananna, ninna-oh!*

3   Paul-Claude Racamier coined the term "maternality", combining the words "maternal", "motherhood" [maternité, in French], and "natality". According to Racamier's definition, maternality includes all the psycho-affective processes belonging to both pregnancy and the post-partum period and should be considered as an existential step in the development of the female identity.

REFERENCES

Bartoli, G. (2006) *Luci e ombre nelle ninne nanne maternità e ambivalenza affettiva*. Milano: Guerini e Associati.

Bergeret–Amselek, C. (2005) *Le mystère des mères*. Paris: Desclée de Brouwer.

Bydlowski, M. (2000) *Je reve un enfant. L'experience intérièure de la maternité*. Paris: Odile Jacob.

Golinelli, P. (2007) "Le ricamatrici: il brillio dello sguardo materno". In: *Atti dei Seminari multipli della S.P.I.*, Bologna. Unpublished.

Marinopoulos, S. (2005) *Dans l'intime des mères*. Paris: Fayard.

Meltzer, D. (1973) *Sexual States of Mind*. Pertshire, Scotland: Clunie Press.

Meltzer, D. & Harris Williams, M. (1988) *The Apprehension of Beauty. The role of aesthetic conflict in development, art and violence*. The Clunie Press for The Roland Harris Library No. 1.

Racamier, P.C. & Taccani, S. (1986) *Il lavoro incerto, ovvero la psicodinamica del processo di crisi*. Pisa: Edizioni del Cerro.

Soulé, M. (1990) "La mère qui tricote suffisamment". In: *Revue française de psychanalyse*, 1992/4 (no 56), pp. 1079–1088.

Chapter 7

In the analysis room

Pregnancy questions the analytic tool

Arianna Luperini

A pregnancy that starts and develops during an analysis offers the analyst the possibility to observe the origins of the mother-child relationship, starting from those stages when the child not only is not concretely present, but also when there is no conscious desire of motherhood in the woman. For this reason, I believe that the analysis room is a privileged vantage point from which to observe the pregnant woman's psychic movements. Pregnancy, as a psychosomatic event of the woman's life, demands, when it occurs during an analysis, that the analyst interacts with an aspect of reality that the pregnancy status imposes with all its evidence. The latter, though, is not easy to manage because of the enormous issue of the psychoanalyst's abstinence in regard to reality. We may wonder whether pregnancy is not, because of this, a micro-trauma for the analyst at work, or rather for the analytic relationship, in terms of its readability and interpretability.

This leads us to the issue of the limit in psychoanalysis that is encountered at many levels. The concept of the limit in psychoanalysis shows many aspects, as it is a structural and genetic concept, but it is also developmental and therapeutic. J.B. Pontalis (1977) suggests that we interpret every progress, whether theoretical or clinical, as something that can be born only by chance based on what he defines as the obstacle or, in other words, the limit. It is the limit that, by showing itself as beyond the threshold of what can be tolerated, becomes a force that generates something new. It is the point where something that is met with resistance that the actual psychoanalytic work takes place, meant not only under the epistemological profile, but also from the point of view of the cure itself, as it puts the analytic couple to the test of transformability. A limit we experience is that of the body: it may be thought of as what lays at the bottom of the psychic and, even as an extreme limit, it may represent the last resistance at the end of an analysis, that which we can call the "remains".

In cases of pregnancies during the analysis, the analyst finds himself/herself having to think of a relationship in which there is a place, besides the psychic reality of the patient-mother, also for another reality – the child's – with "its coming to analysis", who on the one hand somehow makes itself apparent, and on the other hand, "it's not in analysis", as it was not included in the initial contract on which the analysis is essentially based.

In my experience, all this implies a change in the technique, because there are always two levels of listening present: listening to the analytic relationship and listening to the patient's communications in their dimension of reality. It is important to try and not let one eclipse the other. The analyst should always remain, in relation to these two levels of listening, in a condition similar to what occurs during certain times of the day, when the sun is already high in the sky and yet the moon is still visible.

Linda, in analysis for the last three years, is at the fifth month of pregnancy and very much distressed because, even though she had decided to undergo an amniocentesis, she has experienced this exam as if it meant a premature separation from her child. It is a feeling that has deep roots in her history as a daughter, and while I listen to her, I sense many reverberations of a lot of material that filled the sessions of this analysis and, mostly, the memory of counter-transference feelings felt at the beginning of my work with her.

Linda is very worried for the results of the amniocentesis that she will receive during our break for the summer holidays. When at the beginning of August she calls to inform me that she received the results and that everything is fine, I sense that she's very excited to be able to tell me this news (I had given her my phone number so that she could reach me), and I recognize that I am excited, too: "I'm pleased", I tell her. An element of reality powerfully enters this analytic relationship, but this does not exclude the possibility of, later on, using its therapeutic potential by giving a sense to reality.

As an analyst (and perhaps as a woman analyst?), the experience of pregnancies in analysis led me to reflect on the function of the feeling of devotion. Devotion belongs, on one hand, to the position and frame of mind of the analyst at work, and it is a fundamental element of the mother-child relationship as well. It is devotion that constitutes one of the foundations of the feeling of being contained.

By *devotion* I mean the possibility to predispose oneself for listening where nothing is already known and every communication, from smell to words, is listened to; I think about De Toffoli's beautiful words (2003) when she wonders: "Is it possible that the foetus' 'being there', if not acknowledged or forgotten, gets lost, if the emotion aroused by the feeling of existing does not find a counterpart in the maternal psyche–soma?" [own translation].

A few days before announcing to me that she was pregnant, Anna, a young woman in analysis, after telling me about a dream in which she was told that a friend – who in reality had gone through a period of serious psychic suffering – was pregnant, tells me in association to the dream: "She was better because she was pregnant or she was pregnant because she was better, as if by feeling better there was the need to feel a sense of fullness, fullness of devotion, just like it turned out to be".

This young woman, already mother of a little girl, after the first Christmas break since the beginning of the analysis, tells me about the dream she had the night before: "A very long road … there's me, Fabio [her husband] and Giulia [her daughter]; the girl suddenly leaves the car; there's a hole and she is swallowed up, I couldn't even hear her crying". She associates about something being irremediably lost, something that has disappeared completely; it is a feeling of total absence. A few instants later, Anna tells me: "As if the value … as if I needed to give substance to this infantile part by way of another life".

Some time later, Anna tells me about another dream: "I was trying to curl up, my mum was on the sofa, I wanted to be hugged … I was desperately trying to find the niche in her arms". Not much later, Anna announces her pregnancy and tells me: "I've always had the tendency to tone down emotions, but they are surfacing now, as if I perspire them". To use Ferraro's and Nunziante Cesaro's words (1985), "the body that opens up to procreation gives the woman a form of immediate knowledge about the origins, and therefore the unspeakable, impossible to symbolize, from which the man is precluded. Man opposes his own form of knowledge, the knowledge of *logos* based on renouncing, on exiling himself from the place of the origin" [own translation].

In regard to herself in pregnancy, and thinking back about her first experience, Anna tells me: "I'm the one who is different, sometimes I think that is the result of an interaction, not everything depends on me, it is being together with a different person, it is a different being together as opposed to another person".

Luca is born when he was due and when I meet Anna again, she immediately tells me: "You should see him, he's so cute! Children are earthquakes: this child has destroyed all my certainties; he's a passionate child".

The experience with Anna led me to wonder about the extent to which my being a woman analyst has determined the possibility to lend itself to undifferentiating levels that, at a superficial view of this analytic relationship, could be interpreted as an emotional analyst short-circuit, and the extent to which instead the actual female prerogative of "keeping inside" has contributed to the formation of the "nest" in which to be born and give birth. We should not forget that "the woman has always undertaken, during the pregnancy, this 'responsibility' to creatively cross unknown spaces between me and you, and between body and mind, harmonizing them" (De Toffoli, 2003) [own translation].

Busato Barbaglio (2004), quoting Stern and the concept of implicit communication, talks of "a communication that accompanies the whole analysis and that sometimes remains the most important part, that is not always possible or necessary to make explicit and use in an interpretation, but that is, if it occurs, a level of essential communication".

I believe that not only is it not always possible and necessary to make this level of communication explicit, but that, perhaps, it is indeed this impossibility that represents the specific quality of these levels of the relationship, where this same quality is in a close correlation with the possibility, on the part of the analyst, to "ponder" for as long as it is needed about the birth of a thought/child.

But devotion as a predisposition for listening without pre-existing limits may expose the analyst to experiences of fecundation of the mind through the encounter with thoughts never before thought, the encounter with the new in its most radical dimension, a new psycho-biological. I am referring to the experiences I have had in my analytic practice with women who chose assisted reproduction, leading me to unexplored territories of the mind. In these situations, what is not known is not only the child, who comes in analysis as an unknown third, but also all that we rely on as being known; all that we always thought represented the foundations of the psychic life and of the relationship, can no longer be conceived in the same way, that is through known parameters, but needs to be invented, created; as S. Zalusky (2000) observes, a new situation has been created due to new reproduction techniques which make it possible to limit differences that exist between fantasy and action.

With Martina (in analysis for two years at this point), I never took notes while I was listening to her, which I thought impossible up to now and that I attributed to a strong level of concreteness to which this woman clung to. Shortly before she communicated to me her decision to have a child by assisted procreation, I found myself taking a few notes in a notebook. I realized afterwards that I was using the notebook backwards, and I wondered if I was trying to give expression to an "acting out" dimension of this pregnancy, with all the defensive aspects characterizing it, without preventing me, though, to also listen to the expressive-communicative aspects of this acting out. In parallel, I was keeping in mind that "pregnancy is an experience in which one may recognize this two-sided aspect: the attraction towards a backwards path is made explicit in it and at the same time, there is the mobilization of an unsettling form towards differentiation and growth" (Ferraro, Nunziante Cesaro, 1985 [own translation]).

I also wonder to what extent my *lapsus* in the use of the notebook represented a sort of condensation, as an experience of a pregnancy in analysis highlights a parameter of the analytic setting: the circular time, that experience of time promoted by the repetition of the rhythm of the sessions and their regularity. The pregnancy adds a parameter of linear time which is always present, but that in the case of a pregnancy in analysis, becomes prevalent, thus reversing the weights on the scales of these two experiences of time.

If pregnancy, like analysis, finds its place between the new and repetition, then one may think that a pregnancy experienced during the analysis promotes an intensification of the transference where the child itself, with its own characteristics, may act as a modifying factor and thus fecundate the transference. Containing a child, being at the same contained in the therapeutic relationship, may allow the woman who is about to become a mother to experience something she has never experienced before. On the other hand, the analytic work finds its position between repetition and the new where the new is not possible if not within the repetition. It is extended repetition (that permits transformations and accumulated differences) that stimulates new connections. Therefore, it is an important element of change because it permits past situations to become relevant again, and these past situations can be experienced in the analytic relationship under different conditions (*see* Cargnelutti, 1987).

What I was able to experience with the Pre-Infant group was that "nest" made of knowledge and method in which every thought finds a time of its own development and birth. In this sense, it was an experience very similar to the experience of a pregnancy in analysis, where "the arms" of the group held "the me analyst" at work, just like the analyst holds with her mind the "arms" of the woman patient who is experiencing pregnancy.

REFERENCES

Busato Barbaglio, C. (2004) "Setting e disposizione materna dell'analista". In: *Rivista di psicoanalisi*, I, 4, pp. 1149–1166.

Cargnelutti, E. (1987) "I concerti di 'continuo', discontinuo', 'discreto': convenienza del loro uso in psicoanalisi". In: Muratori, A. M. (Ed.), *Il "continuo" e il "discreto" in psicoanalisi*, pp. 79–102. Roma: Borla.

De Toffoli, C. (2003) "Il lavoro somato–psichico della coppia materno–fetale: come 'ciò' diviene 'tu'". In: *Richard & Piggle*, 11, 3, pp. 271–284.

Ferraro, F., Nunziante Cesaro, A. (1985) *Lo spazio cavo e il corpo saturato. La gravidanza come "agire" tra fusione e separazione*. Milano: Franco Angeli.

Pontalis, J.B. (1977) *Frontiers in psychoanalysis: between the dream and psychic pain*. The Hogarth Press, 1981.

Zalusky, S. (2000) "Infertility in the Age of Technology". In: *J Am Psychoanal Assoc.* December 2000, 48(4):1541–62.

Chapter 8

Towards motherhood during the analysis, or in a psychoanalytic consultation

Marco Mastella

In this work, we will try to describe and develop the theme of the internal mother-hood and of being the observed *infant*, in the analysis room, by a male analyst, in difficult situations, such as to require help. Pregnancy is a very interesting experi-ence: for the *woman* directly involved, for the *analyst*, for the transformations of the *analytic field*, and for the work of the *analytic couple*.

The analytic situation is different based on whether the couple is "homosexual" (i.e. with a female analyst) or "heterosexual" (with a male analyst). Interesting studies were carried out on this theme, in particular by Arnoux & Guignard (2003) who led a mixed group of analysts, men and women. The conclusion they came to is that, even though the working through and the analytic process of each case would evolve anyway, the story that developed around the processing of the clinical material, the transference-countertransference resonances, and the trans-formations and interpretations changed completely based on the genders of the patient-analyst couple at work: listening, within the group of male and female psychoanalysts to the analytic material presented by one of them (male or female), highlighted very different resonances and interpretation (and defensive) modes between male and female analysts.

The situation is different when the analyst has a direct experience of mother-hood (or fatherhood), in particular in the counter-transference processing of those situations in which the female patient arrives *too late* to an explicit desire of real motherhood (Chodorow, 2003). However, the choice of one's future psychoanalyst should not be based entirely on any seeming compatibility between patient and analyst, as could innocently occur suggesting a homosexual person to see a self-declared homosexual analyst. Because in this way what is prevented in the analysis is the opportunity to encounter a totally new person, the analyst, who stimulates the patient's phantasies in the transference and is exposed to counter-transference experiences without a protective shield of bias (Argentieri, 2007).

My condition of male analyst in a therapeutic contact with women who have become mothers or who are wishing (to a various degree of ambivalence) to become mothers, and the only male member of the group on the internal motherhood led by Gina Ferrara Mori (2006), put me in a particular situation. I found myself in a state of anxious suspension towards the experiences recalled, so much that little by little I have started sharing a space-time area marked by rhythms that were very different from the ones I was used to.

The *mother* is a woman; becoming a mother is an issue that concerns the woman, who has been before a little girl and then a young woman: it sounds like an enigmatic banality. At times, the baby-to-be can have a sudden sensation of being dispossessed of his/her mother and at the same time of himself/herself in the *rêverie* that escapes him/her and that, even worse, escapes the dreamer herself, the mother. But then perhaps *mater semper incerta est,* from the intrapsychic point of view, because the certainty only concerns the aspects of perception (Semi, 2006). Sometimes, in analysis, it may happen that the analyst is required to suspend words. In this way, the patient (and the couple) may get to the heart of the matter – i.e. experiencing a situation in which feelings are in a *continuum* with sensations – and can also identify with the *silent analyst*, though through a deep, loyal and reliable contact, as well as with the *talking analyst*, who having felt and understood, is able to interpret.

Such a contact is well described in the film "A Common Thread" and analytically commented on by Golinelli (2007): it is a contact, and a look, that allows both "the establishment of the affective relationship of the mother with the body of the child", and the child itself, "to perceive the boundaries of one's own body, of investing it in its functions and erogenous zones, thus determining its future development" [own translation] and to process the separation anxieties, *in primis* from the maternal object.

In modern society, the *hollow space of the woman's body* has been considered as the central place of femininity. Its development may be followed over time and characterized with that particular event that pregnancy is, meant as the saturation of a space that belongs to the body, but that is also the pivot on which the development and sense of the female identity grows (Ferraro, Nunziante Cesaro, 1985). A certain type of attention, sensitivity and reflection, as it emerges from the work of the two above-mentioned authors, could be the result of the work of an entirely female world, even if it is open to the outside, in which man is naturally the other fundamental reference (Micati, 1985) – and man as male can feel dizzy and lost when looking onto this all-female world.

A WINDOW ON THE DAWN OF MOTHERHOOD DURING THE ANALYSIS

A young woman, whose father died when she was little, comes to therapy when she is about to get married and is faced with the discovery of a serious – although curable – disease of her future groom. In addition, the young woman's mother, who has always been severely depressed, has recently decided to let herself be admitted to a sheltered care facility.

The story of a female kitten that was first adopted but who then became unbearable – and for this reason was brought to a villa in the countryside, a

sanctuary for stray cats belatedly set free and returned to the law of the forest –
makes one grasp both the young woman's anxiety (that a part of herself, very little
and needy, becomes unbearable for the couple) and her fear (of not having the
resources to bear deep, primary needs) – needs that could be hers (to be adopted),
or of a future baby.

In the evening, the young woman must now look after her mother's dog, which
stays in her mother's home while the mother is now hospitalized. This situation illustrates the young woman's pressing need to have the chance to still (and
always?) tap into maternal resources (between external reality and internal reality) to look after the animal, who seems to well represent an infantile part of the
self that easily falls ill; the part that in the dream appears as a puppy walking on
two huge milk silos, to then pooh on them.

The young woman is afraid that she will not be able to be a wife, to become
an adult and support the burden attached to it, as well as the emotional and work-
related burdens it entails; she has already thought of keeping a den at some relatives' where she has being staying for a long time now.

> She dreams of arriving too early at the church for the wedding: there is no
> one there yet. She walks but she trips over her dress that is too long; she is
> worried. Then she finds herself in a terraced garden, followed by a man with
> a tube, who wants to make her die pumping out all her blood; she runs away
> terrified ("What a system that man had to go for?!", she wonders). Behind a
> hedge she sees a boy, her first love, observing her. In the everyday reality, she
> says, she is attracted to the birthing process.

The analyst thinks of motherhood, vampire-like phantasies and the return of her
first love, and tells her so. She feels relieved and opens up to the hope of overcoming these contingent (and phantasmatic) difficulties as well as discovering their
origins. The analytic couple finds itself now having to share very violent emotions that can be reconnected to the condensed experienced of very archaic, even
traumatic, sentiments mixed with adolescence-related and youth material. The
analyst also experiences all of this as a possible harbinger and organizer element
of a space for the infantile Self and the maternal.

The *development of femininity*, in its various stages and different aspects – both
more frankly erotic, psycho-sexual, and of tenderness and motherhood (Ferraro,
Nunziante Cesaro, 1985; Guignard, 2002; Schaeffer, 2002) – has been discussed
and analysed in depth, beyond the limits recognized to the original set-up given
by Freud, and likely influenced, in its theoretical formulation, by the difficulties of counter-transference processing provoked by the psychoanalysis with his
daughter Anna (Faure-Pragier, 1993). According to Shaeffer (2002), in the life of
a woman there is a complex conflict between the feminine and the maternal, that
she described specifically in five moments.

We may wonder how it could be possible that the manifold and original contributions by female psychoanalysts still remain in the shadows in relation to the
current psychoanalytic thinking (Yonke, Barnett, 2001), and how this can happen

despite the "black continent" (Freud, 1925) being less black, and the fact that it allows hypothesizing as an important role in the processing of aggressiveness, as suggested by the cases of those innumerable girls and women in analysis, who have difficulties combining choices about their career, family and looking after the children (Tyson, 2003).

On the other hand, the profound social and technological transformations of the last decades deeply affected the new female profiles and identity references. The spread of the contraceptive pill contributed to determine a radical change of the idea of the internal child, with more manifest consequences in those who do not achieve an authentic process of maturity and succumb to unconscious conflicts. Separating the idea of biological fecundation from the sexual experience may give rise to a process of de-symbolization, a splitting movement between body and psyche, an attack against the phantasy of the internal child and the organs that should generate it.

The invigorating effect of the *adult coitus*, as implying a mutual and rich exchange, may be made to refer, according to Ferraro and Nunziante Cesaro (1985), to what Meltzer stated (1973, pp. 67–68): "The foundation, in the unconscious, of the sexual life of the mature person, is the highly complicated sexual relation of the internal parents, with whom he is capable of a rich introjective identification in both masculine and feminine roles. A well-integrated bi-sexuality makes possible a doubly intense intimacy with the sexual partner by both introjection as well as a modulated projective identification which finds its place in the partner's mentality without controlling or dominating".

Pregnancy is the experience of the most intimate and long-lasting bond that may exist between two human beings: the mother and the child she carries in her womb. The intensity of the psychic work that characterizes this epoch of life – which ends, both in its psycho-sensory aspects and in its primeval, intrauterine forms, in a predictable and inevitable way, with the break-up of the bond – is surprising. For this reason, the theme of *separation* is pivotal from the very beginning of the pregnancy. Such separation takes place at various levels, and it conditions the mother's psychic life in her relationships with the parental *imago* and also of her body, with her partner, and with the baby (Lechartier-Atlan, 2001). The latter grows for a long time as an object/foetus – at first partially a stranger, then recognized as a part of the Self and narcissistically, as well as libidinally, invested as a relational object. Because of this, pregnancy may be considered the occasion, offered to women, to play with the two fundamental and contrasting drives of human existence: the need to re-establish the fusional unity and the need to evolve and become an independent individual (Ferraro, Nunziante Cesaro, 1985).

For the *analyst*, the period before and after birth is a fascinating time. It allows an unprecedented access to movements of merging and separation with the object in an adult patient, and it may be studied under three points of view: the identification rearrangements it fosters, the differentiation of the erogenous zones according to the degree of development of the foetus – this strange object – and the conflict of ambivalence between the Ego and the Non-Ego, between love and hate. All of this keeping in mind, in the background, the path of antagonisms between female and maternal, between the working woman (or a woman who is in society) who loves erotically and the woman who procreates (and becomes a mother).

We are therefore very far from the technical preconception for which, during the pregnancy, a woman is less accessible to the psychoanalytic treatment. This is a preconception that has been shared for a long time despite the significant changes in our knowledge on the pregnancy, on the analytic theory and technique, and the extensive clinical evidence – developments supporting the idea that the pregnancy is not a contraindication to analysis but, on the contrary, that it might foster the psychoanalytic progress (Goldberger, 1991).

The concept of *psychic transparency* (Bydlowski, 2000) is a useful one to illustrate the special permeability of the woman's world (and in particular of her deepest desires) while being pregnant. The pregnancy is indeed considered a real *crisis* implying fundamental and irreversible transformations to the fact of being a woman: a proper change of *status*, close to the life-death change.

In this sense, it is important to focus "on the to-be-hoped-for *reconciliation*" "between the female erotic and the maternal" that the young girl who becomes a woman "must try to perform on mother's body". This, "because the two female capacities, remaining in a tension, can be aligned without any splitting in her future body of woman and mother. Because the fact of being penetrated, to receive the penis with sexual joy is not in radical conflict with the fact of looking after, caring for and making the child inside her grow. And that all these pleasures in the same place should no longer be an object of scandal" (Schaeffer, 2002) [own translation].

There are different opinions and conceptualizations in the psychoanalytic world concerning the relevance, for the woman and her surrounding environment (in particular, for her children), of the experience of the *pregnant body*. If on the one hand there are those believing that the pregnant body has actually disappeared from the psychoanalytic theory of the female development – and that this is the case because of the deep anxiety caused, at different levels (Balsam, 2003), by such an image – on the other hand, others have analysed in depth the complexity of the figures representing the female body more or less included in the maternal body (Solis-Ponton, Moro, 2002).

The reflections derived from the transference-countertransference fabric in the analyses in which analyst and patient are women remind one of the fact that the body is a primary plane of psychic inscription (whose central mechanism is identification), and that the role of the mirror of the mother, thanks to which human beings learn to recognize themselves, is fundamental at this proto-symbolic stage of knowledge. It is that mutual space of inclusion (Sami-Ali, 1974) that can be described using the following utterances: "I am – my mother is. My mother is – I am. My body is – my mother's body is".

One may see how this identification is particularly increased when mother and child share the same gender, and that the conflicts that can be referred to the mother can also be conveyed to the daughter. Thus this perspective introduces the *intergenerational dimension*. It is actually within this that these primary identifications can be inscribed.

In the heaviest and most extreme situations of primary relationship dystonia, the result can be a real internal refusal of the female dimension, a *horror vacui*, the anxiety of a limitless empty space. This may have many disorganizing repercussions on the female universe and the existence itself of the woman. "The penetration anxiety combined with the pregnancy anxiety" are actually "intimate consequences" (Vigneri, 2004, [own translation]) of it.

Sexual intercourse may provoke a series of emotions that, going through all the vicissitudes of instinct, create a loss of boundaries of the Self. This is why a rewarding sexual life is a sort of mental feeding, and why it is so important for maturity and the psychic balance (Micati, 1988).

The pregnant body contains *something* that is perceived as both familiar and foreign at the same time: something that as soon as it starts sending the first signs of its presence, the first *autonomous movements*, shifts from being *imagined* to being alive and vibrant. Then the mother progressively compares these *autonomous movements* with sensations and perceptions belonging to her own experience, current but mostly infantile; this leads to an identification movement with the child and with the mother, and with their current, past and future relationship. Let us see now what may happen, specifically.

IMAGES AND MEMORIES CONNECTED TO THE PERCEPTION OF THE FIRST FOETAL MOVEMENTS

S. is a woman close to being 40, at her first pregnancy, in psychoanalytic psychotherapy for some time. When she perceives the first movements of her foetus as rustlings in her womb, she associates them to a sudden, vivid childhood memory: she was about four and in the summer, in the afternoon, she was left by her mother and aunt to sleep in the same room with her younger sister, who was a little older than one year old, while the two women would go to the beach. She remembers the feelings of abandonment, anger and the attempts to comfort herself playing: she used to run her fingertips on the protruding points of the plaster on the wall near the bed, and she recognized various characters of the theatre in the wall imperfections with which she invented stories. In this way, the woman seems to identify with the foetus who feels the womb wall, contained, but destined to leave or also to be left, and to have the chance to comfort himself.

The girl, growing up, became an expert ceramist. She happily became a mother and a few weeks after the baby is born, she offers her son her own hands as a toy, in an extraordinary way: she animates them, in particular her fingers, and the child is fascinated by this game. In his first years of life, the mother has then tried to be very close to him, almost in an attempt to be a better mother, and to be closer to her son than her own mother was to her, as far as she could re-process or remember. The son has then become a person who is very attentive to what the use of hands is.

For the analyst who was listening to the recollections of the pregnant patient, the work with S. provided the occasion to witness, in a participating way, a discovery and a unique experience. As a matter of fact, this called up in the analyst some infantile autobiographical memories of hot summer afternoons spent, at times, in bed with grandfather. Thus the analyst was able to feel towards the patient, about to become a mother, like a sort of grandfather (but also a sort of co-creator or co-dreamer of the child); a bit a small child, who seems to remember the contact of the fingertips with the maternal mammary areola, in identification with the foetus; a bit the mother of that patient who during the psychotherapy has mitigated both the aversions to her own mother and the once prevailing aspects of roughness (also because of remnants of still unprocessed envy and jealousy towards the maternal womb, that had brought out a younger sister) in her memory of the mother-daughter relationship; a bit defining wall (in relation to the residual adolescence phantasies of denial of limits) but at the same time also a wall that can be explored, plastic, malleable and one you can rest on; a bit in identification with the future father, excluded.

Upon S.'s wish, she introduces to the analyst the real child when he is ten months old. He feels a strong bond towards the child, as well as (perhaps in identification with the mother) the desire to entertain him. For this reason, he shows him toys. Among these, there is a dinosaur with a big toothed mouth. The child shows interest, curiosity and hesitation towards it. The analyst holds the toy in his hands so the child can familiarize with it. When the child slowly extends his forefinger towards the dinosaur, the analyst is reminded of the forefinger first exploring the womb wall, and then the breast; so he feels like suddenly uttering "ahm!", which scares the child, who starts crying.

Two years later, S.'s son goes back to the therapy room with his mother. Here he finds a little saw that he uses to play, chasing the analyst to cut his forefinger (example of a residue of the sadistic orality, of union-separation, of castration, enacted).

The *mother-daughter relationship* can be considered as the basis for every love relationship during the rest of life. Through the mother's eyes and hands, the intimate nature of love is transmitted down the generations. The mother-daughter love also is the basis for the heterosexual love and of sensual pleasure. Furthermore, sexuality separates mother and daughter, and as a consequence, the identification of the daughter with the mother becomes the most important factor of transmission of love (Klockars, Sirola, 2001). The mother-son or daughter relationship is the organizing one, with its strength and duration, all the investment of the corporeal in the *infans*. This is based on the development of drives, of psychic sexualities, around the taboo of incest. For the adult woman and mother, the body of the Other is *double*: the lover man, on one hand, the foetus who will become the baby, then child, then adult, on the other. How do the drive investments with feminine, maternal and auto-erotic distribute themselves in her? (Guignard, 2002).

According to the author, as for the psychic development of the female, this revolves around the existence of three places. The space of the *primary maternal*, the one in which from birth the first identification relationships with the mother's capacity for *rêverie* become established. The space of the *primary female*, that organizes itself in relation to the first triangle of the object relationships and the identifications (corresponding, according to Klein, to the primary female stage common to children of both sexes), and which represents the way out from the mutual mother-baby projective identification of the primary maternal. The last "place", the one of *early Oedipus*, finally derives from the primary female. For the little girl, it will mean identifying with the mother herself who deprived her of the omnipotent status of single object of motherly love.

Many suggest the importance of mothers' *ambivalence* towards their children. Often it is referred to as two types of difficulty: one linked to processing the aggressiveness towards oneself and the children, and then to integrate the expectations of self-affirmation in the motherhood experience within one's own family and in society (Hoffman, 2003).

MATERNAL AMBIVALENCE

A beautiful but worn-out woman, still young, asks for a therapy for herself and one for her son. The child, her first born, nearly six, is at times uncontainable: it seems he rejects food (he often vomits), and he is losing weight at a dangerous rate. The mother recalls her troubled life as a woman suffering from anxiety-depression crises. For this she says she has already had two long cycles of psychotherapy. She has become a mother again three months ago. The baby is macrosomic and now, she says, she suffers from gastroesophageal reflux.

The aspects related to a difficult life, the phobic elements, the difficulties in feeling a mother, the remains of a difficult relationship, not yet transformed into a restored one, with both father and mother, are all there. And there is the request to start a psychotherapy in a moment when her husband, who acts as a mother, father and tranquillizer, is no longer enough.

We can only find the space for a short consultation, focused on the crisis. The woman deals with it with relief and gratitude.

Very soon, a deep instability about her emerged: she is a capable, courageous, intuitive, ebullient woman; her ebullience is at times explosive and eruptive, at times switched off. In the patient, what emerged was also a part suffering from a deep (ambivalent) nostalgia towards her mother earth (the primeval mother to whom she feels she cannot go back) and the sense of motherhood, so idealized to become unattainable, both in her daily experience as a mother and as a daughter.

Bursts of sexuality re-surface, leading to a state of malaise, with hypochondriac fears, that will turn out to be the first signs of a third pregnancy, that she is not able to deal with so close to the second delivery.

The biological renouncement to this experience goes hand in hand with a resurfacing of traumatic infantile and adolescence memories, while with an unaware part of the self she continues the mental pregnancy. This leads the woman to suffer with intense separation anxieties at the time when she should have had to give birth; in fact, the mourning for this loss has just started.

The particular "psychic transparency" and emotional fragility make the work to process the transference-countertransference relationship exceptionally delicate. In similar situations, the psychic space is continually occupied by pressing needs and emergencies. They are the expression of anxieties that find a mental container little organized to metabolize them, and make it even more arduous to combine in a harmonious way the issues of a woman who would like to work, love and be a mother, and who feels so fragile and unable to metabolize her anxiety and her children's (besides her husband's, who seems to have been a deprived child).

"It is not easy for the mother to keep in mind in a balanced way her needs and the child's; it is not easy to tidy up between confused impressions of having acquired with motherhood new *potentials* and at the same time having lost *power*. It is certainly a new potential the capacity to identify empathically with the child, understand its needs and meet them, feeling in turn 'capable' and satisfied. But making her satisfaction coincide with the child's puts severely to the test her sense of identity. The only antidote to the risk of effacing oneself in an exclusive bond is to not give up one's own individuation, at the cost of separation, even though partial, from the child; separation that contributes to make the two roles of being at the same time *mother* and *woman* less incompatible" (Bartoli, 2006 [own translation]).

For the *analyst* who finds himself in the analysis room in the presence of a woman, now also a future mother, especially at the initial stages, there can be the temptation to just observe, amazed, rapt or terror-struck, and almost oblivious of his function (but perhaps it is the interpretation suspension). Such temptation is then followed by a recovery of the interpretation function, which may indeed become even more subdued (Roccato, 2003).

The analyst may feel how much the analytic setting can be comparable to inexpressible, pre-verbal, bodily aspects of the mother-daughter relationship, especially when this has been particularly lacking (being an orphan), in the so-called "bent to motherhood". The analytic situation can then allow a patient who had not been a wanted child, and who had lost contact with herself, to re-create herself through the analyst, "to relate to a mother-woman-female body on which to find her new position or another can feel 'looked after'", to "become a daughter to then be able to face life as a woman and now, in her plans, to become a mother" (Busato, 2004 [own translation]), to experience a "good merging" (Tagliacozzo, 1990), to appreciate a "maternal style" (Carloni, 1998).

When the analysis has been going on far too long and has ended up in an impasse, the sudden experience of the pregnancy can be kept outside the analytic context; there may be the temptation to "just do the analysis", as if "nothing had happened", as if "nothing were about to change", bringing dreams and associations regardless of what is happening in the body.

The participation to a study and work group on the internal motherhood (i.e. pre-infant), led with the inspiration from Esther Bick's Infant Observation method, can be of great help in maintaining an internal attitude of *participating observation*, delicate and respectful of the naturalness of the deep processes linked to becoming a mother.

It may happen that more pregnancies, whether continued or interrupted, *have not been mentally processed,* at the price of a huge pain, often kept in a split part of one's own mind, or projected into the surrounding environment, or in parts of one's own body. A psychoanalysis required for symptoms more easily dealt with by the psychiatric language, that thanks to shrewd and at least a little aware choice, may become the occasion, over the years, to process the deep sense of pregnancy and motherhood, realized or prevented, and to start a deep transformation (and construction) process of the internal world and of its boundaries.

PROCESSING WITH HINDSIGHT OF THE PREGNANCY AND THE INDIVIDUATION

Z., a woman close to her forties (but with an apparently endless adolescence), is prone to depressive crises and panic attacks. She becomes pregnant while doing the consultations that precede her request to start an analysis. The pregnancy, feared by the analyst because it is felt as a kind of challenge and resistance to the perspectives of an analytic work, is then followed, for fear of a psychotic breakdown, through a *vis-à-vis* psychotherapy. This allowed highlighting and trying to contain the ambivalences towards the foetus and the future father, giving some form of substance to female experiences, setting some form of limit to a highly undifferentiated internal situation, as well as temporarily dispelling doubts on the fertility, on gender identity and the repercussions of a lacking and confused primary maternal identification. When, two years later, it became possible to start the analysis, one has had the chance to witness the start-up of a processing with hindsight of the experienced motherhood, and of a process towards the integration of split aspects of the personality, such as tenderness and sexuality. This allowed the opening up of a space for the paternal figure (who had been ejected soon after giving birth), the development of a bodily image geared towards the feminine and three-dimensional, a differentiation inside/outside and a progressive reconstruction of an internal and inside world.

The patient was thus able to recover trust in herself, she started feeling more robust, more differentiated in relation to the maternal figure, and more aware of the residues of Oedipal, eroticized enmeshment with the paternal figure. She has been able to visit once again her infantile sexual (and procreation) theories and phantasies, and to cry for lost occasions (also of missed motherhoods). In this way, she has not only entered a more realistic space-time dimension, but she also allowed her daughter to have a space for the father and a relationship with him or, in his absence, with the paternal grandparents.

Thus, when the analyst-patient couple, like the internal mother-daughter couple, can work again because the *attacks on linking* (Bion, 1959) have been mitigated, the working through process can be reactivated without the feared effect of confusion and with the hope to interrupt the transmission of a melancholic nucleus from mother to daughter (Schmid-Kitsikis, 2002).

To have a harmonious psychic development, there must have been the separation allowing to access the *triangulation*. "When the phantasm of the primary scene does not get established, what persists is a fusional mother-daughter linking, depriving the daughter of the necessary space to conceive a child like a work. That the mother appoints a third as the object of her desire appears to be essential for the establishment of the Oedipus. The resolution of the Oedipus itself is an entirely different story" (Faure-Pragier, 2001 [own translation]).

It is important to be able to wait even a long time before giving interpretations. In the presence of an analyst participating observer, who is able to listen in depth, it is then perhaps possible to better tolerate this waiting, which is often filled up with the dread and fear linked to the uncertainty of the unfolding. In the analysis room, it is possible to wait with confidence, in the meantime considering idle thoughts, dreams, fears on the baby-to-be and on the coming status of the mother, who in the end perhaps will be really born: from the belly, from the maternal psyche and then the paternal one.

REFERENCES

Argentieri, S. (2007) "Omosessualità e pregiudizio". In: *Micromega*, 4: 175–187.

Arnoux, D., Guignard, F. (2003) "Significato dell'identità di genere nel setting analitico". In: *Rivista di psicoanalisi*, 4, pp. 739–750.

Balsam, R.H. (2003) "The vanished pregnant body in psychoanalytic female developmental theory". In: *J. Am. Psychoanal: Assoc.*, 2003 Fall; 51 (4): 1153–79.

Bartoli, G. (2006) *Luci e ombre nelle ninne nanne maternità e ambivalenza affettiva.* Milano: Guerini e Associati.

Bion, W. (1959) "Attacks on linking". In: *Second Thoughts*. London, Karnac, 1967: pp. 93–109.

Busato Barbaglio, C. (2004) "Setting e disposizione materna dell'analista". In: *Rivista di psicoanalisi*, I, 4, pp. 1149–1166.

Bydlowski, M. (2000) *Je reve un enfant. L'experience intérièure de la maternité.* Paris: Odile Jacob.

Carloni, G. (1998) "Lo stile materno". In: *Rivista di psicoanalisi*, 4: 753–767.

Chodorow, N.J. (2003) "Too late: ambivalence about motherhood, choice, and time". In: *The Journal of the American Psychoanalytic Association*, 51: 1181–1198.

Faure-Pragier, S. (2001) "Que reste-t-il de leurs amours? Separation mère fille et conception". In: *Revue française de psychanalyse*, lxv, 2, pp. 409–424.

Ferrara Mori, G. (2006) "The interior experience of maternity". In: La Sala, G.B., Fagandini, P., Iori, V., Monti F., Blickstein, I. (Eds.) *Coming into the World: a Dialogue between Medical and Human Sciences,* pp. 85–102. Berlin: Walter de Gruiter & Co.

Ferraro, F., Nunziante Cesaro, A. (1985) *Lo spazio cavo e il corpo saturato. La gravidanza come "agire" tra fusione e separazione.* Milano: Franco Angeli.

Freud, S. (1925) *Some psychical consequences of the anatomical distinction between the sexes. SE*, 19: 248–258.

Goldberger, M. (1991) "Pregnancy During Analysis: Help or Hindrance?". In: *Psychoanalytic Quarterly*, 60: 207–226.

Golinelli, P. (2007) "Le ricamatrici: il brillio dello sguardo materno". In: *Atti dei Seminari multipli della* s.p.i., Bologna. Unpublished.

Guignard, F. (2002) "Mère et fille: entre partage et clivage". In: Bokanowski, T., Guignard, F., *La relation mère–fille: entre partage et clivage,* pp. 11–40. Paris: In Press.

Hoffman, L. (2003) "Mothers' ambivalence with their babies and toddlers". In: *The Journal of the American Psychoanalytic Association*, 51: 1219–1240.

Klockars, L., Sirola, R. (2001) "The mother-daughter love affair across the generations". In *Psycoanalitic Study of the child*, 56, pp. 219–237.

Lechartier-Atlan, C. (2001) "La grossesse 'mère' de toutes les séparations". In: *Revue français de psychanalyse*, LXV, 2: 437–450.

Meltzer, D. (1973) *Sexual States of Mind*. Pertshire, Scotland: Clunie Press.

Micati, L. (1985) "Recensione a Lo spazio cavo e il corpo saturato. La gravidanza come agire tra fusione e separazione F. Ferraro e A. Nunziante Cesaro". In: *Rivista di psicoanalisi*, 4: 587–591.

Micati, L. (1988) "Sulla sessualità femminile: osservazioni sulle forze che ne ostacolano lo sviluppo e sulla loro risoluzione". In: *Rivista di psicoanalisi*, 1: 11–51.

Roccato, M. (2003) "Sogni in gravidanza: immagini delle trasformazioni del Sé". In: *Rivista di psicoanalisi*, XLIX, 1, pp. 179–201.

Sami-Ali, M. (1974) *L'espace imaginaire*. Paris: Gallimard.

Schaeffer, J. (2002) "De mère à fille: l'antagonisme entre maternel et feminin". In Bokanowski, T., Guignard, F. (Eds.) *La relation mère–fille*, pp. 41–50. Paris: In Press.

Schaeffer, J. (2002) "Le parcours des antagonismes entre féminin et maternel". In: Solis-Ponton, L. (Ed.) *La parentalité*, pp. 131–155. Paris: P.U.F.

Schmid–Kitsikis, E. (2002) "Un amour dans la mélancolie: Agnès, de fille à mère". In: Bokanowski, T., Guignard, F. (Eds.) *La relation mère–fille*, pp. 89–103. Paris: In Press.

Semi, A. (2006) "Mater semper incerta". In: *Penser/Rêver*, 9: 19–26.

Solis-Ponton, L., Moro, M.R. (2002) "Des femmes, des mères et des filles. Le rôle du thérapeute femme dans la consultation mère-bébé". In: Solis-Ponton, L. (Ed.), *La parentalité*, pp. 99–111. Paris: P.U.F.

Tagliacozzo, R. (1990) "Angosce fusionali, mondo concreto e mondo pensabili". In: Neri, C., Pallier, L., Petacchi, G., Soavi, G.C., Tagliacozzo, R. (Ed.), *Fusionalità: scritti di psicoanlaisi clinica*. Roma: Borla.

Tyson, P. (2003) "Some psychoanalytic perspectives on women". In: *The Journal of the American Psychoanalytic Association*, 51, pp. 1119–1126.

Vigneri, M. (2004) "Nascere come donna". Speech held at the conference "*La cura delle donne. Un interrogativo all'incrocio tra saperi e terapie*", organized by the Inter-university Centre for Bio-ethical Research, Naples, October 28, 2004.

Yonke, A., Barnett, M. (2001) "Persistence of early psychoanalytic thought about women". In: *Gender and psychoanalysis*, 6: 53–73.

Chapter 9

The "times" of maternality

Fiorella Monti

> *... perchance it might be fitly said. There are three times; a present of the things past; a present of the things present, and a present of the things future.*
> *For these three do somehow exist in the soul and otherwise I see them not.*
> *Present of things past, memory; present of things present, sight; present of things future, expectation.*
>
> *(Saint Augustine, Confessions, XI, 20.26)*
>
> *Psycho-analysis teaches us that the acknowledgement of the past as the foundation of the present is the only means of making the concept of future obedient to reason.*
>
> *(Donald Meltzer, 1998, p. 8)*

INTRODUCTION: THE TIMES OF THE MATERNAL ATMOSPHERE

Our study group, starting from Gina Ferrara Mori's project, began exploring "the territory of the dawn of the mother-child relationships", using as maps the "stories" narrated by "expectant" women and, as the journey tool (Bick, 1964), the observation of the emotional atmosphere. It "has got to do with the climate, the meteorology of emotions and the family mental environment" (Vallino, 2004, p. 156 [own translation]), meaning by family both the enlarged social context (from the partner to the healthcare professionals) accompanying the woman in the pregnancy-birth project, and the internal family that, starting from the conscious or unconscious idea of conceiving a child, undergoes a restructuring, to the point of recognizing itself as both the same and yet different.

The psychic work to become parents is therefore a process of deep transformation that re-activates mental representations strictly connected to the previous relational history, from which past experiences of attachment with one's own parental figures and childhood observation memories re-emerge, from which branch off the threads and wefts to weave a space that will have to host the future representations of the self as a mother, of one's own partner as a father, and the future child. Therefore pregnancy and birth are not just facts, subject to a historical truth, but they are, primarily, *Events*, characterized by the conscious and unconscious representations of those who participate in them, starting with mothers and fathers. Thus they are dynamic Events that have a location in time and are based on a project (Iori, 2006); they are subject to a narrative truth that continuously changes according to time and place. Precisely because of this, they need to be listened to; they need sharing and containment.

In pregnancy, Event elements of one's personal history, the couple's and the social history become intertwined: it is a crossroads featuring genetic code, the code of the individual history and the cultural code (Fornari, 1981). Such complexity thus requires a social dimension that takes on the responsibility and competence of regulating "traffic".

Motherhood is undoubtedly a complex journey. If the symbiotic elements (being a mother, mother-child unit) and the identification-separation ones (making a child, imagining a child other than oneself) become integrated, they confirm to the woman the integrity of her body against the unconscious phantasies of decay or emptiness. They also start a symmetrical mother-child relationship, *vita mea/vita tua* (Fornari, 1981). Were they to remain split instead, they would recall phantasmatic, persecutory and depressive declinations, thus amplifying genetic (Fornari, 1981) and role anxieties, *vita mea/mors tua, vita tua/ mors mea* – steps or missteps in the dance between mother and child (Stern, 1977).

The child is born in the parent's mind and through pregnancy it is "brought" to "light" by thoughts, phantasies, desires, and parental fears thanks to the connection between the mother's biologic system and a sensory nursing provided by the mother, her body and her emotions (Cyrulnik, 1993).

> The woman tells me about two dreams: "One is quite nice, I had it early in my pregnancy: the child was plump, more than this (she turns to her child in the cot). In the dream I couldn't understand that he was my child, then I thought about it and perhaps it was him and he ran after me to hug me. It was one of the most beautiful dreams, the only one maybe, as the others were bad. In the last one, around the eighth month of pregnancy, I was with my eldest and with this child whom I couldn't hold, he slipped out of my hands and I called him … then luckily I woke up. I haven't slept much during this pregnancy" (woman one week after giving birth).

The motherhood work (Pazzagli et al., 1981) thus implies a redistribution of libido and narcissistic investments, a wide and intense fluctuation of the defence system during both the pregnancy and the perinatal period, during which, in the oscillation between phantasmatic, imaginary and real child, a process of re-appropriation of the Self and the baby, in a dimension closer to reality, is activated.

The "earthquake that contains all femininity" and at the same time "makes women's identity vacillate so much" (Bergeret-Amselek, 2005, p. 21 [own translation]), brings about a great transformation potential, although it is connected to an intense vulnerability or psychic "nudity". This psychic transparency, meant both as a "particular relational state [...] of invocation close to a cry for help and almost permanent", that like a "correlation between the situation of the actual pregnancy and infantile memories" (Bydlowski, 1997, pp. 93–94 [own translation]), allows, if adequately supported with respectful listening and awe, the maternal internal look (Ferrara Mori, 2006). Such "dreamy" activity, fostering a gradual regression of the maternal Self to the foetal and then neo-natal Self, leading to a state of "heightened sense of awareness", characterizes the primary maternal preoccupation (Winnicott, 1958), through which the woman will be able to be born as a mother and let her child be born. Therefore, if during pregnancy the woman is supported in her couple and environment context, she can create a physical and mental space for her baby; she can prepare her physical and psychic womb to bring her desire and her need to become a mother to light.

Such space, inhabited by "the mother who knits sufficiently", preparing "a woollen womb" (Soulé, 1990, p. 750 [own translation]), and destined to contain, "stitch by stitch", the idea of a child and the image of herself as a mother, is a place-time whose boundaries are confused with those of more ancient areas that have got to do, in reality and in phantasy, with the image and the memory of her own parents. "We believe that knitting fosters the phantastic production and fosters the phantasmatic interaction: the mother thinks about the child's body, about his/her growth, about how he/she might become, about the child's father, who is always present or has left, about the baby's past, that is, about the mother's sexual life, about her father, grandparents, about the transgenerational task she has been entrusted with. The mother knits the wool, but these ideas as well" (Soulé, 1990, p. 751 [own translation]).

Therefore, there are many subjects that are part of the weaving of this internal landscape: the mother as an adult woman; the child she has been; the mother and the father she has had; the imagined child; the father as a man; the child he has been; the mother and father he has had.

The biological times of pregnancy are very much connected to the psychological, intrapsychic, interpersonal and intergenerational times, in a dimension of innovative continuity.

Therefore, motherhood is first of all "a psychic state, of a psycho-genetic nature, of transference, developmental nature" (Delassus, 1995, p. 138 [own translation]), which needs not so much explanation but listening and understanding. It "is made of social and of private matter, of intimacy and sharing, of silence and announcement" (Marinopoulos, 2005, p. 21 [own translation]); it is deeply imbued with desire and fear of the desire, of known and unknown, "regardless of all technology and scientific knowledge" (Marinopoulos, 2005, p. 9 [own translation]). The strong medicalization and exaggerated use of diagnostic procedures, in collusion with social pressure, often push towards a pre-term motherhood in which the fact of seeing through the "machines", being informed, prevail on feeling and listening.

"I'm a very anxious person, no not anxious, but normally I tend to see ... sometimes I'm not really an optimist, I'm always afraid something will go wrong. For this reason there have been moments when I've experienced this pregnancy in a very serene way and others less so, especially at the time of the ultrasound scans" (woman, 32 weeks pregnant).

The innumerable questions, often implicit and expressed through the changing body, phantasies, dreams, desires and fears, actually concern, in a structuring and/or de-structuring sense, the themes of the child's life and growth, of the primary relationship, of the support matrix, of the reorganization of identity. Such questions, interconnected among themselves, create the new organization of mental life, the motherhood constellation. "The networks of schemas that undergo reworking are the mother's self as woman, mother, wife, career-person, friend, daughter, granddaughter; her role in society; her place in her family of origin; her legal status; herself as the person with cardinal responsibility for the life and growth of someone else, as the possessor of a different body [...] and so on – in short, almost every aspect of her life" (Stern, 1998, p. 24).

In the presence of such "hum" that often may be transformed into internal and external din, so as to make the woman feel alone in the middle of such emotional turbulence, there is a need for an environment that offers sharing, containment and support, because the woman cannot "experience her motherhood alone. Even though it is mainly an individual experience, it requires the collaboration and warmth of other women; mother, sisters, cousins, colleagues, that is, women who represent both her current reality and the reference to the past" (Bydlowski, 2000, p. 20 [own translation]).

> "I had a good experience, I mean I'm happy, I'm happy also for the changes that are occurring: all in all, I like the way I am. I was looking at myself in the mirror and I almost couldn't remember how I was before, that is, how I was without the big belly; also because I've always had quite a flat belly [...]. To tell you the truth, at the beginning I was almost annoyed because people wouldn't notice I was pregnant, wouldn't mention it, also because, being alone, I somehow missed my relatives' pampering, or my mother's, my father's, I mean those people who are normally with me ... I would look at strangers, ah!, she didn't notice! Now I'm all round, when I meet people they notice! [...] anyway, despite the distance, everyone is doing something. So that some friends, or colleagues, have come to visit a couple of times. So, all in all, it hasn't been so ... bad. There have been sad moments, well because I felt lonely" (woman, 30 weeks pregnant).

... the experience of being born (and of giving birth) is lived, every time,
as an extraordinary, exceptional, unique, and unrepeatable event
which storms into ordinary, everyday life and forever modifies people's
relationships and their personal biographies

(Vanna Iori, 2006, p. 25)

THE CRISIS OF MATERNALITY

"There is a state, a process of existential crisis linked to a stage of psycho-physical development of the woman, which I have called maternality. [...] By maternality I mean the stage of affect development corresponding to the biological reality of motherhood. [...] In maternality there are relevant drive fluctuations with phenomena of narcissistic recovery and of object return, a re-activation of Oedipal conflicts and a dissolution and reconstruction of early identifications" (Racamier, 1986, pp. 51–52 [own translation]).

Such a developmental step implies a process of dual self-identification, as the woman ends up being the daughter of her own mother and the mother of her own child (Bibring, 1959; Racamier, 1986): it is a crisis that prepares maturational integration, but that in its transformation path of rewriting allows one to catch a glimpse of possible alterations or fractures.

> "I'm quite emotional. Now I feel weaker, more fragile. Also I happened to cry watching a film, which had never happened to me before. And then, physically, I've gained too much weight" (woman, 32 weeks pregnant).

> "Up until eight months ago I was a daughter and a wife: I was happy. My reaction to the news I was pregnant was to cry. I had erected a high wall around me within which, first alone and then with my husband, I felt serene, sheltered, safe, at ease. It took me 30 years to build it. The arrival of this child has somewhat created a crack in the wall, fears, insecurity, but also a beautiful strong light" (woman, 32 weeks pregnant).

During pregnancy and in the post-partum stage, women experience in their body and their mind a great physical and emotional turbulence, often experienced in loneliness, despite the myths associated with the idea of motherhood and reinforced by social expectations, that equate expecting a baby and being a mother with a state of complete well-being and fulfilment.

> "It was a good time. But not as good as everyone says. Actually at times it was a real nightmare. Because of my tendency to question everything, and so at the time of the most important exams during the pregnancy, even though all went well, I had moments of anxiety … of fear" (woman, 32 weeks pregnant).

> "I don't know why there's this thing of making pregnancy, motherhood, nursing, sound so poetic while actually, after all, it's not really like that, it's … it's great but at the same time exhausting and painful" (woman three months after giving birth).

"Until not long ago, motherhood has almost always been collective. The mother was part of a system that would include not just the family, but also the context and the environment. Currently motherhood tends to become individual, if not solitary. Nothing says this is normal" (Delassus, 1995, p. 190 [own translation]): the commitments of motherhood weigh down on a mother whose feelings of loneliness are often worsened by the collapse of the social *rêverie*.

Through the observation and listening to narratives, it is necessary to understand how often a mother feels lonely and at the same time *split* between often contrasting desires and ideals (Cramer, 1999). On the one hand, there is the need to think and to take care of the foetus-child, on the other, the need to advance professionally, with the accompanying fear of not becoming/being a good enough mother: the difficult and complex cohabitation of the work, female and maternal codes, requires a social and healthcare container (Fornari, 1981).

> "When I discovered I was pregnant, I almost had a heart attack: I was very busy, there was a scholarship on its way. My husband was happy, he was, he wanted a child. Now I'm happy, even though I know it'll be hard" (woman, 24 weeks pregnant).

> "Birth is not merely that which divides women from men: it also divides women from themselves, so that a woman's understanding of what it is to exist is profoundly changed. Another person has existed in her, and after their birth they live within the jurisdiction of her consciousness. When she is with them she is not herself; when she is without them she is not herself; and so it is as difficult to leave your children as it is to stay with them. To discover this is to feel that your life has become irretrievably mired in conflict, or caught in some mythic snare in which you will perpetually, vainly struggle". (Cusk, 2001, p. 7)

The din of the external reality thus becomes an environmental "clash" that leaves the woman, through violent intrusion or deafening silences, alone and hurt: within a vulnerable path, it is a de-structuring loneliness, that in the moment of delivery and *post–partum*, already characterized by a disorganization of the Ego (Lebovici, 1983), because of the massive bio-psychic movements, may lead to a break.

> "The delivery? I haven't realized it, it was very fast, they cut me open [...] I didn't want to see him straight away, I didn't want to be left with a bloody image. During the delivery there were quite many people around, the shift changed as well. And then, you know, I'm a peculiar case, they came to see me [...] One tries to leave issues and shames at home, but even with all those people around I was alone, no one asked me anything" (woman after giving birth).

> "And I gave birth. I was in the labour room for two days and they had injected substances in my veins to accelerate the delivery. Students, doctors, nurses, anyone really who happened to pass by, would come in my room and then leave, would insert their fists inside me, and one after the other they would rape me with gloved hands, shaking their heads over my belly and counting with their fingers the centimetres of dilation [...] Exhausted and humiliated, aching and impotent, I felt like a woman who had been attacked [...] I would have liked to run away, raising from my bed, letting everything behind and crawl into a cave. There, protected by darkness and silence, I would have liked to kneel down and give birth to my child". (Shifra Horn, 2005, p. 188 [own translation])

The woman remembers how she cried during the first few months and the despair of remaining at home alone: "Once it was raining and so I couldn't go out with him. So I took him, dressed him and we went up to the last floor of the block of flats I live in. I was hoping to meet someone ... horrible moments" (woman three months after giving birth).

"When things go badly,
time cannot manage to become
one of the dimensions of existence".

(Antonino Ferro, 2002, p. 11 [own translation])

LATENT CRISES AND DISTRESS DURING PREGNANCY AND AFTER BIRTH

"The latent crises during pregnancy are situations that have a specific char-acteristic oscillating in its emergence and manifestation, in relation to anxiety-provoking events, that are different according to its various stages, or in relation to the announcements of the biologic monitoring, to particular situ-ations of the environment at times depending though on the transformations of the unconscious mental representations (for instance after a dream) [...] For the future mother it is a question of not being contained, understood by her envi-ronment or not able, at times, of containing herself with her more adult parts" (Ferrara Mori, 2007, p. 49).

The turbulences of the "maternal atmosphere" linked to the complexity, and therefore to fluctuations and instabilities, if they are not understood well enough, and shared and contained, run the risk of becoming storms or to become encysted mute "uncanny" nuclei. The risk factors of such perturbations may be identified in the external (poor quality of the relationship with the partner, of the family and social support) and internal containers (a vulnerable personality with presence of anxiety, depression). The woman continuously sends out signals through her verbal and non-verbal "complaints" (feelings of loneliness, self-reproaching, anxiety, sleep disorders, somatic disorders such as rashes and backache). These signals, though, are often not listened to or downplayed, both by the woman herself and by those, from family members to the medical profession, who should act as a *scaffolding*.

"During this second pregnancy my husband has seen me much more anxious and passive, I've often complained. So he told me: 'oh come on, cheer up, it's not a disease objectively, there's nothing that isn't going well, I can't understand why you're like that'. He couldn't understand well my issue with physical tiredness" (woman, 30 weeks pregnant).

"When I go back home from hospital I'm afraid I might be depressed: my hus-band is never there, our home is small, there are problems with my mother and my mother-in-law because they'd like me to do as they say. I'm afraid of staying at home all the time alone with my baby. It's a shame she'll be born in November because autumn is a depressing season" (woman, 30 weeks pregnant).

"I was alone, I'd never been so lonely, my husband didn't notice my sadness, and I couldn't understand why, I had to be happy because my baby was there. Instead I found myself sitting down on the steps and crying, holding her in my arms" (woman three months after giving birth).

In an involutional sense then, the "crisis" during pregnancy may lead to difficulties or the impossibility to go through a developmental process of mourning linked to the redefinition of one's own identity. Such *impasse* may manifest itself through symptoms and depressive distress, meant both as a structural and psycho-pathological neo-formation, characterizing the *post-partum* (Cramer, Palacio Espasa, 1993) – one that often starts during pregnancy, and as the outcome of a combination of factors, including the vulnerability of childhood exacerbated by adult experiences (Raphael-Leff, 2000).

The primary maternal preoccupation can thus be transformed into a primary maternal "persecution": "Submerged in trivia, bogged down in contaminating menial jobs and raw sensations, and starved of intellectual content, a woman experiences herself becoming invisible, taken over by the baby. Living in a timeless world of wasting, wanting, waiting to be saved by the ringing phone, unless she can be rescued from the tedium, she may become deeply resentful and depressed, and feeling devoid of self-expression, sucked dry by the demanding baby she is too exhausted and trapped to be responsive to the infant's emotional communications" (Raphael-Leff, 2002, p. 62).

Maternal depression affects the mother's global psychic functioning, changing her behaviour and responses in the real and phantasmatic early interaction with her child. During pregnancy, such distress, often mute or disguised, can interrupt the dialogue started with the foetus-child and make the maternal representation world more ambivalent or disinvested (Ammaniti et al., 1995). The affection tone of the investment on the imaginary child and on the maternal Self thus tends to become flattened or acute, as if fog or a storm at the horizon prevented her from seeing the route towards internal motherhood.

> "I don't know how to convey to you how I felt: happy, but also a bit ...".

> "At the third month I started swelling up ... and it was terrible. At the fifth month you could already notice I was pregnant ... You no longer understand how you are, there's the perception of not feeling well, you're bloated like a balloon, you've got this belly and you can't really understand whether everything has become wider everywhere: it's terrible ...".

> "It changed completely ... then you start not feeling well, the first few things, you feel blue, you don't feel well, you're at home alone, there's never a soul around, because he works, the others work, your friends work. It's heavy, it was a burden, a bit, quite a lot. And it still is, because it's not over yet ...".

> "I don't know if this child is there, really: I can't feel a thing, besides feeling awful ... Perhaps I'll realize only when I see him, I don't know though ... I hope he'll sleep, so I'll sleep too. This way I'll recover these nine months of insomnia ...".

The maternal agitation during pregnancy thus leads to a failure to assist to both one's own vulnerable parts and the fragile imaginary child, causing a psychic lack of confirmation of one's creativity. In the perinatal "territory", this may affect the relationship with the real child, thus leading to alter the function of stimuli protection, to a thinning out or an alteration of maternal stimulations, to a rigidity of responses, that are not suitable to the developmental potential of the child, to a loss of pleasure in performing maternal cares (Guedeney, 1989): thus the emotional intimacy of the interaction turns out to be compromised.

The depressive distress "empties" these mothers both inside and outside, imbuing them with a strong feeling of helplessness and more strain in relation to the child's caring requests (Monti, Agostini, 2006); it depletes the sensory and the emotional exchanges.

The depressed mother is physically present but psychologically absent, and the changes in her behaviour are experienced in her presence. Mother's depression involves the child because he/she has difficulties experiencing the physical presence in the mother's affective absence, his/her love object: "All of this refers to an absence: absence of memory, absence in the mind, absence of feeling of being alive, all these absences can be condensed in the idea of an emptiness. This emptiness though, instead of referring to a mere absence, or to something that is not present, becomes the substrate of what is real" (Green, 2003, p. 40 [own translation]). In the interactive emptiness, the depressed mother and her child clench at each other in a mute or intrusive way and risk becoming "like the Danaides in the Greek myth who were doomed to carry water in buckets that had holes in them" (Winnicott, 1969, pp. 247–250).

The phantasmatic and real interaction with the child becomes thus permeated by a "silence of affections" that hinders or prevents the mind's capacity, both the mother's and the child's, from creating objects, filling in the internal and external world.

> "I can't even look at her. My poor baby. She never looks at me and I can't look at her. She cries all the time, she cries as if they were killing her. Even the faintest moan terrifies me, I can't get close to her cot. I can't manage to see she's not well. But then I can't keep away from her, I can't do anything. I can't go out ... My whole life is a disaster and will never go back to be like it was before ... I have the impression she looks at me and wants to tell me she's not well ... when she starts crying she never stops ... I can't bear to hear her crying, I don't want to stay alone with her ..." (woman three months after giving birth).

> "I felt anxiety inside. I was without transport, very much slowed down, as if I were in the void. I was afraid of everything, everything attacked me in the street, cars, people; I always felt to be aside, elsewhere; I was there physically but it wasn't me, whether it was a family meeting or with people who were talking outside school [...] I was always distressed. I never said anything, I couldn't remember anything, I couldn't understand anything and then, when I was alone with myself, I would despair for myself; then I would realize I had the children and I had to rear them, look after them [...] One day when someone told me 'your children', I replied 'but they're not my children, they're

children I look after', I can't utter my children, I couldn't, I don't know, but I couldn't say 'my children'" (Manzano et al., 1997, p. 533 [own translation]).

"She wasn't there even when she was" (a depressed woman on her depressed mother) (Bifulco, Moran, 1998, p. 37 [own translation]).

"I've always felt like a machine that must pump oxygen in not to let someone die ... my mother ... who told me many times: 'You're the centre of my life ... the reason of my life ... if you weren't there I'd jump out of the window'" (a [male] patient with a depressed mother).

"I see myself alone, sad, and mother looks at me unmoved, not at all sorry and I wake up in tears" (recurring dream of a patient with a depressed mother when she was little).

Dealing with one's own mother's depressed mood is an impossible task, limiting the chance to start one's own life: "it is like saying that life can be lived in a comatose state" (Phillips, 1988, p. 102 [own translation]). In this sense, the mental experience the very young child goes through is not a depressive experience in the sense of the loss of the object, but an experience that puts at stake his/her very same narcissistic continuity.

"If there is a time for pain, there is a time for life,
for joy, to gallop towards the sun"
(Tonia Cancrini, 2002, p. 184 [own translation])

LISTENING TO INTERNAL MOTHERHOOD

"Prevention [...] may arise only out of listening [...] to the words of every mother. Time and patience are needed to collect, analyse, understand their experience [...] Treating the future mothers requires technique, surveillance, medical guarantees. To look after them though requires adding the word to all of this. Talking to the mothers, supporting them in the expression of a new emotional voice, uncanny at times. It must be there in the cases we work on. It is at the same time a therapeutic and preventive tool" (Marinopoulos, 2005, p. 157 [own translation]).

Pregnancy, because of the psychic transparency, is an ideal moment to open up the dialogue with the future mother; what comes from this is therefore a listening aimed not at "deciphering a symbolic datum, but to render possible the symbolization function, thus opening up the access to the word" (Sami-Ali, 1974, p. 80 [own translation]) to sharing. Therefore, it is a question of including, on a continuous basis, listening in the pregnancy-birth path to bring back the subject (child, father, mother) in his/her own story, and to recreate a space of freedom to prevent that what is upstream goes on absorbing what is downstream (Ansermet, 1999). The generational transmission, that is "the passage from parents to child of themes, ideologies, anxieties, modes that were inherited in a family legacy", bringing with it "both a form of wisdom and oddities that contribute to the symptoms" (Cramer, 1999, p. 32 [own translation]), may represent "an unexpected guest" (Fraiberg, 1999) already in the psychic womb of pregnancy, thus hindering the process of the third identification (young girl, adolescent, woman) (Mastella, 2004).

> "Mine is a long story. This thing is just the latest I've done, the less damaging one, so my parents are happy. And I wanted a boy, my boyfriend too. My mother, on the contrary, after many boys, wanted a girl. I'm the middle child, I have two brothers: one is older than me, the other is younger. As a child I was always dressed like a boy and behaved like one ..." (woman before giving birth).

There is a biologic, genetic, pregnancy-delivery-birth history that requires medical attentions, but there is mostly a relational history that requires an empathic and rigorous attention. One should keep in mind that "the psychic life mainly consists in being able to give oneself a representation of the world, self representations and representations of the relationships one has with the world and with oneself" (Golse, 1999, p. 80 [own translation]). Therefore, listening means fostering, in the motherhood process, the development of the sense of an inner life, of intimacy, understanding maternal and paternal representations to be able to rethink, observe and listen to the maternal tales: "narratives do not get used up, they keep their hidden strengths in themselves, like a wheat grain inside the pyramids that kept intact its germination power" (Benjamin, 1991, p. 75[own translation]).

> "Pregnancy is a new birth for me as well. I've been born again as a person, I've become a mother, I've represented a new life [...] Every day that goes by you experience an emotion ... it's such an emotion, every day that goes by" (woman, 32 weeks pregnant).

If Infant Observation gives back the "little child the meaning of being a person in its full sense, endowed with affection and thinking, and it considers the mental development specific and unique for that person" (Vallino, 2004, p. 222 [own translation]), the Pre-Infant could foster and support the internal motherhood as "the place for fantasies, emotions, desires, dreams, and the place where bonds and affects are formed, new relationships made, and it is the home of this fantasized internal baby, soon to become a real external baby" (Ferrara Mori, 2006, p. 88). The latent crises during pregnancy linked to both the "normal", but not sufficiently considered, complexity of the journey, and the re-emergence of areas of painful vulnerabilities, run the risk of invading "the abode" up to the point of making it inhabitable.

Prevention and treatment cannot be limited to medical monitoring, but they must start from the listening, from the attention paid to symbolic and psychic elements: the mother who cannot affectively invest herself, because she has been invaded by her worries, cannot make the representations of her child alive: "the time of mourning, of distress, of doubt, of pain, but of course also of joy, of amazement, of fullness, does not coincide with the time of technique" (Marinopoulos, 2005, 2006, p. 10 [own translation]). Time is needed to observe, listen, understand the stages and the fluctuations of the maturation process leading to the birth of a child, of a mother and a father. Therefore the process of sharing-containing-narrating plays an important function of "sensebuster" because, by way of the observation, listening to listening, it is possible to achieve a shared reconstruction that recovers the alive and real bond among the parts of the self and between the mother and her child.

"narration lighten up, life sets itself in motion again,
anxieties and fears dissolve when things return in the glow of their childhood,
that is the childhood restored by the narration triggered by memory"
(Gargani, 1988, p. 3 [own translation])

REFERENCES

Ammaniti, M., Candelori, C., Pola, M., Tambelli, R. (1995) *Maternità e gravidanza. Studio delle rappresentazioni materne.* Milano: Raffaello Cortina.

Ansermet, F. (1999) *Clinique de l'origine: l'enfant entre la médecine et la psychanalyse.* Lausanne: Editions Payot.

Ansermet, F. (2006) "Death and Birth". In: La Sala, G.B., Fagandini, P., Iori, V., Monti, F., Blickstein, I. (Eds). *Coming into the World: a Dialogue between Medical and Human Sciences,* pp. 177–184. Berlin: Walter de Gruiter.

Benjamin, W. (1991) *Ecrits francais.* Paris: Gallimard.

Bergeret-Amselek, C. (2005) *Le mystère des mères.* Paris: Desclée de Brouwer Tr. In: *Il mistero delle madri. Un viaggio nel cuore della maternità.* Roma: Magi.

Bibring, G.L. (1959) "Some considerations on the psychological processes in pregnancy". *The Psychoanalytic Study of the Child,* 13, pp. 113–121.

Bick, E. (1964) "Notes on Infant Observation in Psycho-Analytic Training". In: *Collected Papers of Martha Harris and Esther Bick,* edited by Meg Harris Williams, The Clunie Press, Perthshire, Scotland, 1987.

Bifulco, A., Moran, P. (1998) *Wednesday's Child.* London: Routledge.

Bydlowski, M. (1997) *La dette de vie. Itinéraire psychanalytique de la maternité.* Paris: P.U.F.

Bydlowski, M. (2000) *Je reve un enfant. L'experience intérièure de la maternité.* Paris: Odile Jacob.

Cancrini, T. (2002) *Un tempo per il dolore. Eros, dolore e colpa.* Torino: Bollati Boringhieri.

Cramer, B. (1999) *Que deviendront nos bébés?* Paris: Odile Jacob.

Cramer, B., Palacio Espasa, F. (1993) *La pratique des psychothérapie mère-enfant.* Paris: P.U.F.

Cusk, R. (2001) *A life's work: on becoming a mother.* London: Fourth Estate.

Cyrulnik, B. (1993) *Les nourritures affectives.* Paris: Odile Jacob.

Delassus, J.M. (1995) *Le sens de la maternité.* Paris: Dunod.

Ferrara Mori, G. (2006) "The interior experience of maternity". In: La Sala, G.B., Fagandini, P., Iori, V., Monti, F., Blickstein, I. (Eds). *Coming into the World: a Dialogue between Medical and Human Sciences,* pp. 85–102. Berlin: Walter de Gruiter.

Ferrara Mori, G., Mori, L. (2007) "L'ascolto e la comprensione dell'esperienza psichica di gravidanza". *Interazioni,* 2: 43–55.

Ferro, A. (2002) "Prefazione". In: T. Cancrini. *Un tempo per il dolore.* Torino: Bollati Boringhieri.

Fornari, F. (1981) *Il codice vivente. Femminilità e maternità nei sogni delle madri in gravidanza.* Torino: Bollati Boringhieri.

Fraiberg, S. (1999) Il sostegno allo sviluppo. Milano: Raffaello Cortina.

Gargani, A.G. (1988) *Sguardo e destino.* Bari: Laterza.

Golse, B. (1999), "Le prime rappresentazioni mentali: l'emergere del pensiero". In: Cohen Solal, J., Golse, B., All'inizio della vita psichica, Borla, Roma, 2003.

Green, A. (2003) "L'intuizione del negativo in gioco e realtà". In: Bertolini, M., Giannakoulas, A., Hernandez, M. (Eds.). La tradizione winnicottiana. Roma: Borla.

Guedeney, N. (1989) "Le infants de parents deprimes". In: Psychiatrie de l'enfant, XXXII, 1: 269–309.

Horn, S. (2005) Inno alla gioia. Roma: Fazi.

Iori, V. (2006) "Birth: Between medical and human science". In: La Sala, G.B.; Fagandini, P.; Iori, V.; Monti, F.; Blickstein, I. (Eds). Coming into the World: a Dialogue between Medical and Human Sciences, pp. 25–44. Berlin: Walter de Gruiter.

Lebovici, S. (1983) Le nourrisson, sa mère et le psychanalyste. Les interactions précoces, Nouvelle Edition revue et augmentée. Montrouge: Bayard Jeunesse, 2003.

Manzano, J., Righetti-Veltema, M., Conne-Pérréard, E. (1997) "Le syndrome de dépression du pré–partum. Résultats d'une recherche sur les signes précurseurs de la dépression du postpartum". In: La psychiatrie de l'enfant, XL, 2, pp. 533–552.

Marinopoulos, S. (2005) Dans l'intime des mères. Paris: Fayard.

Mastella, M. (2004) Nascita del figlio e dinamica della coppia: una prospettiva psicoanalitica. In: Galli, Arfelli.; Galli, G. (a cura di) Interpretazione e nascita. La nascita dei genitori. La nascita del figlio. Pisa-Roma: Istituti Editoriali e Poligrafici Internazionali.

Meltzer, D. (1998) The Kleinian Development. Freud's Clinical Development. Book 1. London: Karnac Books.

Monti, F., Agostini, F. (2006) La depressione postnatale. Roma: Carocci Editore.

Pazzagli, A., Benvenuti, P., Rossi Monti, M. (1981) Maternità come crisi. Roma: Il Pensiero Scientifico.

Phillips, A. (1988) Winnicott. London: Harvard University Press.

Racamier, P.C., Taccani, S. (1986) Il lavoro incerto, ovvero la psicodinamica del processo di crisi. Pisa: Edizioni del Cerro.

Raphael-Leff, J. (2000) Spilt milk: perinatal loss and breakdown. London: The Institute of Psychoanalysis.

Raphael-Leff, J. (2002) "Where the wild things are". In: Raphael-Leff J. (Ed.) (2008), Parent-Infant psychodynamics. Wild Things, Mirrors, and Ghosts, pp. 4–69. London: Anna Freud Centre.

Sami-Ali, M. (1974) L'espace imaginaire. Paris: Gallimard. Tr. it. Roma: Magi, 1998.

Sant'Agostino (1979) Le confessioni. Roma: Edizione Paoline.

Soulé, M. (1990) "La madre che lavora sufficientemente a maglia. Apologia del lavoro a maglia: il suo ruolo nella capacità fantastica della madre". In: Psichiatria dell'infanzia e dell'adolescenza, 57, pp. 749–753.

Stern, D.N. (1977) The First Relationship: Infant and Mother. Cambridge: Harvard University Press.

Stern, D.N. (1998) The Motherhood Constellation. A Unified View of Parent-Infant Psychotherapy. London: Karnac Books.

Vallino, D. (1998) Raccontami una storia. Dalla consultazione all'analisi dei bambini. Roma: Borla.

Vallino, D. (2004) Essere neonati. Questioni psicoanalitiche. Roma: Borla.

Winnicott, D.W. (1958) Through Paediatrics to Psycho-Analysis, London: Tavistock Pubblications.

Winnicott, D.W. (1969) "The Mother-Infant Experience of Mutuality". In: Anthony. E.J., Benedek, T. (Eds.), Parenthood: Its Psychology and Psychotherapy. Boston: Little, Brown and Co.

Winnicott, D.W. (1989) Psycho-Analysis Explorations. London: The Winnicott Trust.

Chapter 10

Having or not having a baby

Internal movements searching
for new balances

Gabriella Smorto

"The mother was not people
neither nothing, nor any thing
She was the origin
Of what was about to happen
And she was thought
and memory"
Anonymous pre-Columbian civilisation

In a group that acted as an Observatory for the internal motherhood, we were
bound to come across material on the observation of women who decide to interrupt an unexpected, unlooked-for pregnancy on the scenario of their external and
internal world. The psychological assistance I have been providing for many years
to women and couples in the context of an out-patient clinic for the voluntary
pregnancy interruption is a privileged vantage point for this.

The activity is carried out, upon referral, by gynaecologists and nurses in a cultural context, oscillating between the desire that women are supported in the possibility to rethink about their request and the respect for their right to decide for their
future and the child's who could be born. In this emotional context, I substantially
share with the operational group an understanding attitude towards the particular
condition in which the women find themselves, as may be summarised by a statement by the gynaecologist in charge of the service: "It seems to me this is one of the
few ways to really help those who seek help" (Pippi, 2001, p. 31 [own translation]).

THE MEANINGS OF A REQUEST

"I wanted this child, but now that I'm pregnant I'm no longer sure I want it ... I
don't know if I could manage!", Marta exclaims as she steps into the room where
I see the women the gynaecologist refers to me.

"I don't know why, but I never thought I would have had children ... I thought
I was unable ... but now that I'm pregnant, I can't think of an abortion ...", Irene
whispered, almost to herself.

"I'd like to have a child … I've always liked children … but I can't", Maria finally confessed. Some of them cry for a little while, before uttering any of these things, or even exclaim, grieved, like Lia: "But are you aware that you can see their heart beating?!".

Like them, many women appear uncertain, sorrowful, and confused in relation to a choice that they have actually already taken, and they talk of their conflict between desire and refusal. The interruption of the pregnancy contains in itself an ambivalent desire towards motherhood: "I'd like but I can't". It is always hard to talk about this topic. It was so also within the group for the observation of the internal motherhood. Too painful, exploring the transparency of the internal motherhood, analysing its less transparent corners! It is no accident that the literature on this topic is meagre and rather recent as well (Meltzer, Bydlowski, Bergeret-Amselek, Marinopoulos).

Nonetheless, if one thinks well about it, fertile women lose every month the possibility to have a child. As Bergeret-Amselek (2005) observes, every monthly occurrence of the menstrual cycle can be experienced as a missed pregnancy, a little loss for that child who could have been born, for that maternality[1] that could not come true. Women may even develop the phantasy of having eliminated a child. We know very well also that refusal accompanies desire during every pregnancy. Contraception itself could be seen as an expression of the refusal of conceiving. As Marinopoulos (2005) observes, in our historical epoch, characterized by the possibility of controlling births, the common point of view could be turned upside-down completely considering that non-conception is the norm, and starting a pregnancy is considered the odd, the unusual, the irregular. Many women even declare openly they do not wish to have children, and they believe their choice should not be criticised and that it, on the contrary, shows a great sense of responsibility. I found the following statement in a popular women's magazine:

"I'm not maternal, at all … I don't know how to behave with my friends' children, actually to be honest, they bore me. I'm bored by what they say about their children, the couples with children. … Perhaps, thinking about it, I don't want children because I still feel very much like a little girl myself. … Perhaps I'm a little egoist, self-centred, narcissist, an old girl unable of too many shows of affection or big responsibilities. But I'm fine like this even though people don't understand me …".

Nonetheless, even these days, there are still women who become pregnant without desiring it and decide to interrupt the pregnancy. As Bergeret-Amselek and Marinopoulos underline, the desire for motherhood acts in the female unconscious producing enactments to which other enactments follow. The desire has escaped control. As the deepest objective of a woman's identity is motherhood, the voluntary interruptions of a pregnancy may be seen as crises in the path to achieve the maternal condition: accelerations of a process of getting closer to motherhood, internal movements, actions seeking new balances. We are dealing with a woman wishing to have children but who feels incapable of having any, who does not feel to be in a condition to have any, not yet psychically ready, when we deal with a woman who asks for a voluntary interruption of her pregnancy.

In truth, carrying on with a pregnancy means taking on a huge psychic responsibility, coming to terms with the fact of taking on a parental identity, with the ensuing risk of a failure, and because of this, one is not always in the internal and external condition to take on that responsibility. When I brought my work to the group, I told them about a dream I had had the previous night: "I could see a tiny and tentacular being that once it had nested in the host's body quickly developed". The group linked it to that *monster-child* that all pregnant women fear of generating. Fornari (1981), analysing pregnant women's dreams according to the coinemic method, links this generalized fear "of giving birth to a deteriorated child", this "genetic anxiety", to the theme of the "death which is in the original relationship between the child and the mother", to that "total persecution" that, in a manifest way at the moment of the delivery, the mother feels coming from the child and the child from the mother, and that becomes neutralized during the pregnancy by the symbiosis that develops between them[2] (Fornari, 1981, pp. 270–278 [own translation]).

The risk of failure represented by the monster-child is always lurking if one decides to carry on with the pregnancy. It is a monster both because the woman may fail in her attempt to give life but also because it absorbs all her energies, like a parasite with its host. This is more or less what Marta said during the interviews she agreed to have, after the first one, to be helped to take a decision: "Everyone will be focused just on him, everyone will think of him and no one of me anymore … me, who grew him inside me, … I can't bear it … I hate him, if I think about this!".

Again, as Fornari states, the maternal code, the development of the capacity to be a mother, clashes against the female code, the identity of the woman, and unconsciously links up with the life-death alternative, life of the mother and the child as opposed to the death of the woman and her sexual identity and vice-versa (see also Chapter 8). Based on my experience, the alternative may be also between maintaining an infantile state and moving towards an adult condition, between the possibility of a growth towards a new identity (that of motherhood) and remaining in the regressive condition of eternal little girl. This is illustrated is Ornella's case, who was seen before and after an interruption of pregnancy.

> In the meeting before the elective abortion, Ornella declares of being uncertain although she immediately clarifies it is not possible to question the family's pressures to interrupt a pregnancy arising from an extra-marital affair with a married man "one can't be sure of". When she returns, after the abortion, she reveals her own partner could not have had a child. Not just that, while her partner is cold and distant, the other is passionate and eager to be close to her. The woman though was afraid of this and still is, together with a great desire to be with him and to become a mother. Again, like before the interruption, she complains because she cannot let her voice emerge, that she always lets others interfere.

By giving her, thanks to the meetings, the chance to express herself, her thoughts turn to herself, in particular the conflict between the need for dependence, safety and the need to have to make choices if she wants to go on: remaining with her current partner and give up the dreams of a pregnancy or go and live with her new lover who would like to have child with her but whom she does not know well enough yet? It is clear that the problem laid, and lays, in the present as well, in the conflict between the possibility to grow and remain in her condition of considerate young girl, sister, partner. Also it is clear that perhaps it is necessary for her to go on working on herself to decide what she really wants.

The woman thinking about conceiving or who has got pregnant and has decided to go on with the pregnancy understands that what is growing inside her is a child but also a modified image of herself. It may be her maternal capacity but also not yet developed parts of the self, infantile parts, or parts not yet integrated with her conscious self. These internal movements have been highlighted by the research on pregnancy and may determine a conflict between the self and the child, between one's own need to be looked after and to look after the baby. The conflicts, if they are not made explicit or if they are not processed in other ways, can also become manifest through the somato-psychic phenomena typical of pregnancy[3] (sickness, vomiting, etc.) and at times even cause unexpected miscarriages. It is no accident that about 80% of women have a miscarriage in the first few months of the first pregnancy and that this experience makes these women become more mature.

The conflict is present and continuous since it is a condition of the pregnant state, but it may find a solution over time through the progressive identification of the mother with the child who is developing in her.

At times, though, not even many pregnancies brought to their due term are enough to establish this internal state. Annalisa, mother of two children, who has had previous interruptions of pregnancy, separated from her husband, may be an example of this.

Annalisa is pregnant within a very new relationship and she would like to have an abortion both because her new partner is not in favour of it and because "she is ashamed in relation to her children and her mother". The interview with Annalisa is characterized by mutability and duality: despite her age she looks like an adolescent and she wears a rather serious jumper over bright pink trousers. The interview starts with Annalisa crying because of the necessity to have an abortion, then she has some strong expressions of refusal towards this pregnancy. As her partner too does not want to keep this baby, Annalisa has decided to abort that "something of him inside me". After the abortion she wished him to never be able to have other children while she starts a new search, that she does not want to give up, for her "Prince Charming".

In the counter-transference, I see many "characters" in her: wild woman, then a little peasant girl, a gypsy, a mother, a lover, an adolescent. In the transference, I can feel the various roles Annalisa gives me: first psychologist, then witch, finally mother. In her path, it is clear the woman has experienced the child as assimilated to the lover; her situation, like the one of a woman competing against another woman, with a parental couple, and finally her need that I look after her like a little girl. In the group discussion, Annalisa's internal state is described as the state of a little girl excluded from the procreation capacity of the parents and who experiences the child in her like an intruder, like the other's child: the Oedipal couple's in her psychic reality, the boyfriend's or fiancé's, whatever he is, in the external reality.

Of course these are not the only mental states that are connected to an interruption of pregnancy. Besides the women who are unsure about taking on the new maternal role, the women who are still looking for their psychic stability, we may encounter women who use a conception to defend themselves from painful moments of their life.

> Angela, who has never wanted children and does not want any now because too busy with her job, is referred to me. She cries and goes on also with me, for a while, before she manages to say something. She tells me this pregnancy has arrived unexpectedly a year after her father's sudden death and also after her mother falling ill. I suggest that perhaps this pregnancy may be a way of bringing something vital right in the middle of a mournful, sad situation, and Angela observes that perhaps if her father were still alive, she could have now thought to bring about the pregnancy but that now, in such conditions, even though she is suffering for this, she does not think she has a choice!

It is not unusual to come across couples who make mistakes as far as contraception is concerned in periods when they are going through a crisis or are about to separate, as if to partially give back life to a relationship that is ending.

> Maria "has always loved children". She thinks they come "from the Divine Father" and that "one shouldn't say no to them"; this child, though, has been conceived while she is separating from a man who mistreated her. Talking about it, the woman can accept the idea that the pregnancy may represent the expression of her extreme wish to keep him with her, to go on with a "relationship that can't work and one that would kill her", and she decides to take on the responsibility to "kill" – her, a believer, that child.

Among the women asking to have an abortion, one should not forget the mothers who already have too many children and cannot have physical and psychic space for additional children. In these cases, the internal motherhood has been achieved and simply the painful choice is made to give up the conceived child.

During the first part of the interview, Rosanna cries, expressing all her guilt for the request she just made. When I try to explore with her what prevents her from continuing the pregnancy, she tells me she already has two children and the youngest is just a few months old. "I wouldn't really want to give up this new child, now that I know what it means, how great it is to have children, but how am I supposed to manage?! How could I look after the other two who are there already?! They need so much looking after ...!", she concludes, recovering a more reflexive state.

There are also women who deprive themselves of the possibility to be mothers for the first and only time for an open renouncement to develop their motherhood.

Margherita got pregnant shortly after separating from a former partner, within a too recent, new relationship. She comes to us because it could be her last occasion to become a mother and she would be very tempted to go on with the pregnancy but she does not feel she can count on this relationship, or just on herself. Faced with my attempts to attach meanings to this pregnancy of hers in terms of a wish to give life to something, she reacts stating that "the interruption only equates to giving up on motherhood". This renouncement of hers is even more needed now as her sister, too, has recently become pregnant, and because of this she thinks that: "Both for my mother and my sister, it would be a problem if I had a child, too, now".

There are also instances featuring women who decide not to interrupt the pregnancy. Here is Irene's case.

Starting from her observation that "she can't think about having an abortion", Irene develops a reflection on herself and the relationship with her family, her mother, so that she ends up revealing to herself the reality of her own condition: while working for her mother, she doesn't even make her pay a salary! During the short but intense interview, the acquired awareness allows her to take in the thought that she is still very much linked to her mother, perhaps even merged with her, and she comes up with the idea that it is because of this that she felt unable to become a mother. Supported by the image of a partner wishing to become a father, she decides to develop the newly-found maternal potential; she accepts not to interrupt the pregnancy and plans to separate from her mother.

Defining the psychic dimension of the interruption of pregnancy and the different types of women is emotionally demanding. Authors like Bydlowski (2000) observe the phenomenon from a single point of view, while others, like Bergeret-Amselek (2005) or Arcidiacono (1996), group in a different way the situations the women find themselves in. It is a multi-faceted phenomenon that because of its own nature does not lend itself to too rigid rationalizations, even though it understandably stirs them. I think that, precisely because of this, it is not helpful to proceed with too many codifications and that, conversely, it may be helpful to go on exploring the state of the women with the tools we have at our disposal in the attempt of helping them.

HOW TO BE HELPFUL WITHIN ALL THESE DIFFERENT SITUATIONS?

The group wondered about possible ways to be helpful in a context that rapidly leads one in contact with the deepest levels of the psychic functioning, in unusual setting conditions as compared to our usual work as psychotherapists. As a matter of fact, often women come for a single interview but they bring something and they must receive something, they are entitled to use the opportunity that fate or the unconscious offered them "for the occasion" (Arcidiacono, 1996). In the group, we discussed how to help the woman reflecting on her situation, how to integrate her personal history with the fact of having conceived a child, how to think about what was there before the pregnancy and how she arrived to her present condition.

The technique must necessarily be more active and the length of the interview more flexible. Given the space-time characteristics of the organization set-up (a room for a few hours) and the characteristics determined by the users' needs (women who must take a decision in a short time frame), the way of working that may be used is the "short psychoanalytic consultation" – actually very short. During a 45–50 minute meeting, the woman is offered the opportunity to be listened to, to identify and reflect on the meaning of her emerging anxieties.

Simonetta M.G. Adamo (1990), who has been active for many years in a consultation service for adolescents, writes that it is "an experience of coming closer to one's own anxieties and of reflection on their possible meaning [...] a meaningful experience of listening to and understanding, within the limits of a setting having a pre-defined timing" (p. 10 [own translation]). This intervention does not hold a therapeutic function because it cannot intervene on structural intra-psychic conflicts, but it may contribute to the recovery of the developmental movement which at that point is experiencing a critical moment, a passage, a turning point, as Bianca Iaccarino (Adamo, op. cit., pp. 171–188), in charge of a similar service underlines, and at times it may help the woman to take a decision.

Some of the technical features used are the following: the alliance with the adult functions, for instance reducing the expectations of elimination of the psychic suffering connected to the interruption of the pregnancy; the use of countertransference to grasp the underlying anxieties; and avoiding the use of transference for interpretations, referring to what happens outside, in the external relationships, rather than in the here and now.

During my experience, I noticed that the characteristics of this setting led the consultant to attach a great deal of relevance to every detail: all the barely visible movements of the patient are considered and are used to give form to the invisible movements of his/her counter-transference, widening the view on the woman's internal world. The discussions in the group and the thinking that develops inside it, with its associations and questions recalling to the consultant's mind other details, may further expand the view.

Within this context, the experience of the Infant Observation takes on a fundamental role because it allows on the one hand to take note of every little detail and on the other to identify their underlying psychic elements. These elements may create in the consultant's mind an interpretation of the woman's state that remains silent as such but that may be expressed through questions, observations on reality data, and also actions like those that are used in a child psychoanalytic psychotherapy, or those described by Sylvain Missonnier (2003) when he talks about the perinatal therapeutic consultations (CT).

Referring to Lebovici's thinking, Missonnier writes: "It is in this translation into an inter-body communication (a language of the action) [...] that the richness of the CT's metaphor-creating enactment emerges [...] The analyst identifies empathically with the various protagonists of the scene [...] When he/she feels empathically the need that one or the other of the protagonists feels, he/she becomes allied with his/her cause and acts accordingly; he/she therefore creates a metaphor of the interactive situation" (op. cit., p. 204). All of this is made possible by a setting that sees the therapist offering himself/herself as a "metaphorical maternal womb enveloping the future mother (or the parents)" (ibidem, p. 215 [own translation]).

If the counter-transference of the professional is then the best compass to understand and contain the woman's or the couple's state, the questions and the observations on the story recalled by the woman and also the analyst's actions represent the interpretative means. Again, as Missonnier says, in the consultation it is "essential to be able to launch interpretation probes" (op. cit., p. 214 [own translation]) giving back the user/patient something that concerns her. In this way, even a single meeting, instead of being experienced as an "abortion" of a therapeutic act, akin to offering someone something without having a feedback, may become an occasion of thinking, akin to gathering seeds that may grow inside and even blossom.

In relation to the contents of these possible interpretations, I believe that a statement by Meltzer (1973) is suitable to summarise the central problem of those who have to help a woman who is uncertain on whether or not to have a child: "In the instance of any particular pregnancy and its proposed termination, the problem could be stated [...] 'Whose baby and whose judgement'? [...] In so far as a woman experiences her pregnancy as her own, she is free to rescind the 'gift of life' and to mourn" (p. 168).

To again use Meltzer's words, it is a question of understanding whether the pregnancy is experienced "from the point of psychic reality" or not (p. 168). That means undersanding whether in the future mother there is, or is developing, an identification with her own mother, and the extent to which the pregnant woman manages to plan a development of herself together with the development of her child. The pregnancy may instead be experienced "as a delusion of pregnancy". That means understanding the extent to which the shown maternal capacity is just a fraud, a fake, motivated more by a competition with other women, with her own mother, rather than by the desire to become a mother like her.

In other words, in that moment it becomes necessary that the woman is helped to become conscious of the mental state she is in, the meaning this pregnancy has for her, with whom she is identifying or with whom she is trying to. If for instance it is a woman in search of her own motherhood but she is uncertain, unsure or already a mother and too busy in her task, then she may decide for the interruption and mourn. If there is uncertainty and confusion on the role she is playing, if she is in the state of a child still wishing to have a child by her father, if she is in the state of an adolescent who is only trying to feel reassured about the possibility to become an adult, if she is in the condition of a young adult woman who is trying to soothe a temporary pain with a pregnancy, then the experience may become an occasion to reflect on her condition and possibly start a process to cure herself.

In some cases, those characterized by a traumatic situation amplified by the pregnancy and those "in which the interpretation probes intensify a paralysing archaic anxiety", according to Missonnier (op. cit., p. 214, own translation), it is important to maintain a psychological support. Bergeret-Amselek (2005) as well believes that in some situations it may turn out to be very important for the woman to be seen until the moment when the child should have been born, or contacted on that occasion, because in that period, something may happen to the woman that may be connected to the delivery that could have taken place.

CONCLUSIONS AND DEVELOPMENTS

As early as 1920, Freud, highlighting the consequences of failure to process such an experience that he assimilated to the loss of a love object, wrote: "One is also amazed at the unexpected results that may follow an artificial abortion" (Freud, 1920, p. 367). Nonetheless, it is always hard to talk about it, reflect on it and be of help. It is a sector of intervention which is not considered enough and is still full of consequences for many women's psychic health.

As already mentioned, I believe it is very important, opposing and processing cultural and personal resistances, to continue exploring women's experiences and refine the technical tools that are helpful to contain them and transform them into elements that can be used by the women themselves and by us all.

To refine the technical tools that are helpful to contain women's experiences, already in the waiting room, in 2009, an exploratory questionnaire on the possible risk factors was introduced with the idea of conveying, straight away, to the woman the attention of the service for her particular situation, and to convey the message that the service is ready to talk about what she is experiencing. The experiment has had almost immediate results both as for the increase in the number of women who accepted to meet the psychologist, and the quality of the relationship they showed during the consultation and therefore the transformation potentials of the experience. The service, too, has benefited both in terms of relieving the anxiety burden of the staff involved and the improvement of the collaboration among the various professionals, thus strengthening the holding of the group container. The experiment is continuing so to be able to collect useful elements to further improve this tool in its routine use.

NOTES

1 As for the concept of *maternality,* see Chapters 6 and 9.
2 See Chapter 9.
3 The results of the studies of the multidisciplinary team of the Paris Centre for Foetal Medicine, which Michel Soulé is part of, give us confirmation of what has been described about the biological dimension. The results led to the surprising discovery that at the beginning of a pregnancy, the biological body of the mother tries to reject the embryo, releasing a hormone; this, though, in turn releases another hormone and opposes such rejection. If the body-embryo balance is not adequate, very early miscarriages can occur. In this context, sickness, vomiting, fainting, still mysterious phenomena, might be an expression of this "immunological paradox" (Soulé, 2000; Soubieux, Soulé, 2005).

REFERENCES

Adamo, S.M.G. (1990) *Un breve viaggio nella propria mente.* Napoli: Liguori.
Arcidiacono, C. (1996) *Identità femminile e psicoanalisi.* Milano: Franco Angeli.
Bergeret-Amselek, C. (2005) *Le mystère des mères.* Paris: Desclée de Brouwer.
Bydlowski, M. (2000) *Je reve un enfant. L'experience intérièure de la maternité.* Paris: Odile Jacob.
Fornari, F. (1981) *Il codice vivente. Femminilità e maternità nei sogni delle madri in gravidanza,* Bollati Boringhieri, Torino.
Freud, S. (1920) *The Psychogenesis of a Case of Homosexuality in a Woman.* Penguin Freud Library: Volume 9, Case Histories II.
Marinopoulos, S. (2005) *Dans l'intime des mères.* Paris: Fayard.
Meltzer, D. (1973) *Sexual States of Mind.* Pertshire, Scotland: Clunie Press.
Missonnier, S. (2003). *La consultation thérapeutique périnatale. Un psychologue à la maternité.* Ramonville Saint-Agne, Èditions érés, 2005 (1ère édition 2003).
Pippi, E. (2001) "I.V.G.". In: *Malvagia,* XVIII, 56.
Soubieux, M.J., Soulé, M. (2005) *La psychiatrie fœtale.* Paris: P.U.F.
Soulé, M. (2000) "La vita del feto: studio per comprendere la psicopatologia e gli inizi della psicosomatica". In: Righetti, P. & Sette, L. (Ed.) *Non c'è due senza tre.* Torino: Bollati Boringhieri, 2000: 343–364.

Chapter 11

Being received in consultation

Cristina Pratesi

It is already widely known that pregnancy is a process, a "crisis" that on one hand mobilizes old, unresolved or latent conflicts and new anxieties, and at the same time leads the woman to maturity, as it is a fundamental step in the construction of her female identity.

As a maturity crisis, it entails a "dismantling" of one's identity (similar to the one that takes place during adolescence); the changes in the organization of the Self, that consequently may occur, require the capacity to deploy the dual identification with the foetus and one's own mother about which we talked in Chapter 3.

Pregnancy is characterized by a particular mental functioning that many authors[1] have previously described, consisting of: a dilation of the permeability between the somatic sphere and the psychic dimension, a lowering of usual defences and resistances towards the repressed unconscious, in addition to a peculiar relational state, often characterized by a cry for help, a call to a responsible and caring person, that "conditions a transference capacity" (Bydlowski, 1997).

The period of pregnancy reveals itself as a privileged one in which, thanks to the reactivation of original phantasies, the "resurgence of the most archaic conflicts that stage the primitive vicissitudes of the containment" (Missonnier, 2005 [own translation]), emerge from the unconscious to consciousness without encountering the barrier of repression. In this psychodynamic context, the pregnant woman's need for a positive maternal image to be idealized and with which to identify is fundamental: a sort of point of reference to whom to convey memories and representations that might sometimes turn out to be pathogenic in the relationship with the future baby. The consultation therefore may also play a primary prevention task for early relationship imbalances and parenting disorders.

In my work experience in the Italian public health service, pregnant women come to consultation through different channels and in different ways. Generally, participating in the antenatal course allows them familiarizing with figures such as the psychologist who would be otherwise looked at with suspicion, or even be perceived as "threatening" – perhaps because they are wrongly believed to deal exclusively, like their colleague psychiatrists[2], with mental illnesses. Furthermore, as we know, during pregnancy women may show aspects acknowledged as being personal, internal, while in other cases, they are not well known, denied and placed outside oneself. For instance, it occurs with feelings of aggressiveness and hatred towards the internal parental figures, towards whom the pregnant woman may enact defensive splitting and projective mechanisms. Doctors, obstetricians, echographists, psychologists, and all the healthcare system staff may then be perceived as dangerous for oneself and the child and become, in the woman's perception, the embodiment of these negative, persecutory aspects. It is therefore undeniable that participation in the antenatal course fosters the possibility to have a meeting; women, though, can use, in any moment of their pregnancy, additional other ways of accessing the service, that is:

- the spontaneous and direct request of the Health Service-customer;
- a referral by professionals (for instance, gynaecologists, obstetricians and GPs) whom the woman, aware of a difficulty, may have gone to;
- a referral, after a routine visit during which the professional has noticed a difficulty or problem not made explicit.

The woman may also seek consultation at the beginning of her pregnancy, in the period called "*blanc d'enfant*" (Soulé, 1982), that is a period still characterized by the absence of mental representations of the child.

Very frequently, the conscious reasons for the request concern problems linked to the pregnancy and the foetus' health, body changes, or couple and family relationships. It is interesting, though, to notice that often what emerged is the theme of rivalry among women and death-related anxiety, even though disguised.

Birth and death, opening and closure of the life cycle, are indeed closely connected in the unconscious. The fear that the birth of a person "requires" the death of another, the phantasy that every "new self" that emerges must leave behind an "old self" – like a snake shedding its skin – and the idea that giving life literally means losing one's own, are always present in the pregnant woman's mind, just like in the staff's (Birksted-Breen, 1992; Del Carlo Giannini et al., 1981; Barletta et al., 1982; M. Roccato, 2003)[3].

The fear of dying while giving birth, or to somehow lose the child, that recurs so often in the phantasies mentioned by the women in consultation, appears intimately linked to the fear of punishment for damaging one's own mother or for having usurped her role of "life creator". However, if the pregnant woman manages to find inside herself the original pre-Oedipal link with her "early" loving and tender mother, the rivalry and envy issues must come undone, thus opening her to the feeling of gratitude and paying off the "life debt" (Bydlowski, 1997).

Jolanda has just turned 20, and she is about six months pregnant. Since her parents separated when she was 13, she has been living with her mother and two sisters, with whom she says she does not get on well. Then her father moved abroad and stopped any contact with his three daughters.

During a study and work trip to Great Britain, Jolanda started a relationship with a Jamaican boy and she got pregnant. She is against abortion; she decides to continue with the pregnancy and comes back to Italy, where she can count on the support "at least of her mother tongue". She sent money to her boyfriend so that he could join her, but he has not done it – nor will he ever do it. She feels lonely and lost, faced with "this experience that is bigger than her", while the baby girl she is expecting only represents a means to keep the young father close.

During the interviews she manages to talk about her parents' separation, and her current separation from her boyfriend, as terrible experiences that made and make her feel fragile, vulnerable.

She compares her present situation with the past one, her mother's. In external reality the relationship with her and her sisters improves. She gave birth and went back to England so that her partner could meet the baby, then she settled for good in Italy, without him.

In analysing her own experience and comparing it to her mother's, Jolanda was able to identify with her mother's pain, and this allowed her to feel closer and no longer hostile towards her. This also allowed her to mobilize her own resources and tolerate the separation from her partner.

Being as Jolanda is an adolescent, the path she made in just a few interviews was particularly significant because in this phase, the restructuring of the self image typical of adolescence became intertwined with the complex dynamics of pregnancy.

A VERY SHORT CONSULTATION

Joan Raphael-Leff believes that among the advantages of psychotherapeutic intervention during pregnancy, "[...] can serve as a healing experience for deficits in an expectant parent's own childhood, offering an opportunity to break transgenerational patterns by working through unconscious conflicts and revitalized issues, rather than enacting them with the next generation" (Raphael-Leff, 2001, p. 175). Therefore this author formulates a few, precise guidelines for pre-natal and perinatal treatments, providing for differentiated interventions according to the nature of the disorder: the focal intervention to deal with a crisis, including between one and six sessions; brief therapy (between three and ten sessions); and proper psychoanalytic psychotherapy.

The consultation, too, has been proven to be a helpful support to face in a more constructive way the crises during pregnancy, and may eventually become a more structured psychological support, longer in time, or a psychotherapy, for those situations that are different from the "normal complexity" of becoming mothers, in which one may notice signs of loneliness, fragile aspects that are difficult to be processed, down to an outright pathology.

During a relatively short time span, between one and a maximum of four sessions, the consultation work may actually become a toll to bring about a rebalancing and to quickly reactivate personal resources.

Susy, a woman in her early thirties, is 39 weeks pregnant; she lives alone, as her father died when she was eight years old and her mother when she was 20. Her partner is a 55-year-old man, separated, but who is still living with his ex-wife and a son, same age as Susy.

She asks for an interview in a cryptic way "because", she says, "I hope it'll help me take a very important decision".

She recalls she has spent these past nine months trying to make the father of her baby accept this pregnancy. Since the beginning he has stated he does not want anything to do with it; more than once he confessed to her he is ashamed for getting her pregnant at his age, and that he cannot accept the idea of having another child. He will take on all the legal responsibilities towards this child, but he does not feel he will be able to be a father to him. Susy talks about how humiliated and wounded she has felt: one day, while they were together in a shop, the man literally ran away so not to be seen by a relative of his. For Susy, who has always tried to make her partner feel emotionally closer to her pregnancy so to build a new family, all of this is a cause for a deep suffering.

The woman says she feels guilty, for wanting to keep the child against his will. She no longer knows whether she wants the man to legally recognize the child and for him to have his surname: this is the difficult decision she is faced with today. She adds she could not enjoy her pregnancy in a serene way like mothers normally do; she realizes she has not had a moment to think about her child, and now she would not like him to be born anymore and she does not know whether she will be able to love him.

She gave birth a few days after this single meeting and she gave the child her father's name. She called the Service to inform me about the birth and to ask me to go on with the sessions and to tell me that her son "is beautiful".

In this case, even with one single interview, the initial request for help, at first unclear and confused, then took form and Susy was able to "find" her baby, starting a positive and differentiated relationship.

THE DELIVERY AS A "WATERSHED"

In the experience of our Observatory, the moment of the delivery seemed to us to be a watershed, an event that, with the appearance of the real child and the emergence of its concrete presence, decrees the change.

A new psychic change of the woman corresponds to this situation that involves and absorbs the mother in a complete way: Bydlowski (2000) talks about an amnesia after the delivery, that goes hand in hand with the task to meet the needs of the newborn baby in terms of attention and looking after[4]. The state of psychic transparency disappears and thus that condition which has facilitated the contact of the pregnant woman with her deepest parts goes missing.

So, if it is rather common for the therapeutic relationship started during pregnancy to be interrupted, in some cases, the fact that an internal reflection process has been started will act upon the woman and she might feel motivated to go on with the therapeutic path. Birksted-Breen (1992) considers the continuity of the relationship to mitigate the sense of caesura caused by the delivery and the new life-style important: she believes it is greatly helpful to mourn the depressive feelings linked to the loss of pregnancy, of the child inside-the-belly and the phantasized child, and in dealing with that particular condition of vulnerability and fragility – very similar to an illness, although being normal – that emerges in the *post partum*[5].

In the cases dealt with by our Observatory, it was actually possible to confirm the extent to which this *continuum* of the therapeutic relationship is fundamental, and the transformation functions, often thought as exclusively part of the analytic or psychotherapeutic session, in reality also belong to the consultation setting.

As a matter of fact, a few authors characterize the consultation sessions as a *uterus* – "metaphorical uterus"[6] (Missonnier, 2005) or "imaginary uterus" (Roccato, 2003) – as this may be experienced by the pregnant woman as a practice that allows the discharge of unconscious drives, and one that helps her stabilize her emotional movements, to relax her defences, to feel contained in a therapeutic relationship, in which the face-to-face modality turns out to be a fundamentally important tool. The eyes "in the interrelation moments [...] play a unifying function, integrating the other sensory modalities [...] fundamental for the structuring of the Self" (Haag, 1985 [own translation]). Together with the voice of the therapist, they are the vehicle for the emotions and they create a shell, a container, an "*enveloppe*", visual and for sounds as well, malleable but at the same time solid enough (Maiello, 1993; Cresti, Lapi, 1996).

The consultation encounter thus becomes a time and a place to experience being welcomed, listened to, supported "in the expression of a new emotional formulation, at times uncanny" (Marinopoulos, 2005). As a matter of fact, the pregnant woman is encouraged to talk, to reveal herself, starting from a reflection, so to start the creation of a mental space able to take in the representations of herself (as mother), her partner (as father), and the baby about to be born: a "becoming" child, who may be thought, imagined, so as to establish a psychic continuity of the link to him/her.

Tatiana is nearly 40 and expecting her second child, a boy like her first; she is 32 weeks pregnant.

She asks to have a meeting "to know how to behave" with her first born, Marco. The child, who is 7, a few months ago started being aggressive with his schoolmates and hostile towards his future little brother, whom he says he does not want. Tatiana is sincerely worried for these behaviours and she believes they are caused by jealousy. Her words, though, show the absolute "no presence" of the baby she is expecting: she only wants to receive practical suggestions to make Marco change his behaviours.

Almost at the end of the interview, incidentally, she recalls having had, about a year before, another pregnancy that ended at the third month. The couple became aware of the sad news of having lost the baby at the first ultrasound scan, to which Marco too was present.

Tatiana recalls she had been very upset and terribly anxious because her son had discovered about the death of his future brother in that way. The child, though, had never mentioned that event afterwards, and she had relaxed, thinking he had forgotten. In a very cursory and hasty way, and only upon an explicit request, she talks about their sorrow, hers and her husband's, for the loss of their child.

She also recalls the moment when Marco was told about the new pregnancy: he was apparently indifferent and only after a long time he started saying: "This one too will die like the other, you'll see. I wanted that other brother, not this one". He then resumes the aggressive behaviours he had had in kindergarten, when he used to bite and hit the other children; and other behaviours, like putting his lips close to his mother's breast and the refusal to clean himself, much more infantile than his age.

Before saying goodbye, it is the woman who asks to come again: "This time to talk about me", she adds. In the meetings that followed, only when she was able to tell her story as a little girl who had lost a sister in a car accident, the future child had the chance to start appearing in her words.

THE SHADOW OF DEATH IN THE CONSULTATION

Even though a pregnancy might have been desired and actively sought, with great awareness, it is anyway always accompanied by hostile, latent and expulsion feelings. In addition, it is characterized by a conflict between getting rid of the baby and protecting it, that invests not just the woman but also the other people around her[7].

In our work experience, we noticed that the maternal ambivalence towards the foetus and what it stands for may be strengthened by the presence of losses that have not been mourned. They may concern previous interrupted pregnancies because of an intrauterine foetal death or an elective abortion even[8]. They can also refer to the loss of a parent or a significant relative. Squires (1999) talks about "pregnancies in the shadow of the child in limbo" to define those "projects-child" and those gestations that start to repair the endured narcissistic wound and cover with the presence of a new baby the ghost of the unborn or prematurely dead one.

During the meetings of the antenatal course, the emergence of themes linked to death is very frequent. It is often the experience of "coming closer" and sharing, in a group, these problems that are so painful and dramatic that makes it possible for the pregnant woman to ask for a consultation.

If it is clear that the possibility to contain a baby implies for a woman the fundamental experience of having been contained herself, which influences the maternal experience in relation to the permanence of the child inside her and then at the birth, in the situations when there are unresolved Oedipal conflicts and losses not mourned, sometimes the pregnant woman may feel a refusal for the pregnancy that is underway[9].

Barbara is 34 and has been married for almost two years. She works in a company and she is in charge of the administration. She is very much appreciated for her professional competence. She has various interests and hobbies, a very reward-ing and intense social life. She has become pregnant despite using contracep-tives, but she has decided not to have an abortion to not displease her husband.

She decides to have an interview with the psychologist, after meeting her at the antenatal course: this was a difficult choice for her, conflicting, implying a lot of pain, about which she has reflected for a long time and one that she finally managed to take, but only after postponing the appointment a couple of times and without informing anyone about it.

She is good-looking and well-groomed, she often smiles and makes jokes. Her eyes though betray a deep anxiety: she cannot accept her changing body, she is afraid this pregnancy will make her lose her beauty and youth, will make her age, will "mess her up". She is afraid her husband, and men in general, will no longer like her. Most of all, she cannot tolerate the idea of having to breastfeed: she wonders how the other women who seem to accept the thing in a natural way and even happily can manage. The simple idea of breastfeeding disgusts her and makes her think about the future baby as a "little monster who'll suck me alive".

Precisely because she feels the other women are so different from her, she has never confided these thoughts to anyone, not even her partner. She recalls how for the first six months she would wear clothes that hid the pregnancy, she was very attentive not to gain weight, she enrolled at the swimming pool and is still attending a Caribbean dancing course.

She even got to the point of secretly wishing herself a miscarriage, she imag-ines the birth of the child as a disaster that will drive her husband away and will prevent her from doing all the things she has always liked to do until now: her job, travels, evenings out with her friends.

She imagines also that she will be very jealous of the relationship between her partner and her son, because she would really like this child not to be there: when her husband talks about the imminent birth, she feels a pang of pain, which she has learnt to conceal, though. She is desperate and she feels trapped.

At the end of the meeting, she starts talking about her own mother, who was beautiful when she was young, and the way she, as a little girl, would look at her adoringly, spying her way of walking, talking, moving, smoking, to try and become like her. At this point she recalls, crying, of the tumour that "sucked her alive" and brought her to death, when she was an adolescent.

A few days after the meeting she asked to start a psychotherapy.

Barbara's dramatic recollections stir up in the therapist's mind the thought of an unwanted parasite-child, who has nestled in mother's body and lives at her expense: the refusal of the pregnancy could then be the consequence of this persecutory experience, probably linked up to an attempt of working through the Oedipal con-flict, "aborted" also because of the illness and the loss of the real mother.

Barbara is terrified at the idea of the very close mother-child relationship during the breastfeeding. This intimate and exclusive union between the two conjures up in her the image of an insatiable greed, so big as to be compared to a devouring tumour that sucks the life away (Wittenberg, 1987; Sontag, 1978).

Nonetheless, together with these persecutory aspects, the delivery and the birth of the child also seem to call up in this woman the experience of abandonment and rekindle in her intolerable separation anxieties. Perhaps it is precisely because of this reason that she can get to the consultation and finally manage to ask to be helped.

The possibility of tolerating her own feelings of rejection also seems, for this mother, influenced by the possibility to "maintain other objects of desire and investment, so not to be reabsorbed in a mutually paralysing symbiotic orbit" (Ferraro, Nunziante Cesaro, 1985 [own translation]).

FINAL CONSIDERATIONS

As we have been able to witness in our Observatory on the internal motherhood, the consultation during the pregnancy is a particularly efficient intervention level to allow the pregnant woman to express her experiences and needs, fostering reflection on underlying conflicts, fostering insights helping to overcome difficult moments and possibly make her aware of the need for further work, more structured and in depth, such as a psychotherapy. Therefore it has a prevention purpose in relation to the risk of *breakdown* in the couple, in the future mother-child relationship, in the woman herself.

Within the setting of the consultation session, "the most primitive part of the personality is projected" (Bergeret, 1974 [own translation]), while the therapist finds himself/herself in the position of metabolising the contents that Missonnier calls "placenta function": "The attempt will be made to make the rigidity of the discordant anticipation (idealizing, depressive, obsessive, persecutory, delusional) [...] more elastic" (2005 [own translation]).

Therefore let us not be deceived by the seeming simplicity of this type of intervention, which in fact requires a specific training and a sound experience, never neglecting the transference dynamics of the pregnant woman towards the therapist and the foetus "virtual child" and able to favour, always and without exceptions, her internal reality, keeping an atmosphere of intense, empathic participation.

NOTES

1 Deutsch, Bibring, Pines, Winnicott; Racamier; Pazzagli; Ammaniti; Ferraro and Nunziante Cesaro; Bydlowski just to mention a few.
2 See Chapter 4. *Vox populi* tends to level the two professions under the same description of "*shrink*", a term that recalls, in a manifest way, the idea of violent, painful, unpleasant and unwelcome practices: so, to be avoided at any cost!
3 See Chapters 4 and 12.
4 Such amnesia is also present in the popular tradition: in Tuscany, for instance, the labour pains are called "*mal scordone, che rimane tra materasso e coltrone*" [own translation: "Forgettable pain, that remains between mattress and quilt"], meaning a type of pain that is quickly forgotten.

5 See Chapter 9.
6 See also Chapter 10.
7 See Chapter 12.
8 See Chapter 10.
9 According to Soifer (1973), the refusal obeys to terrifying ghosts linked both to the child itself (as a representation of the woman's hostility towards the parents) and to the parents themselves (as carriers of threats and reproaches for the woman's sexual activity). Ferraro and Nunziante Cesaro instead underline how the imminence of the delivery may stir feelings of hostility and refusal, and the re-emergence of the phantasy of a damaging, persecutory child.

REFERENCES

Barletta, G. et al. (1982) "Il vissuto della maternità nell'esperienza clinica delle donne in gravidanza". In: *Età evolutiva*, 13: 64–66.
Bergeret, J. (1974) *La personnalité normale et pathologique. Les structures mentales, le caractère, les symptômes.* Paris: Dunod, rééd. 1996, 2003.
Birkted-Breen, D. (1992) "Fantasia e realtà in gravidanza e nel periodo post natale". In: Ammaniti, M. (Ed.) *La gravidanza tra fantasia e realtà.* Il pensiero scientifico editore, Roma,1992.
Bydlowski, M. (1997) *La dette de vie. Itinéraire psychanalytique de la maternité.* Paris: P.U.F.
Bydlowski, M. (2000) *Je reve un enfant. L'experience intérièure de la maternité.* Paris: Odile Jacob.
Cresti Scacciati, L., Lapi, I. (1996) "Dall'osservazione alla psicoterapia once-a-week". In: *Contrappunto,* 19: 15–27.
Del Carlo Giannini, G. et al. (1981) "Lo sviluppo del feto". In: *Età evolutiva*, 10: 93–99.
Ferraro, F., Nunziante Cesaro, A. (1985) *Lo spazio cavo e il corpo saturato. La gravidanza come "agire" tra fusione e separazione.* Milano: Franco Angeli.
Haag, G. (1985) "La mère et le bébé dans les deux moitiés du corps". In: *Revue de Neuropsychiatrie de l'enfance*, 33, 107–114.
Maiello Hunziker, S. (1993) "L'oggetto sonoro: un'ipotesi sulle radici prenatali della memoria uditiva". In: *Richard & Piggle*, I,1: 31–47.
Marinopoulos, S. (2005) *Dans l'intime des mères.* Paris: Fayard.
Missonnier, S. (2005) *La consultation thérapeutique périnatale. Un psychologue à la maternité.* Ramonville Saint-Agne, Èditions érés, 2005 (1ère édition 2003).
Raphael-Leff, J. (2001) *Pregnancy. The inside story.* London: Karnac.
Roccato, M. (2003) "Sogni in gravidanza: immagini delle trasformazioni del Sé". In: *Rivista di psicoanalisi*, XLIX, 1: 179–201.
Soifer, R. (1973) *Psicología del embarazo, parto y puerperio.* Argentina: Ediciones Kargieman.
Sontag, S. (1978) *Illness as Metaphor.* New York: Farrar, Straus and Giroux.
Soulé, M. (1982) "L'enfant dans la tète, l'enfant imaginaire: sa valeur structurante dans les échanges mère-enfant". In: Brazelton, T.B. et al. *La dinamique du nourisson.* Paris: ESF, 1982: 135–175.
Squires, C. (1999) *La grossesse à l'ombre de l'enfant des limbes.* Augsburg: Mikrofiche.
Wittenberg Salzberger, I. (1987) *"Consultazioni brevi con genitori di bambini nel primo anno di vita".* Unpublished work read at the Psychoanalytic Psychotherapy Florentine Association on May 22, 1987.

Chapter 12

Training childbirth professionals

Isabella Lapi

Working in that initiation place (Bydlowski, 2000) of the motherhood area is something special. It is packed with surprise, happiness, fear, and pain, because every new life that is born is the renewal of a mystery that will never be completely unveiled, despite the technology. It is the beginning of a new story, always different from any other.

If in the rest of the healthcare system medicine aims at repairing the damage, in obstetrics the medical intervention is aimed at assisting a life taking shape: from conception onwards, to the birth of a new being, the obstetrician gives the "care that is the work of supporting life, the place where a sense of being starts" (Mortari, 2006) [own translation]).

The emotional impact is very intense and peculiar. For childbirth professionals, after conception, pregnancy, and delivery, the beginning of the relationship of the mother with the newborn has, to a certain extent, the quality of an act of love, in which one shares the deepest joy, a joy that is not contaminated because it is still free from all the painful experiences that life will later on bring. The mother and her child are precious good objects to be lovingly preserved and taken care of.

For childbirth professionals, early and internal experiences connected to their infantile self and the original bond with their own mother are stirred up: good and idealized objects that one would like to keep safe inside oneself and repair in the moment when one takes care of the mother giving birth to her baby. The love circulating around birth lays on these intense experiences but it is never completely free: the early experiences that one goes through again unconsciously are often not exempt from the pain of a separation or an unrewarding nourishment, or from narcissistic wounds to be repaired; the stronger the pain, the more the idealization grows, defensively. Disturbing feelings are intertwined with unselfish love, and forced towards a stronger idealization. In the attempt to expel the difficulties and keep the anxiety at bay, they may even spill over into omnipotence, in the desire of possession, in envy.

There is a thought looming over all of this which makes the emotional participation even more intense: the thought of death. The two extreme moments of the beginning and end of life are closer than one would expect them to be: death, like birth, contains in itself a mysterious element that cannot be commanded and that hangs over man, defying the possibility of control and understanding.

Death is "present in a latent way in every life project" (Negri, 2006, p. 13 [own translation]): perhaps Piero della Francesca felt it as well, as he wanted his *Madonna del Parto* placed in the cemetery where his mother was buried. Or so much that Chagall, seeing it, grasped this feeling and exclaimed: "It's the symbol of life that is about to be born from the maternal womb in the place of death, but this is an outstanding idea!" (Ferrara Mori, 2006, p. 86). Both at a phantasmatic (as thought and anxiety) and at a physical level (as real possibility), death is present in the choice to procreate, in the time of the pregnancy, in the delivery, in the risk of malformations and anomalies. Professionals are deeply touched: working with life means also coming to terms with the possibility of death.

In relational dynamics, the professionals' intimate psychic mobilization becomes intertwined with mothers' projective identifications, which are intense, coloured with love and anxiety, and ambivalent. Extremely close relationships get established: they shift from being professional to becoming personal, and at times even burdensome and hard to manage.

Among childbirth professionals, those who are more engaged at an emotional and relational level are obstetrics, as they are closer to mothers.

The care provided at the moment of the birth has always been "an event in which two women act together" (Duden, 2006, p. 93 [own translation]). This special relationship between women remains and should be preserved in our era as well, where technology seems to be dominating and depriving the birth of its natural course. The historian Duden addresses an invitation to obstetricians: that despite their technical training they could apply "the approach of the old midwives [...] of caring for the women" they accompany during the pregnancy and the delivery with "an affection today more needed than in the past" (Duden, 2006, p. 94 [own translation]).

Obstetricians are indeed aware of their need to be competent, updated professionals, able to embrace the beneficial possibilities offered by technological developments. At the same time, though, they know they must defend themselves – and the mothers as well – from the excesses and risks inherent in these technologies, offering them a personalized psychological assistance: from midwife to woman, from woman to woman. Their desire to understand the professional psychic dynamics and to acquire a psychological and relational training is based on the awareness of this complicated task.

At a deeper level, this desire derives from a great psychic sensitivity and willingness to let oneself be involved and to look inside oneself. Just like the pregnant woman experiences a mental state of "psychic transparency"' (Bydlowski, 2000), in which the psychic, unconscious contents can have more easy access to consciousness, we can think that in a very similar way obstetricians, too, find themselves experiencing a specific psychological state of "transparency". In this mental state the unconscious reasons, linked to the choice of this profession, might more easily become conscious: coming to terms with one's own internal motherhood, the ensuing emotional ambivalence and all the emotions, including the most disturbing ones, provoked by the fact of staying close to the creating subject, i.e. the pregnant woman who gives life. In the encounter of all these transparencies, the special relationship among women becomes a way of feeling the same, the capacity to be in tune and understand one another.

To recognize, manage, and professionally use the intense emotional tangle circulating around procreation and birth, professionals need a specific training.

The training methodologies inspired by the Infant Observation according to Esther Bick teach how to feel and mentalize emotions, and to look for their meanings as an "internal, necessary condition to encounter the other" (Mazzoncini, 2007, p. 147 [own translation]); the various experiences conducted with these methodologies have already proven efficient in introducing in healthcare contexts the "mental variables promoting positive processes of transformation and integration of that body-mind split that too often characterizes the healthcare work" (Lapi, Stefanini, 2001, p. 171 [own translation]) and one that, faced with the anxiety implied in professional tasks and in healthcare relationships, produces rigid, defensive and dysfunctional reactions, already well known and studied (Menzies, 1970; Druon, 1996).

By extending the Infant Observation technique to the observation of pregnancy, our Observatory for internal motherhood uses a working methodology based on group discussions and processing of observation clinical material as a basis for theoretical-technical reflection. This methodological organization that we use is an extremely helpful training tool for those working in the area of childbirth: it actually facilitates a better understanding of the psychic processes of becoming a mother, grasped in the liveliness and immediacy of the clinic and in their impact in the professionals' minds. At the same time, it allows one to experience sharing, containment and support in a working group.

By using this observation method, some of us have led training groups with obstetricians working in different services (hospital wards, family consulting units, antenatal courses, after-birth out-patient clinics, and home visits after the birth of the child), with the possibility to include in a complete way the path of care for motherhood to birth.

Our training proposal aimed at the deeper aspects of the relationship with the mothers has been welcomed with great interest and followed with authentic participation. The course mirrored the Observatory methodology: in the group meetings, every obstetrician, in turns, would bring a written protocol about a case she had dealt with, describing the story, and then in detail she would discuss about one or two meaningful interviews. The material was discussed using all the inputs coming from the group, as if it were an Infant Observation protocol. Then a synthesis of the discussion was drafted. The last meeting of the training cycle was then devoted to a summary of the work produced and a reflection on it.

The obstetricians experienced a group mind at work on the internal aspects of the relationship with the mothers and so they understood and accepted the fact that encountering the internal motherhood means encountering one's own feelings, ambivalence, limits and new or unknown aspects of the Self as well. During the meetings, the obstetricians of the groups accomplished two steps: the first was grasping and expressing their own emotional experiences, trying to understand how much of these experiences was linked to their re-awakening, because of the contact with the mothers' experience and their emotional experiences, their own internal experiences, and how much on the contrary was due to projections of the mothers onto them. From this the subsequent step was to use the understanding obtained through the filter of the emotions to re-orient their professional behaviours. All of this work produced the result of stimulating and strengthening their capacity to become empathic and offer containment.

During the meetings, an intense atmosphere developed and the group mind was able to express and contain personal emotional experiences, also producing psychic relief.

From the group work material, very rich and presented with great participation, a few general themes have emerged which are particularly compelling and which exemplify typical and recurring emotional movements. Here we discuss some of them.

THE CHOICE TO WORK WITH LIFE

Today the choice to become an obstetrician may still be linked to a family tradition and the identification with an obstetrician mother or grandmother. In other situations, the choice is made serenely, as part of regular study path in which young women make the choice out of sheer interest and more or less awareness of personal motivations.

Often, though, the choice derives from much deeper reasons: they are related to facts pertaining to personal history, in which a strong juxtaposition has occurred between life and death. In these cases, choosing to become an obstetrician carries the meaning of choosing life against dominating death anxieties. It may be a reparatory choice in relation to early traumatic experiences linked to one's own or a sibling's birth – difficult births, that caused losses, handicaps, deaths – or again, a reparation choice in relation to narcissistic wounds or risks of death linked to one's serious diseases.

The encounter with death and the will to escape it is also clear in the motivation of those who decided to become obstetricians after working for a period as a nurse in wards where they were in close contact with death (resuscitation, E.R., ICU). In a very touching way, even though with a degree of idealization, these obstetricians recall how, at one point, they felt overwhelmed or crushed by the pain and a sense of impotence, and for this they chose "the role of giving life".

> "The limit of death couldn't be won". "I needed to breathe … just like the baby who needs to breathe to live". "I fled towards life". "Only by getting away from the pain I could go on working". "I felt I wanted to deal with life"[1].

MAKING CONTACT WITH ONE'S OWN INTERNAL MOTHERHOOD

Inevitably, the conscious and unconscious contact with one's own maternal experiences, or lack of them, occupies front stage.

The identification processes are very strong. It often happens, when talking about a case, that similarities with personal motherhood experiences surface, or also with aspects of one's own personality. Such projective and introjective identifications, if they remain unconscious, can, as one may imagine, make it more difficult to bear the relational impact and avoid colluding with defensive aspects in the mother.

When it is possible to achieve a high enough level of awareness, this identification game allows the obstetrician to become more empathic, up to the point of it being "a professional tool", one of them says.

However, what creates the biggest emotional difficulty is the absence of personal experiences of motherhood. The experience of non-motherhood seems to remain at the forefront of the mind as an unprocessed element (for instance, during the first meeting of the group, the first obstetrician to introduce herself declares, spontaneously and without any request, that she has no children). In others, there is a clear envy for mothers, perceived as custodians of something powerful and inaccessible (one obstetrician who has no children tells the group how she feels "paralysed, belittled and attacked" when the mothers ask her whether she has children or not). *The envy and the persecutory anxiety can be felt also towards other colleagues.*

Another obstetrician with no children who feels hurt attributes to the rest of the group the thought that she is not able to do a good job because she is not a mother herself; therefore, she cannot really understand mothers.

ENCOUNTERING MATERNAL AMBIVALENCE

Encountering maternal ambivalence is quite different from dealing with the idealization of motherhood and of one's own profession. It often stirs up in the obstetrician's intense defensive reactions to avoid anxiety. The capacity to empathize with the mother disappears and the identifications focus on the child, with the effect of leaving the mother even more lonely and in difficulty.

A sudden hospitalization of the newborn baby seems to break the idyll of the mother-child relationship ("Absolutely perfect up to that moment", the obstetrician comments): the mother starts experiencing her child as a fragile, spoiled object, no longer attractive as before, and she has difficulties managing breastfeeding and bearing the baby's crying, which becomes more frequent and prolonged, altering the sleep-wake rhythm. The obstetrician tries to make the woman understand "in every possible way" how much the child might be stressed by the hospitalization and the separation from her; but she only obtains more anxiety from the mother. Finally the mother resorts to a milk formula and asks the paediatrician for a medication to make him sleep: "After all my efforts! At that point I gave up!", the obstetrician exclaims.

USING EMPATHY

If obstetricians can manage to interpret the ambivalence as an expression of difficulty and a request for help, there is a positive empathic response that allows them to offer understanding and protection, and to be, in a sort of female gender identification, "the champions of women".

A woman with a very unpleasant and hostile behaviour immediately declares she did not want this pregnancy. The obstetrician recalls: "I felt that behind her harshness there was a great need for help, I felt she was very lonely. So I sent her to the antenatal course but then I immediately realized that if she went there with that attitude, my colleagues would have treated her coldly. So I was worried about her and I ran after her down the corridor to walk her there myself".

Another case illustrates how empathy produces well-being.

An obstetrician is faced with a very anxious woman who, despite a regular and abundant production of maternal milk, cannot put her baby to her breast. At first, to feel more at ease and competent in supporting the anxiety of this mother, towards whom she feels a strong involvement, the obstetrician tries to rely on the techniques learnt during a course she had attended. Soon she realizes those techniques that seemed to be good are in reality insufficient; only by letting herself be guided by what she feels and her own personal experience she manages to become attuned to the mother's needs and give her a good piece of advice to help her relax. The obstetrician recalls: "As soon as I realized she was having difficulties, I thought about using what I had learnt during the communication course: I looked at her straight in the eyes and I repeated her words: they had told me it worked this way … like this; but she kept on crying. I felt lost, more and more anxious, then I thought she must feel the same, and despite everything that they had taught me about the advantages of breastfeeding, I suggested she could try the bottle: she immediately calmed down, she familiarized with her baby, little by little, and now … she has resumed breastfeeding!".

THE PAINFUL IMPACT OF INTRAUTERINE DEATH

When real death occurs at birth, it invests everyone with great despair, without any possibility of being prepared or of representing it in one's own mind because everyone expected life: "Death at birth – and with good reason, above all, death before birth – adds to the inexpressibility of death and of our origins" (Ansermet, 2006, p. 177). The pain is extremely strong, the narcissistic wound difficult to repair, and the psychiatric risk is high.

Childbirth professionals have the delicate task of accompanying the mother and the parental couple in separating from the child and to begin mourning, but it is – as it may be easy to guess – a painful and heavy task to bear because one must come in contact with the most fragile and needy part of the Self. Such personal involvement is less controllable and felt to be more dangerous. When death occurs in the labour room, the obstetricians' vital professional role is damaged because death before birth is not compatible with their mission of giving life.

One obstetrician asks the group, in an anxious way, whether she has not been very professional, meaning not "detached" enough, with a mother who had lost her child because she hugged her and she cried with her. She finally manages to tell the group that during that period her sister was going through a difficult pregnancy and she was worried for her: "I really had to make an effort not to run away from this mother". That death made her think about her own experiences of loss, feared or actually experienced, so much that unbeknown to the mother, she had gone, alone, to the cemetery where the dead child was buried and brought him flowers. She had thus managed to have her own moment to alleviate a grief that had indeed become personal.

Managing to share the pain of death is a relief not just for the mothers but also for the professionals themselves, who feel they are of help and they, too, can express their painful emotional participation, thereby mitigating it. On the contrary, the emotional retreat that often one encounters in the mothers and the families hit by the loss stirs in the obstetricians a feeling of impotence due to the impossibility of repair that leaves them sad and unsatisfied.

One obstetrician phones various times to a mother who has given birth to a child who died in uterus and she offers to go and visit her at home and to take care of her. Although the woman accepts to talk about herself over the phone and shows to appreciate her interest, she is evasive about setting a date. The obstetrician bitterly comments: "Of course I respected her resistance, I took a step back. What else could I have done!? Now I have the problem!".

Abandoning preconceptions and idealizations, being more aware of one's own identification movements, managing to mentalize emotions and searching for meanings beyond the appearances of the concrete and the visible: these are the objectives and the targets of a training that helps and supports the professionals in understanding internal motherhood – a training that, as opposed to what happens in an adhesive ways of learning, in the certain as well as mechanical techniques, helped them to observe, listen, give value to what they feel.

The last meeting of the groups was devoted to reflecting about the experience they had had and to highlight which results, of the training they had carried out, they could bring with them as a benefit for their work experience. It was extraordinary for all of us to see how many "fruits" were picked. And they were not virtual fruits found in books, but fruits born and ripened thanks to the actual experience of the cases they had encountered. The reports of the last meetings illustrate the way the experience of Infant Observation works by integrating cognitive and emotional aspects.

In the report of the last meeting of one of the groups – which follows as an example – one can clearly see the process of learning from experience, of accepting reality (as opposed to the temptation of idealizing), and managing, without fear, to tell oneself that it is not wrong to make use of one's own emotions.

REPORT OF THE LAST MEETING

In light of the clinical cases that were discussed, we reflect on what it may mean to take care of the mother from the psychological and relational point of view: in our services, as it often happens within families, the attention is all on the newborn baby. The mother, though, still needs a lot of attention and care. For us obstetricians, taking care means "keeping the mother at the centre", taking care of the child through caring for the mother without losing sight of the relationship, accepting the mother for who she is, without imposing what one would like her to be. Next to the know-how of our professionalism, it is important to be able to be present: there is no technique without the relationship. Even if the relational requests and the feelings expressed by the mothers invest us and involve us intensely, it is useful to use one's emotional reactions to understand their mood. This is often characterized by anxiety – for instance, to lose control, the denial of the difficulties (up to the exclusion of reality), the hyperactivity or the impossibility to get in touch with one's own feelings. Therefore, it is essential to be able to detect the signs of crisis, such as excessive dependency, the extreme need for rules and prescriptive behaviours (sign of uncertainty); one should pay attention to those traumatic and stressful elements, whether small or big, troubling the pregnancy, because those elements will trouble the relationship with the child. In addition, it is essential to grasp mother's positive emotional energies that, like good engines, can help her. How to relate effectively? Containment plays a fundamental role: finding an adequate physical space and time for the relationship, but also the mental space, that is, being willing to take in the other person's mental contents, observing and listening, as well as offering continuity to the presence. Even though the care tasks also imply active offers of help, prescriptions and being directive, it is important to be present; at times it is even more important than words. We thought about how to reassure: for instance, it may be helpful to put into words that we have understood the difficulties and that we accept them (conveying empathy); legitimating the fact that mothers may also have negative emotions and not to feel guilty for that; never deny difficulties, never belittle or behave in an untruthful way, never joke when faced with pain. Finally, in the situations of emotional retreat and/or of rigid defence, when active interventions do not seem possible, the best thing to do seems to be to remain next to the person in order to be in the position of noticing moments of opening up, and anyway show that we are there. Sometimes, we encounter aggressiveness in mothers, disguised as different behaviours: from the analysis of the cases we saw, aggressive and hostile behaviours in the mothers are almost always reactions to a state of need and fear. For this reason, they may be interpreted as a request for help. But we also saw that aggressiveness makes us professionals feel offended, let down, betrayed, just like aggressive answers, thus preventing empathy and understanding from occurring. For all of this, containment is necessary for us as well: it is team work that offers support and containment, that helps us overcome loneliness. The group is ready to take in the mind.

NOTE

1 Material collected by Cristina Pratesi.

REFERENCES

Ansermet, F. (2006) "Death and Birth". In : La Sala, G.B.; Fagandini, P., Iori, V., Monti, F., Blickstein, I. (Eds.) *Coming into the World: a Dialogue between Medical and Human Sciences*, pp. 177–184. Berlin: Walter de Gruiter & Co.

Bydlowski, M. (2000) *Je reve un enfant. L'experience intérièure de la maternité,* Paris: Odile Jacob.

Druon, C. (1996) "Réseaux d'identification dans une situation à haute risque". In: *Contrappunto,* 18, maggio 1996.

Duden, B. (2006) *Il gene in testa, il feto in pancia. Sguardo storico sul corpo delle donne.* Torino: Bollati Boringhieri.

Ferrara Mori, G. (2006) "The interior experience of maternity". In: La Sala, G.B., Fagandini, P., Iori, V., Monti, F., Blickstein, I. (Eds.) *Coming into the World: a Dialogue between Medical and Human Sciences,* pp. 85–102. Berlin: Walter de Gruiter & Co.

Lapi, I., Stefanini, M.C. (2001) "Tra il corpo e la mente. Il difficile percorso dell'osservazione con il personale sanitario". In: Cresti, L., Farneti, P., Pratesi, C. (Eds.), *Osservazione e trasformazione,* pp. 171–180. Roma: Borla.

Mazzoncini, G.M. (2007) "Prima della lettura dei lavori". In: Cresti Scacciati, L., Nissim, S. (Eds.), *Percorsi di crescita: dagli occhi alla mente,* Roma: Borla.

Menzies, I. (1970) *The functioning of social systems as a defence against anxiety,* London: The Tavistock Institute.

Mortari, L. (2006) *La pratica dell'aver cura,* Milano: Mondadori.

Negri, R. (2006) "Prefazione". In: Aite, L. (Ed.), *Culla di parole,* Torino: Bollati Boringhieri.

Addendum

The crisis of "internal motherhood" and its impact on the "consultazione partecipata"[1]

Dina Vallino

FROM THE CONCEPT OF INTERNALIZATION TO THE CONCEPT OF INTERNAL MOTHERHOOD

Gina Ferrara Mori is a reference figure for Italian child psychoanalysis. Her specialization in paediatrics, which precedes her specialization in psychoanalysis, has directed her attention to the development of babies starting from their first few weeks of life and the mother-child relationship.

In a paper dating back to 1980, *Correlazioni fra la relazione analitica e la relazione madre-bambino* [Correlations between the analytic relationship and the mother-child relationship], presented with Lina Generali at the 4th National Conference of the Italian Psychoanalytic Society (S.P.I.), she illustrated the absolutely pioneering idea, for the eighties, that real mothers' maternal competences help us understand the analysts' symbolic maternal functions. An analogy is established between the mother-child relationship and the analytic situation: "just like mothers learn from babies and from their children ... the analyst may learn from the patient when he/she interprets too much or in an insistent manner without giving the patient the possibility to assess, decide and say his/her 'no'" (Ferrara Mori & Generali, 1980 e 2007, pp. 213–5). The analytic situation is based on the concept of internalization which can transform a real, affective experience into a mental, internal experience[2]. This mental process may be considered inclusive of all the other processes and mechanisms, including incorporation, introjection, and introjective identification. All of these aspects are structural derivatives from the theory of object relations, through which the internal psychic world comes into being (Napoletano, 2006).

The concept of *internal motherhood* derives from the relevance that Gina Ferrara Mori attaches to internalization. It is an extremely valuable concept for the definition of internal psychic relationships, related to the project of "taking care of a child and, more in general, of someone". Gina Ferrara Mori (2006) writes that *internal motherhood* is a process in which female identity and mental representations develop, a place for phantasies, emotions, desires, and dreams, where bonds, affections and new relations reside. It is the container of a phantasied internal child who will become the external, real child.

Gina Ferrara Mori shows us images of motherhood from the religious or non-religious iconography (*Madonna del Parto*, Young woman cradling a child baby by Odoardo Borrani and others) with which many artists, in their works, created "an extended observatory of motherhood" (Ferrara Mori, 2006, p. 86). Their paintings lead us to contemplate that mysterious something inherent to the spiritual strength of an expectant mother. The emotional sensation of *internal motherhood* is expressed in some Madonnas with a series of signs: the gesture of the hands lying on the belly "as if to reassure herself of the baby's presence and to protect him" *(Madonna incinta di Piero)* (Ferrara Mori, 2006, p. 87). Even the absorbed look of the Madonnas of the Annunciation, together with a hint of a movement turned the inward, a sort of withdrawal of "demure awe", reveals the woman's internal contact with the creature inside her that she begins to think about. Only the internal perception that the mother has of the child may make us aware of his presence: in other words, it is the *maternal atmosphere* that leads us closer to the mysterious beauty of motherhood and, implicitly, its labour.

DEVELOPMENTS OF THE CONCEPT OF INTERNAL MOTHERHOOD

The concept of internal motherhood and the correlations that are added thanks to the continuous work carried out by Gina Ferrara Mori's research group is a sort of "map" that can be of help in defining the world of the mother's internal relation with her child (Stern's *motherhood constellation*, 1995). It starts when she conceives him, to continue when she feels its full foetal life, to the birth and her intimate, daily caring for the newborn child. Therefore, the disappearance or lack of emergence of the *internal motherhood* is a significant prognostic sign. During the pregnancy, if the future mother is bombarded by an excess of technological explorations, in particular ultrasound scans, the future mother could end up feeling lost and inadequate for the future task of *merging* with her own internal child. Objectification of the foetus (her internal child) does not respect the *maternal atmosphere,* within which her being the main witness gets established, as an expectant woman, of the experiences about the child inside her body[3].

With the aim of supporting pregnant mothers in their precious merged relationship with the foetus, Gina Ferrara Mori has created, with her group, the Observatory of the Internal Motherhood, extremely important also for the prevention of pregnancies at risk (Ferrara Mori, 2008).

INTERNAL MOTHERHOOD AND LATENT CRISIS

The value of the concept of internal motherhood developed by the important research carried out by Gina Ferrara Mori and her group helps us define in retrospect many situations of motherhood. These are combined in an alternated way, all along the mothers', fathers' and children's lives, with the phenomenon of *latent crisis*: a concept, derived from observation, to which I refer to indicate an invariant in the motherhood situations[4]. A *latent crisis* is a type of crisis that occurs between the mother and her child in relation to the fact that the child feels his/her needs are not met by mother and then realizes that either she has not understood those needs or that she has imposed something different from what her child was expecting from her. It is an "old" story that starts at birth, while the Pre-Infant Observation tells us that it starts before birth, that is, during pregnancy. The newborn, when the mother is unable to acknowledge his/her experiences, cannot internalize a comforting maternal object. The *latent crisis* is part of the mother-child relationship, but its intensity and frequency might impair, in the baby, the matrix of trust in him/herself and the first nuclei of personal identity (Vallino, Macciò, 2004, p. 178 [own translation]).

For the child it is a question of bearing, possibly not in a stormy way, these moments without good containment and without being understood, to finding again the mother or the father, perhaps with the support of symptoms or alarm signals for the parents. For the mother, who is not perhaps helped by the father or the family environment, it is a question of learning once again to feel able to carry out her maternal tasks: comforting, understanding, foreseeing, loving, educating. The repetition of latent crises between mother and child, and the concept of internal motherhood, allow us to signal the difficult moments in the life of a mother, calling them *"crises of the internal motherhood"*.

This concept, at the moment of the child consultation, that sees both parents joined together in their request for advice and understanding for their child, grants therapists the possibility to deeply deal with the crisis of the internal motherhood and bring it to the fore.

THE CRISIS OF INTERNAL MOTHERHOOD

Having analysed in detail many mother-daughter/son consultations, I have observed that *"crisis of internal motherhood"* means a form of maternal suffering that is symmetrical with the child's, painful intrapsychic and interpersonal events, almost as if the child's story resonated mother's own story inside her. Young women as well, undergoing analysis, and having difficulties **imagining** themselves as mothers, lead me to explore their infantile relationship to their own mother and to often discover that these young women did not feel intimately recognized by an internal mother with whom they were identified. The Pre-Infant Observation is based on the same evidence derived from the attachment theory (Fonagy, 1992) in regard to these aspects. As a matter of fact, if a woman still has unresolved conflicts and remote emotional tensions with her own "internal" mother, this may be critical for her future motherhood to be realized or not, once the young woman becomes an adult.

The *Observatory of internal motherhood* is made up of a group of psychoanalysts and psychotherapists who offer future mothers the possibility to be listened to and cared for, with Pre-Infant Observation, with antenatal courses, with psychoanalysis or psychotherapy projects; all these passages allow pregnant women to become aware of their past history and plan the dawning of the psychic process that will lead them to a new maternal identity (Ferrara Mori, 2006).

The "consultazioni partecipata", in particular, show us how the events of the children's neurosis and psychosis become, in the mother's histories, something that hinders the development of the maternal identity and that therefore must be taken into consideration as a part of caring for the child. With the request for a psychological consultation for her child, a mother may be highlighting her personal crisis of internal motherhood, when her son's or daughter's malaise or outright psychic illness resonates in her a symmetrical and complementary problem.

CLINICAL VIGNETTE: CARLA, SEVEN YEARS OLD

Carla's mother is a very busy professor of economics and her father is a physician. Carla has developed a bitter and painful identity that leads her to surly silence, to a closure in the relationship with her parents, to a quasi-autistic isolation – such a serious presentation, in fact, that after ending a participated consultation with both parents as well, I decide to see her for a participated consultation with her mother once a week in my office.

> Carla is seven years old, she attends a private school and has excellent results. Carla's everyday life has a managerial style, she is basically busy every afternoon: language schools, swimming-pool, piano lessons, karate, Religion classes. Her main symptom, that is the reason why her parents contacted me, is the following: in the evening, when her parents come home from work, she often accuses herself of having been the cause of some accident that may have occurred to her brother or a schoolmate and she asks to be punished. Punishments are typical of the education given to Carla by her parents, who impose rules and discipline to their children. Despite the strictness of their educational system, Carla's parents ask to be helped to understand what is happening to their daughter. They feel that she is upset and not really connected. They are afraid their punishments and strictness have damaged her. After a few meetings, both mother and father realize that their daughter complains because she "works too much", and after reconsidering things, Carla is allowed to have some time free from structured commitments. In the sessions with the parents, I think I was able to help them enhance their internal perception of the affective relationship with Carla, the reasons for her emotional detachment. I still sense, in the mother, especially when Carla is more upset and withdrawn, a crisis that is symmetrical to the one their daughter is expressing (*crisis of internal motherhood*). The mother has anyway accepted with relief the idea of being able to do something for her daughter. She is making changes for Carla, too: she devotes more time to her, she accompanies her to the sessions.

> I plan a continuation of Carla's consultation with her mother, considering that mother and daughter need to talk and to understand each other, and to overcome a persistent mutual misunderstanding.

I will now illustrate with a vignette the typical way in which this mutual misunderstanding occurs. There has been Carla's birthday party, organized by her parents, with entertainment activities the mother chose, about a month before. She invited children, friends and the neighbours of the countryside house where the family spends their weekends.

At the beginning of the session of the day after the party, mother walks in and announces that "today Carla is very tired" and that she did not want to come. She adds that the day before something happened. Carla forces the mother to be quiet. She is sitting stiffly with her head bent down and her pullover over her eyes, she puts her hands in front of her face as if to hide herself, as she withdraws more and more. I talk about her difficulty in telling me simple things that have happened during the week. I ask her whether she might like her mother to talk on her behalf, even though I am quite sure she could tell me what happened because she is able to do it. Carla whispers something that I can hear: "I didn't have fun at the party but I don't know why". Again she puts her hands over her mouth, ears and eyes. The impression is that she has closed down, as if she wanted to communicate to me and her mother that she has no intention whatsoever to engage in a dialogue with us. I feel powerless as I cannot help her and at the same time I feel bothered by a sense of isolation between mother and daughter. I tell her something about the fact that I am not expecting to know "the reason why"; regardless of what happened at her party. I remembered she had been looking forward to it, we had talked here about it. The mother tries to go back to the events of the party: "Carla blew the candles on her cake, there was a game she enjoyed, she liked the piñata game", she says. Initially Carla seems to feel she can continue telling what happened but then she closes down, she puts her hands over her eyes again, her pullover is all twisted on her face and addressing me she says: "As you're so curious why don't you let her tell you!" (pointing at her mother). I tell her I am sorry she experiences my questions as if they come from a "witch" [the word witch condensates my feeling of something malignant that Carla is afraid of], I am not that curious about the party itself, but rather I am interested in how she is.

The mother looks downhearted, she warmly addresses Carla, all closed down, trying also to explain to me what had happened: "I understand", she says, "it happened to me as well when I was a child: it was my birthday party; a lot of friends had been invited and there were many toys, but I wasn't having any fun because nobody cared for me. Perhaps yesterday as I was so busy organizing the activities I haven't realized that you'd gone to your room, where dad went to call you. Is this the reason why you're so upset?". With this intervention, mother has shown a sensitivity based on her own experience as a child and I feel I could seize the opportunity to link up with what mother has just said and continue telling her that in my office Carla also withdraws into herself (I address her directly). I remind her, as well, of what happened last time, when she told me: "You two talk", but she knows very well that her mother and I talk, while it is she, Carla, who has to learn to speak for herself. A dense silence follows and I conclude by saying that the time has come to start attending the sessions alone with me, making it easier to play and talk together. "I have thought about this, what do you think, do you feel you can stay in here alone, during the session? What does mummy think about it?"

After a short while mother says, "Perhaps it's better if you see the doctor by yourself because there's no need for me". The woman looks mortified as if she felt, on the one hand, that the efforts to make her continuously unhappy child happy did not hit the target, while I sense she may feel the danger linked to me as someone who might take her place.

COMMENT

These exchanges from the consultation allow us to understand how and why it is not suitable to hastily anticipate an individual psychotherapy project when a mother-daughter relationship is not serene.

What happened in the subsequent session was good in terms of the daughter offering a solution to her mother's experience of inadequacy. Carla had completed a first drawing featuring a tree that was dominating the whole sheet and underneath she had written something, hardly legible because it was covered by a red stain. Carla hands me a magnifying glass that is on the table to decipher the words. It says: "Sorry Doctor Vallino from Carla because I didn't want to talk to you before and you were disappointed about it".

Mother intervenes once again: "You see, I know too well this mechanism that Carla uses. At times I also don't feel like doing things, but then in the end I have to apologize and this means I have twice as much to do". I reply to both saying I interpreted this drawing as a token of Carla's friendship towards me, the evidence of trust in mother's advice. In her second drawing, Carla's experiences are portrayed. There are two faces, one on each side of the sheet. One image features a girl blowing a raspberry, she is called Carla "happy tangerine" with the initials of her father and her mother's surnames; the other is the "pirate" girl, all covered in black with scratches and wounds. They are both self portraits: she either feels like one or the other.

In relation to this clinical illustration, I wish to underline that the mother senses her daughter's symptom, her suffering, as something that she recognizes as her own: the same happened to her and, to a certain extent, regaining contact with her daughter allows her recognizing how she could have felt as a little girl, and as a consequence, allows her to empathically understand what happens to Carla when she withdraws into herself.

The crisis of internal motherhood in this consultation emerged when the mother had a clear internal perception of an eclipse, a sort of shadow falling over her relationship with her daughter. She had done whatever she could think of to make her happy, organizing a party with many people, and everything had gone very wrong. This mysterious and silent spiritual contact between mother and daughter, a presence that is imperceptible to the senses, had started during the pregnancy and continued after the birth. Mother's history and what happened after Carla's birth showed us that the mother had been separated from her daughter by a German Swiss nanny, Celestina, a very strict woman. Carla's photographs of when she was little portray her desperately crying with this nanny. I had the chance to analyse with the mother the fact that she had not been allowed to let herself go, following Carla's "messages" when she was a newborn baby, and that it was essential recovering a relationship between the two, which both needed and wanted. The two faces in Carla's drawing, raspberries and scratches, illustrate the little child's anger and desperation that had finally found a way to surface from her closure.

SHORT SUMMARY

My intent has been to analyse in depth the aspect of internalization present in the concept of the *internal motherhood*. It includes fundamental human feelings that had not found a name yet: we must be aware of the difficulties in expressing the sphere and the extent of the meanings linked to the experience of giving birth and maintaining the affective mental life. Therefore the *internal motherhood* is a complex concept that, thanks to Gina Ferrara Mori, encompasses the concepts of *rêverie*, primary maternal preoccupation, maternal responsiveness, containment, holding, etc., as such concepts share a similarity, that is, they all refer to adjacent observation fields, relating to various aspects of the mother's relationship to her baby. As a model of observational facts, of female identity aspects, of mental representations processing, the internal motherhood allows exploring other adjacent fields. This is precisely what I attempted to do, trying to apply the notion of *crisis of the internal motherhood* to the field of the child treatment and, more specifically, the "consultazioni partecipata" with parents (Vallino, 2009).

The clinical vignette, starting from the concept of *crisis of the internal motherhood*, helped me in illustrating the way in which a mother becomes meaningfully aware of her impossibility in making her son or daughter modulate his/her own suffering. Only then can the mother accept with relief the collaboration with the analyst to rely on the therapy with her daughter/son. This occurs through a painful sense of awareness of the crisis and of the need to help her daughter or son. At the same though, it entails strong emotions and an empathic capacity to identify with her own daughter/son and her/his difficulties, with renewed hope about herself and her capacities to love.

NOTES

1 Dina Vallino proposes what she calls "consultazione partecipata" (Vallino, 1984, 2002, 2004, 2009) for parents and their child (from infancy to puberty) that explores the difficulties that emerge during the first meeting, followed by a more complete study in order

to program future sessions. The setting includes various sessions that proceed in the following manner: a first session with both parents; a second session with the parents and their child; another session with the mother and the child followed by a session with the father and the child; a session with the parents during the child's psychotherapy; and a final session. It is a clinical extension of the Infant Observation that, besides Esther Bick's and Martha Harris' inputs, also makes uses of inputs from children and adolescents psychoanalysis. Authors such as Annette Watillon, Michel Haag, and Gianna Polacco have developed in Europe different types of parents-children consultation as clinical extensions of the Infant Observation. Another modality is the Tavistock model.

2 Internalization: at times used as a synonym for introjection, it is better used to designate only that process according to which the objects of the external world acquire a permanent, mental representation, and the perceptions are converted into images that become part of our mind's baggage and structure (cf. C. Rycroft, 1970).

3 The objectification occurs through the progressive medicalization, the ultrasound scan images, the many choices and decisions to be made (amniocentesis or chorionic villus sampling, yes or no, delivery at home or in hospital, epidural, yes or no, etc.).

4 For instance, adoptions, in various countries and environmental contexts, oftentimes highlighted the situation of maternal pre-maturity. Later on, we will get to know that if motherhood proceeds with a hasty constellation of foetus objectification manoeuvres, the mother may encounter a state of "prematurity" that will not allow her to modulate the new representations of herself as mother of the future child and could also lead her to reject her child.

REFERENCES

Bick, E. (1964) "Notes on Infant Observation in Psycho-Analytic Training". In: (*International Journal of Psychoanalysis*", vol. 45 8 1964, pp. 558–566) *Collected Papers of Martha Harris and Esther Bick*, edited by Meg Harris Williams, The Clunie Press, Perthshire, Scotland, 1987.

Ferrara Mori, G., Generali Clemens, L. (1980) "Correlazioni fra la relazione analitica e la relazione madre-bambino". In: *Quaderni di psicoterapia infantile*, 2007, 55: pp. 211–227.

Ferrara Mori, G., et al. (1982) "L'osservazione dell'interazione madre–bambino nel primo anno di vita: presentazione di una esperienza, riflessioni e testimonianze". In: *Quaderni di psicoterapia infantile*, 4: pp. 179–200.

Ferrara Mori, G. (2002) "Pre-Infant Observation: una estensione della metodologia di Esther Bick", speech held at the 6th Infant Observation International Congress following Esther Bick's method, Cracow, 2002. Unpublished.

Ferrara Mori, G. (2006) "The interior experience of maternity". In: La Sala, G.B.; Fagandini, P., Iori, V., Monti, F., Blickstein, I. (Eds.) *Coming into the World: a Dialogue between Medical and Human Sciences,* pp. 85–102. Berlin: Walter de Gruiter & Co.

Ferrara Mori, G. (2008) "Introduzione". In: Ferrara Mori G. (Ed.) *Un tempo per la maternità interiore. Gli albori della relazione madre bambino.* Roma: Borla.

Fonagy, P. (1992) "La genesi dell'attaccamento: la relazione della donna al feto durante la gravidanza". In: Ammaniti M. (Ed.) *La gravidanza fra fantasia e realtà.* Milano: Raffaello Cortina Editore.

Napoletano, F. (2006) *Voce: Identificazione/introiezione, interiorizzazione.* In: Barale, F., Bertani, M., Gallese, V., Mistura, S., Zamperini, A. (Ed.), *Psiche. Dizionario storico di psicologia, psichiatria, psicoanalisi, neuroscienze.* Torino: Einaudi.

Rycroft, C. (1968) *A critical dictionary of psychoanalysis.* New York: Basic Books.

Stern, D.N. (1995) *The Motherhood Constellation*. New York: Basic Books.

Vallino, D. (1984) "L'avvio della consultazione partecipata". In: Algini, M.L. (Ed.) *Sulla storia della psicoanalisi infantile. Quaderni di Psicotererapia Infantile* n.55. Roma: Borla, 2007.

Vallino, D. (1992) "Atmosfera emotiva e affetti". In: *Rivista di psicoanalisi*, XXXVIII, 3: pp. 617–637.

Vallino, D. (2001) "Estensione dell'Infant Observation ad altre discipline". In: Cresti Scacciati, L., Farneti, P., Pratesi, C. (Ed.), *Osservazione e trasformazione*. Roma: Borla.

Vallino, D. (2002) "La consultazione con il bambino e i suoi genitori". In: *Rivista di Psicoanalisi,* 2002, XLVIII, 2: 325–343.

Vallino, D. (2004) "La consultazione partecipata: figli e genitori nella stanza d'analisi". In: *Quaderni di psicoterapia infantile*, 48.

Vallino, D. (2009) *Fare psicoanalisi con genitori e Bambini*. Roma: Borla.

Vallino, D., Macciò, M. (2004, 2006) *Essere neonati. Osservazioni psicoanalitiche*. Roma: Borla.

Index

abduction of the baby, phantasies of 75
Abécassis, E. 28
abortion *see* interrupted pregnancy
Adamo, S.M.G. 126
aggressiveness in mothers 146
ambivalence, maternal 15, 102–4; affective
   84–5; artistic portrayal of 27; denial
   of 85; mobilized by comparison
   between women 46; in obstetrician
   143; during peri-natal period 98–9;
   popular cultural expressions of 84–5;
   pregnancy interruption and 121; role
   of 5; unmourned losses and 135–7
Ammaniti, M. 24
amnesia, post partum 50, 133, 137*n*
analysis during pregnancies 90–4; changes
   in listening techniques in 91; concept of
   limit in 90–1; implicit communication
   in 92; intensification of transference in
   93; origins of mother-child relationship
   observed in 90
analyst: gender of xvi, 95; peri-natal period
   and 98–9; responses to pregnant client
   103; silent 96; talking 96
analytic couple, "homosexual" *vs.*
   "heterosexual," 95
analytic field 95
Angelico, Beato 25, 26
Anne, Saint 53, 63*n*
announcement in pregnancy xiv, 24–36;
   in ante-natal group meetings 55–6;
   in artistic iconography 25–8, 32;
   comparison with other female figures
   accompanying 32; derived from medical
   investigations 24; emotional impact of
   25; in Infant Observation and in therapy
   28–31; moment of 83–4; by mother-to-
   be 24, 28–9; narrative dimension of 30;

phantasies associated with 30–1; salient
   aspects of 28; signs-announcements
   24; as source of anxiety 30–1, 35–6;
   technology and 33; transformation
   processes triggered by 32–3; during
   ultrasound scan 33–5
"Annunciation and Two Saints, The"
   (painting) 25, 27
ante-natal groups for pregnant women
   48–64; announcement theme in 55–6;
   death themes in 135; discussion of
   gestation experience 55–60; dissonant
   voices in 58–9; encounters with
   conflictual motherhood in 60–3; on fear
   of pain 59–60; re-discovering the Self in
   51–5; on search for significant maternal
   figure 56–7
anthropology of the foetus 66
anxiety(ies): announcement in pregnancy as
   source of 30–1, 35–6; damage 18; death-
   related 131; defence against 20; genetic
   14–15, 34, 108, 122; of limitless empty
   space 100; maternal 14–15; Oedipal 39;
   penetration 100; pregnancy 100; role
   108; separation 14–15, 18, 102; of the
   stranger 15–16; types of 14–15
après-coup 18, 19
artistic iconography 25–8, 32, 40, 149;
   of maternal identity 3; for visualizing
   intra-psychic path to motherhood 52–5
assisted reproduction xvi, 92–3
atmosphere, maternal 1, 52, 107–10, 149;
   recovery of 58–9; turbulences of 113–14
Augustine, Saint 107
automatism, repetition 75

baby-in-the-mind 51
baby-in-the-womb xv–xvi, xiv